AXEL OXENSTIERNA AF SÖDERMÖRE

By David Dumostier

Svenska Porträttarkivet, Stockholm

THE LIVONIAN ESTATES OF AXEL OXENSTIERNA

BY

EDGARS DUNSDORFS

ALMQVIST & WIKSELL INTERNATIONAL
STOCKHOLM, SWEDEN

1981

ISBN 91-22-00363-0

Publication partly financed by
Swedish Council for Research
in the Humanities and Social Sciences
and by the
Committee on Research and Graduate Studies
of the University of Melbourne

Printed in Australia 1981 by
Impress Printing Pty Ltd
Melbourne

PREFACE

The author became interested in the Livonian estates of Axel Oxenstierna while, on his postgraduate studies in Sweden in 1933/1934, he read a document at the Riksarkiv. It stated that in 1848 the Riksarkiv had purchased all documents 'of importance' of the Chancellor Axel Oxenstierna's archives at Tidö. There were in the Riksarkiv some fragments of the accounts of the Oxenstierna's Livonian estates and the author deduced that at Tidö castle there should be more of this material which in 1848 was regarded as unimportant.

With the help of Captain E.Malmberg the author was able to obtain an invitation from Baron Herbert Schinckel to visit Tidö. Here the author worked at the Tidö private archives enjoying the hospitality of Baron Schinckel in 1934 and again in 1935. The result was a book published in 1935 in Latvian about the Axel Oxenstierna's Livonian estates, covering the period from 1624 to 1645. After the war this book was translated into German and the unauthorized translation is deposited at the Royal Library in Stockholm.

The rest of the archives, which remained at Tidö castle after the acquisition in 1848, were purchased by the Riksarkiv in 1968, and the valuable manorial accounts and other documents were put in order by archivist Arnold Soom from 1968 to 1970. Now, after 45 years, the author returned once more to the topic of his first book and the result is the present volume.

In writing the final chapter of the present book at Stockholm during autumn 1980 the author was fortunate to enjoy the hospitality of Mrs Dagnija Šleiers and Mr Juris Šleiers, who relieved him of all everyday worries and to whom he would like to express his gratitude. Complementing his research at the Riksarkiv, the author spent one week at the Library of the J.G.Herder-Institut at Marburg in Germany.

The material published in 1935 has been incorporated into the present volume in a condensed form. The period discussed has been extended to the end of the seventeenth century and the beginning of the eighteenth century. In this way the entire period when the Livonian estates, which were called the 'bishopric', were in the possession of the Oxenstiernas af Södermöre has been covered, not only the period until the death of Axel Oxenstierna in 1654, as in the first book.

The author regards the present volume as an introduction to further research on Axel Oxenstierna's economic activities–to be effected probably not by the present author, but by someone else.

Finally the author wants to express his appreciation and gratitude to all those who have shown interest and have been helpful in various ways since he started to consider publication of the present volume. They are so numerous that being afraid to miss someone the author has to refrain from naming them. His special thanks go to his wife for her assistance in publishing this book.

E.D.

Autumn 1980 in Stockholm and Spring in Melbourne

PRONUNCIATION OF LATVIAN PHONEMS

VOWELS

A dash over a vowel denotes a long vowel:
ā as in father,
ē as in there and Italian credere,
ī as in machine,
ū as in rude;
o is a diphthong that starts with a u (as in put) and finishes with an a (as in hut);
ie is a diphthong which starts with an i (as in bit) and finishes with an a (as in hut).

CONSONANTS

c is an affricate consisting of t and s,
j as y in year,
s as in sip,
z as in lazy,
č as in child,
dž as in bridge,
š as in ship,
ž as in pleasure,
ķ, ļ, ņ, ŗ are palatalizations of consonants by a following j.

PASTOR HERMANN SAMSON GREETS KING GUSTAV ADOLF
at Riga on 16 September 1621

Stained-glass window of the Riga Cathedral

CONTENTS

ILLUSTRATIONS

MAPS

CHARTS

TABLES

SOURCES AND LITERATURE

ABBREVIATION	SOURCES AND LITERATURE
Ādamovičs	Ādamovičs, Ludvigs, *Vidzemes baznīca un latviešu zemnieks 1710–1740* (Rīgā, 1933; Sējējs, USA, 1963).
Aghte	Aghte, Adolf, *Ursprung und Lage der Landarbeiter in Livland* (Tübingen, 1909).
Ågren	Ågren, Kurt, 'The reduktion', Michael Roberts (ed.), *Sweden's Age of Greatness, 1632–1718* (The Macmillan Press Ltd, 1973).
Ahnlund	Ahnlund, Nils, *Axel Oxenstierna intill Gustav Adolfs död* (P.A.Norstedt & Söners förlag, Stockholm, 1940).
Almquist 1930	Almquist, Johan Axel, 'Den civila lokalförvaltningen i Sverige 1523–1630, III, 7. Jordebok och förläningsregister över Livland', *Meddelanden från svenska riksarkivet* 19 (Stockholm, 1930).
Almquist 1931–1947	Almquist, Johan Axel, 'Frälsegodsen i Sverige under storhetstiden' 1–3, *Skrifter utg. av svenska riksarkivet* (1931–1947).
AOB	*Rikskansleren Axel Oxenstiernas Skrifter och Brefvexling* (Stockholm, 1888–).
ARL	Dunsdorfs, Edgars (edidit et recensuit), *Actus revisionis Livoniae 1638*, Pars Latviae. Fontes historiae Latviae (Editio Instituti Historiae Latviae, Rigae, 1938–1941).
Axelson	Axelson, G.E., *Bidrag till kännedomen om Sveriges tillstånd på Karl XII: tid* (Visby, 1888).

Buddenbrock 1802	Buddenbrock, Gustav Johann von, *Sammlung der Gesetze* (1758–1821), welche das heutige livländische Landrecht enthalten, kritisch bearbeitet. Erster Band (Mitau, 1802).
Buddenbrock 1821	*Ibid.* Zweiter Band (Riga 1821).
Broocman	Broocman, Reinero, *En Fulständig Swensk Hus-Hålds-Bok* I–II (Norrköping, 1736, 1739). Copy from Kungliga Biblioteket, Stockholm.
Dorošenko	Dorošenko, Vasilij, 'Riga i jeje hinterland v XVII veke' [The hinterland of Riga in the seventeenth century], *Latvijas PSR zinātņu akadēmijas vēstis* 3/392 (1980).
ED 1935	Dunsdorfs, Edgars, *Uksenšernas Vidzemes muižu saimniecības grāmatas 1624.–1654.* [The manorial accounts of Axel Oxenstierna, 1624–1654] (Rīgā, 1935).
ED 1936	Dunsdorfs, Edgars, *Vidzemes zviedru laiku finances* [The public finances of Swedish Livonia] (Ramave,Rīgā,1936).
ED Außenhandel	Dunsdorfs, Edgars, 'Der Außenhandel Rigas im 17. Jahrhundert', *Conventus primus historicorum Balticorum* (Rigae, 1938).
ED 1938	Dunsdorfs, Edgars, *Vidzemes arklu revīzijas 1601–1638* [The uncus revisions in Vidzeme, 1601–1638] , Acta Universitatis Latviensis, oec. & iur., IV, 1 (Rīgā, 1938).
ED 1954	Dunsdorfs, Edgars, 'Zum Hakenproblem', *Commentationes Balticae* I (Bonn, 1954).
ED 1962	Dunsdorfs, Edgars, *Latvijas vēsture 1600–1710* [Latvian history, 1600–1710] (Daugava,[Stockholm], 1962).
ED 1964	Dunsdorfs, Edgars, & Arnolds Spekke, *Latvijas vēsture 1500–1600* [Latvian history, 1500–1600] (Daugava, [Stockholm] , 1964).

ED 1950, 1974	Dunsdorfs, Edgars, *Der grosse schwedische Kataster in Livland 1681–1710*, Kungl. Vitterhets Historie och Antikvitets Akademiens handlingar. Del 72 (Stockholm, 1950). *Ibid.*, Kartenband (Melbourne, 1974).
ED 1979	Dunsdorfs, Edgars, *Pirmās latviešu bībeles vēsture* [The first Latvian Bible] (Latviešu ev.lut. baznīca Amerikā, 1979).
EKA	Eesti Keskarhiiv Tartu [The Estonian Central Archive at Tartu].
Elgenstierna I–VI	Elgenstierna, Gustav, *Den introducerade svenska adelns ättartavlor* I–VI (P.A.Norstedt & Söners förlag, Stockholm, 1925–1931).
Endzelīns	Endzelīns, Jānis, *Latvijas vietu vārdi* I, Vidzeme [Place names of Latvia, I, Vidzeme] (Rīgā, 1922).
Fries	Fries, Ellen, *Erik Oxenstierna.* Biografisk studie (P.A.Norstedt & Söners förlag, Stockholm 1889).
Gardberg	Gardberg, John, *Kimito Friherreskap* (Helsingfors, 1935).
Generalstaben	Generalstaben, *Sveriges krig 1611–1632,* Bd II. Polska kriget (Stockholm, 1936); Bilagsband I (Stockholm, 1937).
Gubert	Gubert, Salomon, *Stratagema Oeconómicum* Oder Ackerstudent [. . .] (Riga 1645).
Heckscher	Heckscher, Eli F., *Sveriges ekonomiska historia* I, 2 (Albert Bonniers förlag, Stockholm, 1936).
Hornborg	Hornborg, Harald, *Konspiratören Johann Reinhold Patkul* (Holger Schildts förlag, Helsingfors, 1945).
Isberg	Isberg, Alvin, *Karl XI och den livländska adeln 1684–1695* (Lindstedts Universitetsbokhandel, Lund, 1953).

Johansen	Johansen, Paul, *Die Estlandliste des Liber Census Daniae* (H.Hagerup, Kopenhagen; F.Wasserman, Reval, 1933).
Lamond	Lamond, Elizabeth (ed.), *Walter of Henley's Husbandry* (Longmans, Green, and Co, London 1890).
Liljedahl	Liljedahl, Ragnar, *Svensk förvaltning i Livland 1617–1634* (Uppsala, 1933).
LR	RA, Reduktions- och räfstemyndigheternas arkiv, Livländska reduktionskommissionen.
LTR	Latin-tysk registratur.
Meurling	Meurling, Anna Christina, *Svensk Domstolsförvaltning i Livland 1634–1700,* Bibliotheca Historica Lundensis XIX (CWK Gleerup, 1967).
Neydenburg	Herrmann von Neydenburg, *Liefländischer Landmann* (Riga, 1645).
Ogg	Ogg, David, *Europe in the Seventeenth Century* (Adam and Charles Black, London, 1948).
Ottow & Lenz	Ottow, Martin, und Wilhelm Lenz, *Die evangelischen Prediger Livlands bis 1918* (Böhlau Verlag, Köln, Wien, 1977).
RA	Riksarkivet, Stockholm.
Richter	Richter, Alexander von, *Geschichte der dem russischen Kaiserthum einverleibten deutschen Ostseeprovinzen* II, 2 (Riga, 1858).
RR	Riksregistratur, Riksarkivet, Stockholm.
Seuberlich	Seuberlich, Erich, *Stammtafeln Deutsch-baltischer Geschlechter* (Riga, 1938).

Slicher van Bath	Slicher van Bath, B.H., 'De oogstopbrengsten van verschillende gewassen, voornamelijk granen, in verhouding tot het zaaizaad, ca. 810–1820', *A.A.G.Bijdragen* 9 (Wageningen, 1963); 'Yield ratios, 810–1820', *A.A.G.Bijdragen* 10 (Wageningen 1963).
Schirren	Schirren, Carl (ed.), *Die Recesse der livländischen Landtage aus den Jahren 1681 bis 1711* (Dorpat 1865).
Soom 1954	Soom, Arnold, *Der Herrenhof in Estland im 17. Jahrhundert* (Lund 1954).
Soom 1970	Soom, Arnold, 'Inledning', Tidö arkivet (Riksarkivet, 1970).
Stryk	Stryk, Leonhard von, *Beiträge zur Geschichte der Rittergüter Livlands* II. Der lettische District (Dresden, 1885).
Švābe	Švābe, Arveds, 'Livonijas senākās bruņinieku tiesības' [The oldest Livonian knights' law], *Straumes un avoti* III, (ed.) Lidija Švābe (Pilskalns, 1965).
TA	Tidö arkiv, Riksarkiv, Stockholm.
VA	Valsts archīvs, Riga, Latvia.
Webster	Gove, Philip Babcock (ed.), *Webster's Third New International Dictionary of the English Language* II (G. & C. Merriam Company, Springfield, MA, USA, 1963).

GOVERNMENT AND SOCIETY OF SWEDISH LIVONIA

On 11 August 1621 King Gustav Adolf of Sweden laid siege to Riga and thirty six days later, on 16 September, at the head of his troops entered on horseback through the gates of the partly devastated Riga. Although the war with the Commonwealth of Poland and Lithuania lasted a further eight years, until the armistice of Altmark on 15 September 1629, with the capture of Riga, Sweden was on its way to not only acquiring Livonia, but also becoming the master of the Baltic Sea and Northern Europe. In his wars in Livonia and later in the Thirty Years' War in Germany, King Gustav Adolf was assisted by his friend and trusted servant–Axel Oxenstierna.

AXEL OXENSTIERNA

Axel Gustavsson Oxenstierna was one of the most remarkable statesmen of Sweden. Born 1583 he was educated at the universities of Rostock, Wittenberg, and Jena. In 1605 he joined the Royal court and in 1606, while entrusted with a diplomatic mission in Meklenburg, he was appointed senator. In 1610 he became a member of Gustav Adolf's Council of Regency and in 1612 was appointed Chancellor. After the capture of Riga and the Swedish expedition to Kurzeme (Courland) in July 1623, Axel Oxenstierna negotiated a truce with the Commonwealth. In the meantime in Livonia, the Swedes took over the estates possessed by the Commonwealth and those of noblemen who had sided with the enemy. The revenue of the estates was used for supplying the Swedish forces and the peasants were taxed mainly in kind. (The accounts are preserved in RA, Livonica, Östersjöprov. Godshandlingar.)

In 1622 the King started donating the Livonian estates to the Swedish dignitaries. One of the first to receive a grant was Axel Oxenstierna, who on 16 August 1622 was donated the so-called bishopric of Cēsis (Wenden), though Cēsis itself was not yet in Swedish hands. Axel Oxenstierna received the largest donation of all the Swedish dignitaries. According to data calculated for 1638 (ED 1938, p.192 and ARL, pp. DXXVIII, DXXXVI), in terms of the area of Latvian Livonia (the southern part of Livonia) he had received 12.5 %. Judging from the taxation unit called the uncus (see Appendix), according to official figures for 1638, he had received 18 % and in terms of peasant farms his share from Latvian Livonia was 15 %. From the total arable he had received 17.8 %. While the average of the arable from the total area was 0.98 %, in the Chancellor's district it was 1.4 %. This shows that the Chancellor had received the best part of the land.

In comparison with Axel Oxenstierna's grants of 276 ½ unci in 1637 (which after the revision of 1638 were counted for 1641 as 425 ¼ unci) the other prominent dignitaries who had received land in the Latvian part of Livonia were in order of the number of unci: Gustav Horn (Alūksne, Gulbene, Vainiži) 99 ⅝ unci for 1637 and 150 ⅝ for 1641; Svante Banér (Rauna, Smiltene, Dzērbene) 88 ¾ and 129 ⅜; Johan Banér (Bērzone, Ļaudona, Lubāna) 90 ⅞ and 114; Gabriel Gustavsson Oxenstierna (Allaži, Sigulda) 48 and 95; Karl Karlsson Gyllenhielm (Piebalga, Skujene, Dubinska) 63 and 85 ¾; Nils Brahe (Cesvaine) 36 ¼ and 52; Jasper Mattsson Krus (Rūjiena) 26 and 50 ⅜; Gabriel Bengtsson Oxenstierna (Krimulda and two small estates) 27 ⅛ and 43 ¾; Nils Stiernsköld (Turaida) 24 and 40; Axel Banér (Gaujiena) 31 ¼ and 37 ⅞; Kristofer Assarsson Mannersköld (Nītaure) 24 and 35 ¾; Wilhelm De la Barre (Ērğeme) 41 ¼ and 35; Hans Wrangel (Lugaži) 19 ½ and 27 ¾, and Nils Assarsson Mannersköld (Mālpils) 21 and 27 (ARL and Almquist 1930, pp. 315–333).

When fighting between Sweden and the Commonwealth of Poland and Lithuania started again in 1625 (Generalstaben 1937), Axel Oxenstierna was busy organizing supply–from Riga and his possession in Livonia–for the King Gustav Adolf (Ahnlund, pp. 317 ff.).

After the conquest of Prussia, Axel Oxenstierna was appointed its Governor General. The truce at Altmark on 15 September 1629 was successfully negotiated by him, and Livonia was kept by Sweden. In 1629 Chancellor Oxenstierna was appointed *legatus* in the Rhine-lands. After the death of Gustav Adolf at Lützen 16 November 1632, Axel Oxenstierna reorganized the Swedish government and organized the Protestant League (1634). In 1636 he returned to Sweden and for the next nine years was in charge of the Council of State.

Gustav Adolf was succeeded by his daughter Kristina. During her minority the factual ruler of Sweden was the Chancellor. In 1644, Kristina was crowned Queen of Sweden. On 19 November 1645 Axel Oxenstierna was created Count of Södermöre by the Queen. This was in recognition of his successes at the peace negotiations with Denmark, which ended the war of 1643. Sweden obtained freedom from toll in the Öresund also for ships of her foreign possessions and gained the provinces of Jämtland and Härjedalen, the islands of Gotland and Saaremaa (Ösel) and for 30 years Halland. On 27 November 1645 to Axel Oxenstierna and his successors was granted the county of Södermöre which was significantly situated to the north of Brömsebro where the peace negotiations had taken place. Despite the honours received by Count Axel, disagreements which had developed over a period of time between him and the Queen deepened. Though the Chancellor was not happy when Kristina abdicated. Not only this, to the horror of all Swedes, Kristina, the daughter of Gustav Adolf, the defender of the Protestant faith, went to Rome and became a Roman Catholic.

Kristina was succeeded by King Karl X Gustav, but on 23 August of the same year (1654) Axel Oxenstierna died (Elgenstierna V, p. 606 ff.). The estates of Axel Oxenstierna were inherited by his two sons and after their untimely death were managed by guardians of his two grandsons: Axel and Karl Gustav.

THE GOVERNMENT OF LIVONIA

Beginning in 1622 Swedish Livonia was ruled by a governor general appointed by the Crown. The first was Feldmarshal Count Jakob de la Gardie followed in 1628 by the councillor and former teacher of Gustav Adolf, Johan Bengtsson Skytte, who in his turn in 1634 was succeeded by Bengt Bengtsson Oxenstierna. In 1643 Herman Hansson Wrangel was appointed Governor General, but after his death the same year, in 1644 he was followed by Erik Eriksson Ryning. The next governors generals appointed were: 1645 Gabriel Bengtsson Oxenstierna, 1649 Count Magnus Gabriel Jakobsson de la Gardie, 1652 Count Gustav Karlsson Horn, 1655 again Count M. G. de la Gardie, 1658 Count Robert Patriksson Douglas, 1661 Count Axel Gustavsson Lillie, 1662 Count Bengt Gabrielsson Oxenstierna, 1665 Count Klas Åkesson Tott until 1671. Afterwards the Governor Fabian von Fersen was acting. From 1675 the Governor General was Krister Svantesson Horn, from 1686 Count Jakob Hastfer, from 1696 Count Erik Dahlberg, from 1702 to 1706 the Acting Governor was Karl Hansson Frölich and the Governor General was Count Nils Strömberg (Richter, Appendix). On 4 July 1710, with the capitulation of Riga to the Russians, Swedish rule in Livonia came to an end.

The Swedish governor general of Livonia and Estonia governed with the assistance of a governor in Riga and a governor in Tallinn. In each circuit a commissioner was in charge. The two circuits of Riga and Cēsis were inhabited by Latvians and therefore in official documents called Lettland (at present called Vidzeme—a province of the Republic of Latvia; the other provinces are Zemgale, Kurzeme, and Latgale). The other two circuits of Pärnu (Pernau) and Tartu (Dorpat) were inhabited by Estonians as was Estonia proper, further to the north (now united in the Republic of Estonia).

Among the duties of the governor general was supervision of the courts, the clergy, and the schools. He had to provide for the collection of taxes from the peasantry and to look after the defence of the country. His office consisted of two secretaries, one Swedish and one German, and an accountant *cum* treasurer. On 1 September each year he was required to send a report and the accounts to Sweden. He had the sole responsibility for the government. The nobility had no say in governmental affairs and therefore at the end of the Swedish period considerable disagreements between the Crown and the nobility developed.

THE NOBILITY

Among the Livonian nobility three distinct groups are discernible. The first was the Swedish aristocracy who had received large grants of land from the Crown. The second group was the Swedish petty nobility with small grants. The third group were the members of the indigenous, mainly German, nobility who had not sided during the war with the enemy and consequently had received confirmation of their estates from King Gustav Adolf or Queen Kristina. In the 1680's, the Swedish high aristocracy possessed 45.4 % of the estates, measured in unci (42.3 % of Vidzeme), the petty Swedish nobility held 12.2 % (10.2 %), and the local nobility possessed 34.9 % (38.4 %). The rest was possessed by the towns, the Crown, the clergy, and others (ED 1962, p.105).

In 1634 a Royal resolution permitted the Livonian nobility to elect a head called the Landmarshal thus granting to them the status of a corporation. The nobility elected a candidate from each of the three, later four, circuits (Riga, Cēsis, Pärnu, Tartu); from the ranks of these candidates the Governor General appointed the Landmarshal. In addition the nobility elected four delegates and a secretary. These, together with the Landmarshal and the Landmarshal's candidates, constituted the diet (Landtag). From 4 July 1643 the Livonian nobility was permitted to elect a council (Landesrat) of six members subject to confirmation by the governor general. Three of the members of the council had to be elected from the Swedish nobility, and the other three from the indiginous nobility. The council could not participate in the government, which was in the hands of the governor general. The council could submit to him only complaints; its main functions were to prepare deliberations of the diet and to assist officials of the Crown in reviewing the retainers' forces.

On 5 September 1647, the diet was reformed and the standing order of the diet received Royal assent. The reformed diet consisting of all noblemen was called annually, by the order of the governor general in conjunction with the councillors. The diet had to be compulsorily attended by all noblemen in possession of land. Because the city of Riga had also estates, it was granted permission to send its representatives to the diet (in 1646). Stewards and leaseholders had no vote in the diet. The diet elected the Landmarshal in the following way. Each circuit elected two candidates and from those elected the diet presented two to the Governor General who selected from these the Landmarshal. The Landmarshal presided over the diet, presenting to it the propositions of the Governor General and at ballots counted the votes. He had to execute the decisions of the diet after their approval by the Governor General.

In 1648 the number of councillors elected from the circuits was doubled to twelve persons, and one from each circuit became an assessor of the High Court (see later). The office of the Landmarshal was extended from one year to three years. From 1653 onwards one of the councillors, taking turns, resided permanently in Riga.

For the privilege of holding estates the nobility had to provide retainers (militia men). The retainers were provided with abandoned peasants' land which was tilled by peasants' statute labour. The nobility had to elect from their ranks, in each circuit, a captain, a lieutenant, an ensign, and four corporals. The Livonian nobility had no other obligations, and for these certainly not excessive services they had the benefit of freedom from taxes, except that their duty was to collect taxes in kind from the peasants and to deliver these to the Crown, carted free of charge to the destination by statute labour of the peasants.

THE CLERGY

In its standing in society the clergy was on par with the dignity of the nobility, but its economic position was inferior. The estates of the pastors were small in comparison to the estates of the nobility.

In Sweden, the Lutheran faith was very orthodox. Neither Catholics nor Calvinists could hold any offices and worshiping by non-Lutherans was not permitted. Within the Lutheran church pietism, which started to develop at the end of the seventeenth century, was prosecuted. All this was very pronounced and pushed to its limits in the Swedish province of Livonia. The monopoly of the Lutheran church was supreme. The only exception was the sect of the Old believers of the Greek Orthodox faith; for political reasons it was tolerated in Riga where Russians adhering to this faith sought refuge from prosecution in Russia. To a certain degree also, members of the Reformed church were not prosecuted.

To centralize the Lutheran church Gustav Adolf in 1622 appointed Pastor Hermann Samson to the office of 'Superintendent General', which in fact was a bishop's office. Samson was a friend of Axel Oxenstierna. Their friendship dated from common studies at the University of Wittenberg. As the senior pastor of Riga, Hermann Samson had preached at the first service attended by Gustav Adolf in Riga. On 2 January 1626 Gustav Adolf donated to Samson the estate Vestiena (Festen), which was confirmed to him by the Swedish State Council on 25 February 1633 (ARL, p. 1100). In 1638 the estate had 26 peasants with 14 unci, by the revision estimated 9 unci for the year 1641. In 1640 the councillors, obviously on the suggestion of Axel Oxenstierna, elevated Samson to the nobility with the name of von Himmelstierna.

The town of Tartu, still under Polish government, in 1628 refused to follow the directions of Superintendent Samson, and Governor General Jakob de la Gardie had to explain to the municipal authority that the task of Samson was only to safeguard the true faith and to eliminate Popish superstitions. This shows the endeavour of the Swedes to use the office of the superintendent preparing annexation of districts still under Polish suzerainty.

Despite frictions between the Superintendent and the Governor General, the latter vigorously assisted the Superintendent in his endeavour to rebuild churches destroyed during the war and to supply them with pastors. In the year 1633 the Governor General ordered the preparation of a provisional consistory statute and in the following year the ecclesiastical court called Overconsistory was established. At the same time two subconsistories were established–at Riga and Tartu–and in 1636 subconsistories were established at Pärnu, Koknese (Kokenhusen), and later at Cēsis. Independently of these subconsistories there existed town consistories at Riga, Tartu, and Pärnu, and in two cities of the Estonian governorship.

Samson von Himmelstierna died at the age of sixty four on 16 December 1643. He was followed by the Swedes–Johan Stalen in 1648 and Zacharius Kling in 1650. In 1660, the Swede, Johan Georg Gezelius, was appointed Superintendent of Livonia. He initiated the translation of the Bible into Latvian, but his time of office (to 1665) was too short to accomplish this task.

After Gezelius, the former Superintendent of Saaremaa (Ösel), Georg Preuss, was appointed as the Livonian Superintendent. In 1673 Livonia was divided into two church districts. Georg Preuss remained the Superintendent for the Estonian circuits of Livonia, but Johann Fischer was appointed Superintendent of the Latvian circuits (1674). In the following year Fischer became Superintendent General of Livonia. During Fischer's term of office, the Latvian Bible was translated by Ernst Glück. He worked on the translation from 1682 to 1689. Printing of the Latvian Bible was started in 1685, but because of various complications release of the Bible was permitted by the King of Sweden only in 1694. Fischer left for Germany in 1699 (ED 1979, p. 79).

The constitution of the Overconsistory was changed several times during the Swedish period. From 1633 to 1648 it was a *collegium ecclesiasticum mixtum* with a president appointed by the Crown from the laity and the superintendent as the vice-president. From 1648 to 1662, the Overconsistory was a *collegium purum ecclesiasticum* with the Superintendent General as president. From 1662 to 1683 it again became a mixed institution but with the Superintendent General as president. In 1693 the consistories were entitled to deal only with strictly ecclesiastical matters (*consistoria mere sive pure ecclesiastica*), and all other matters were transferred to the competence of the courts. Subsequently subconsistories were liquidated and their functions taken over by the newly established Dean's Courts, one in each circuit (ED 1962, pp. 83–84; Ādamovičs, pp. 3–6; Ottow & Lenz, pp. 1–2).

At the beginning of the Swedish period the circuits were divided into castle districts. The nobleman who had received the grant or confirmation of the castle had advowson of the church of the district. Together with the nobility of the district he appointed the pastor of the congregation. At the end of the Swedish period parishes became the territorial division of the circuits.

The revisions of 1630 and of 1638 required among other things to collect information as to who held the advowson of the church and about stipends of the clergy. The replies about the stipends show a very great variety. The main form of remuneration was in kind. Firstly, the pastor received land, usually an abandoned peasant farm. This was tilled either by the labour of peasants assigned to the pastor or in turns by peasants of the nearest estate. Secondly, the pastor received grain and other produce from the lord of the estate up to 3 tons of rye and barley. Thirdly, peasants paid one kilmet (one twelfth of a ton or a sixth of a leap) of each grain. In some rare cases pastors received payment in cash from the lord. The largest amount recorded in 1638, 40 riksdollars (ARL, p. 237), was jointly paid by Sigulda (Segewold) and Allaži (Allasch).

In the estates of Axel Oxenstierna there were five pastors and the annual stipend was on the average 10 to 15 tons of rye and the same amount of barley. They received further malt, butter, and animals for slaughter. Whether peasants also paid to the clergy cannot be seen from the records, but it must be assumed that each peasant farm paid the customary one kilmet of each grain.

In 1640 the Governor General decreed that peasants should pay to pastors, from each uncus, a quarter of a ton (or approx. 33 litres) of rye and the same amount of barley. This meant an increase of some 20 % compared with previous payments. The nobility was not too happy with this decree, being afraid it could diminish the customary dues they themselves took from the peasants.

THE TOWNS

The towns in Latvian Livonia were Riga, Valmiera (Wolmar), Cēsis, Valka (Walk), Limbaži (Lemsal), and Koknese. Only Riga deserves the name of a town, while Cēsis and Valmiera were nothing more than fortified villages and the remainder were even more humble. According to one contemporary estimate the inhabitants of Riga numbered 6000, while another contemporary estimate gives their number at 20,000. A figure of 10,000 inhabitants could probably be near the truth. The other towns together had at best a total of 2000 inhabitants. The total of inhabitants of Latvian Livonia in the two circuits of Riga and Cēsis, including the towns, can be estimated at 142,000 (ED 1936, p. 177).

The townspeople fell roughly into two classes: the burgesses and the town-dwellers. The burgesses were merchants and artisans, the town-dwellers—workers, servants, agriculturists, and fishers. Some of them were wealthier than the burgesses, for instance, the transport workers at Riga, but socially they were still in an inferior class. The government of the towns was in the hands of the burgomasters and the council. In 1660 the Swedish Crown granted nobility to all existing and future council members of Riga. In cases of death the council itself appointed successors to the office of councillors from the ranks of burgesses, usually from the same families. The merchants were organized in a guild, and the craftsmen had their own various guilds in Riga and a common guild in the smaller towns.

The city of Riga was situated on the banks of the river Daugava (Düna), some 14 km from the mouth of the river at the Gulf of Riga of the Baltic Sea. The Daugava was the main artery of commerce of the city, reaching deep into Polish and Russian territory. The toll levied on Riga export trade, and to a lesser extent on its overseas imports, was an important source of revenue for the Swedish Crown. Riga, as a city of the Crown, and Cēsis and Valmiera, as towns of the Chancellor Oxenstierna, had to maintain defence installations with artillery. There is also an indication that Koknese, like Valmiera, had a Finnish garrison, but not much is known about it while there are nominal rolls and other records about the Finnish garrison of Valmiera. At the mouth of the river Daugava there was a fortress garrisoned by Swedish forces.

The inhabitants of the towns were of mixed nationality: German and Latvian in Riga, Finnish, German, and Latvian at Valmiera and probably at Koknese, German and Latvian at Cēsis, Latvian and Estonian at Valka. The Latvian population of Riga was growing because of the attraction of this commercial city with its demand for workers and the prescription period of one year and one day for fugitives, which, following the insistence of the nobility, eventually was extended to two years (ED 1964, p. 417).

THE PEASANTRY

The majority of the population were peasants. They were a semi-servile class. To the Livonian peasantry of the seventeenth century the term 'serf' can be applied only in a limited way. The status of a medieval serf was fundamentally different from the status of a seventeenth century Livonian peasant. The services of the former were uncertain while the services of the latter were fixed. Contrary to a serf, during the period of review the Latvian peasant could give his daughter in marriage without paying merchet. His holding went to his eldest son without paying a fine. The term denoting the peasant who had inherited his land from his ancestors was the Latvian *dzimtcilvēks*, German *Erbbauer*, Swedish *arvbonde*. One could translate this term into English as 'hereditary peasant'.

After the First Northern War the legal position of the Livonian peasant started to deteriorate and with the ordinance by the Swedish Governor General, Klas Tott, of 1671 a new definition of the term *Erbbauer* was launched, denoting his dependency. This term could now be translated into English as 'inherited peasant'. After 1671 the legal position of the Livonian peasant became more precarious, and during the eighteenth century he became not only a serf but, in actual fact, a slave.

The economic obligation of the peasant, who was a landholder, towards his lord was two-fold. Firstly, the peasant had to pay customary dues in kind and money. Secondly, he had to perform statute labour on the fields of the demesne with his own implements and own traction animals, providing his own food as well as feed for the working animals. These services were performed by farmhands of the peasant and only rarely by the peasant himself. In addition, the peasant had to pay taxes to the Crown in kind and in money. He also paid customary dues to the clergy, and the clergy had the benefit of specially assigned farms with an obligation to render statute labour. All these obligations were fixed by custom. In cases of extraordinary seasonal demands the lord was entitled to request from the peasants boon work, and then it was customary for the lord to provide a feast for the workers at the end of the task.

The main market where the peasant could sell the produce of his farm, which was in excess of his customary dues and his own sustenance, was in Riga. Over the centuries a peculiar form of bondage had here developed. Every peasant was assigned to a Riga merchant and was obliged to sell his produce only to this particular merchant. The bond was established by granting credit which was entered in a special booklet in the hands of the peasant. The booklet was endorsed in the name of the farm. In cases when the ownership of the farm changed hands, the new farmer was obliged to trade with the same merchant as his predecessor. The nobility was fighting in vain against this firmly entrenched custom. Thus in addition to the developing bondage of the peasant with his lord, the peasantry was also in bondage to the merchants of Riga. Significantly when the municipal government of Cēsis approached the grandson of Axel Oxenstierna, Karl Gustav Oxenstierna, asking that he granted to Cēsis the same rights as Riga enjoyed, he decreed that settlements of debts should be demanded from the heirs of peasants and not people living on the land who were not heirs (LR, Del 2, 22, F II: 1, Strödda handlingar, 12 October 1673).

CHAPTER ONE

ACQUISITION AND CONSOLIDATION OF ESTATES BY AXEL OXENSTIERNA

DONATIONS TO AXEL OXENSTIERNA

One of the first measures of the King of Sweden in Livonia, even before conquest was completed, was to confiscate the manors of his enemies–the estates possessed by the Crown of Poland and Lithuania and those of the nobility who had sided with the Polish cause. The confiscated manors were donated to Swedish noblemen and the choice went to Axel Oxenstierna–the Chancellor of Sweden and chief advisor of the King. On 16 August 1622, the King issued a writ (AOB II, 1, p. 193, no. 163): 'We, Gustavus Adolphus etc., declare that in this war through God's providence we have seized the city of Riga and a great part of Livonia subject to us and the Crown of Sweden. In order that our servants and subjects, whose faithfulness, obedience, and willing service we always have experienced, also may utilize this from God us granted fief and thus promote even more faithfulness and service for us and the fatherland, we have decided to enlarge and improve their fortunes with castles, land, and wealth from the acquired and conquered Livonia.' After this preamble the King expressed his appreciation for Axel Oxenstierna–the Baron of Kimitho (Finnish: Kemiö), Lord of Fiholm and Tidö, Knight, the Councillor and Chancellor of the King and of Sweden. He granted to Axel Oxenstierna, his wife, and male descendants, according to the Norrköping rules the Livonian 'bishopric' and specified this in naming the castle (slot) and town of Valmiera (Wolmar), the castle (hus) of Burtnieki (Burtneck), the castle (hus) of Trikāta (Trikaten), the benefice from Cēsis (Wenden), and in addition the nobleman's manor (adelshus) Mujāni (Mojan). The donation included everything within the precincts of the 'bishopric'–the estates, land, farms, villages, fields, meadows, forests, woods, seas, rivers, fishing rights, inns, hunting rights, rents, revenues, and incomes, which were valid during the bishop's time and what could be legally acquired.

The term 'bishopric' used by the King refers to the former Roman Catholic diocese established by the Polish King, Stephan Batory, in 1582 in order to recatholicize protestant Livonia and the estates granted for the upkeep of the bishop. The grant according to Norrköping rules is a reference to a decision of the Swedish parliament assembled at Norrköping on 16 February 1604. This decision was binding on all Swedish kings and it stipulated that all grants of land could be inherited only by male descendents of the grantee with provisions should there be no male heirs. Before selling or mortgaging of the grant it had first to be offered to the ruler. Confirmation of the grant had to be requested from each new ruler of Sweden. In other words, the grants according to Norrköping rules were fiefs (*iure feudo masculini*).

Axel Oxenstierna received a further grant from the King, on the same conditions as previously, on 7 July 1627 (AOB II, 1, pp. 341–342, no. 277). With this grant Axel Oxenstierna received the castle and town of Cēsis. The enumeration of the accessaries was the same as in the grant of 1622 with the addition that this time peasants were also mentioned–obviously by error omitted in the previous grant. Under conditions of prevailing quasi-serfdom in Livonia it was rather important that peasants should be mentioned in the royal writs.

In response to a request by Axel Oxenstierna of 18 January 1631 (AOB I, 5, p. 69, no. 18) a further grant was signed by Gustav Adolf on 8 February 1632 (AOB II, 1, pp. 750–752, no. 548). Nine months later, on 16 November 1632, Gustav Adolf was killed at the battle of Lützen. The grant of 1632 confirmed the previous grants of the bishopric and the starosty (administrative district during the Polish-Lithuanian period) of Cēsis. In view of the considerable expenses of Axel Oxenstierna in buildings and in the upkeep of a garrison, and other expenditures, the King promised to grant to Axel Oxenstierna, within the precincts of the bishopric and starosty, all noblemen's estates which had not yet been donated or which Axel Oxenstierna, or his heirs, could acquire by purchase or by redemption of mortgages. The King further granted to Axel Oxenstierna jurisdiction within his Livonian estates in the first instance, empowering him to appoint judges.

FURTHER ACQUISITIONS

Within this legal framework of royal grants the Chancellor Axel Oxenstierna expanded and consolidated his Livonian estates in Latvia. During 1622 he could not take possession of any of the granted estates because all of them were occupied by Swedish troops consuming the revenue. During the years 1623 and 1624 he drew revenue only from the estate of Valmiera and a part of Mujāni–the Mode hundred (*pagasts*).

In the Valmiera district was situated the town of Valmiera, the estate of Valmiera, and two estates which, in the previous century, the bishop had incorporated–Kokmuiža (Kokenhof) and Mūrmuiža (Muremoise). The official revision of 1638 mentions four more estates: Völkersams Hoflage possessed

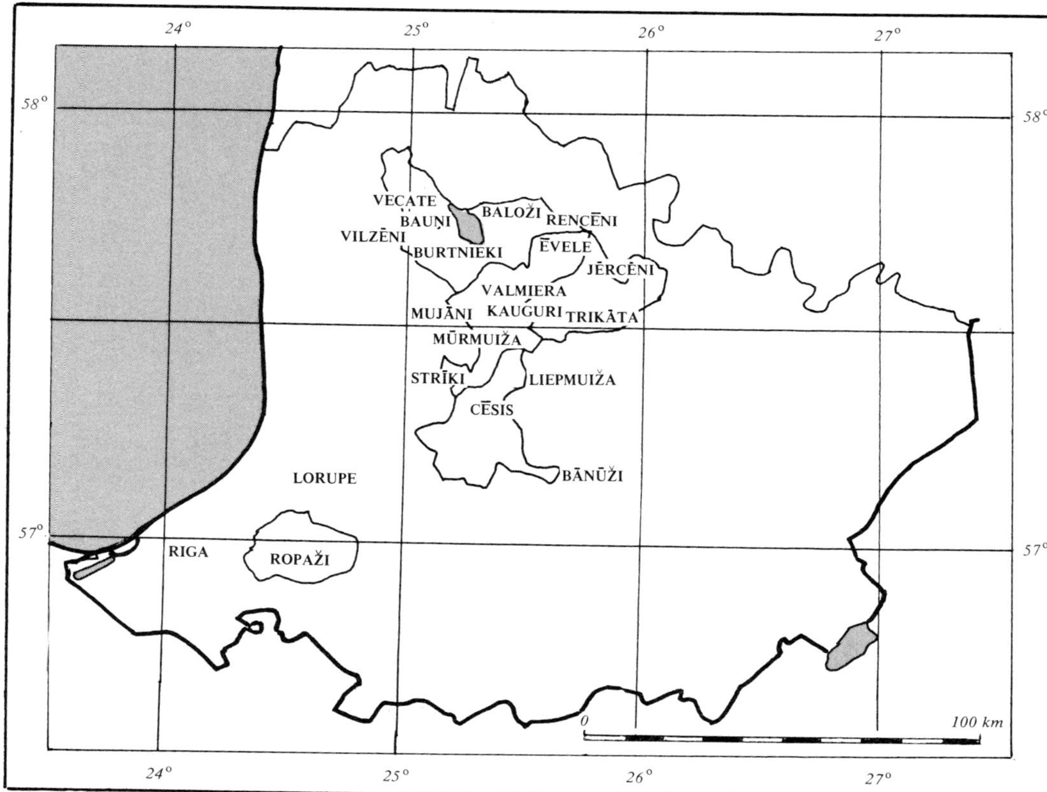

THE BISHOPRIC: AXEL OXENSTIERNA'S LIVONIAN ESTATES

by the steward Ledebohrn (ARL, pp. 500 and CCLXII), Strīķi (Strikenhof), assigned to the retainer (trooper) Berend Mortenson (ARL, p. CCLXIII), Tarnisa (Turneyhof), which cannot be located in the 1638 register but is an estate in the 1652 manorial list, and Kauguri (Kaugerhof) that was established on peasants' land just before the 1638 revision (ARL, p. CCLIX).

In the cash account of the Oxenstierna estates of 1626 (ED 1935, p. 388) the amount of 1000 Swedish dollars, equivalent to 474 riksdollars (Rd) 6 groschen, was paid to Catherine König. This could be for Ķoņi (Königshof) mentioned by Karl Oxenstierna to the reduction commission (LR, F I: 10, p. 897) as a purchase by his grandfather Axel Oxenstierna. In the revision of 1638 Ķoniņš is a peasant's homestead (ARL, pp. 518 and CCXXI). The above mentioned document (LR, F I: 10, p. 897) also states that Axel Oxenstierna had *iure caduco* acquired Doctormoise (Doctorshof) and the nobleman's estate of Skaņkalne (Kolbergshof).

Mujāni was taken into possession by the Chancellor only after he had paid a dowry to Judge's Wolmar Schlippenbach's mother (*ibid.*, p. 913). Regrettably the amount paid could not be established. An annex of Mujāni was Lenči (Lenzenhof). It was granted by the Chancellor to the retainer Hans Lenz (ARL, p. CCXCVII). Within the boundaries of Valmiera was situated the Ēvele estate (Wohlfart or Hövelshof). On 5 January 1622–the day after Valmiera was taken by Gustav Adolf–this estate had been granted to Fieldmarshal Herman Wrangel (RA, Livonica II, 713). On 2 July 1636, at Stralsund, Herman Wrangel and Axel Oxenstierna agreed on an exchange of estates. Wrangel received Otepää and Prangli in the Tartu district, which had been granted to Oxenstierna by the King. Wrangel on his part gave to Oxenstierna the estate of Ēvele. Queen Kristina confirmed the exchange (AOB I, 15, pp. 607–608, no. 534).

The Chancellor had some difficulties in taking possession of Burtnieki which was mentioned by name in the King's charter of 16 August 1622. The King had mortgaged Burtnieki, for the duration of five years, to the burgomaster of Riga, Nichlas Eke, for an amount of 6031 Swedish dollars paid in marks. On 14 December 1622 the Chancellor came to an agreement with the burgomaster that on St. John's day 1623 he would pay half the amount–3015 dollars and 3 marks, or the equivalent in ordinary dollars in case the Swedish dollars were less in value. The Chancellor promised to pay the second half of the mortgage by Christmas 1623. The agreement stipulated that, if the first amount was not paid at St. John's day or at least a fortnight later, the mortgage remained in the possession of the burgomaster, but the Chancellor would be granted a moratorium for one year and he could pay half the mortgage the following year at St. John's day. The first amount was paid by the steward of the Chancellor, Captain Anders Munck, on 1 August 1623 (ED 1935, p. 158).

Not having sufficient liquid funds Anders Munck requested the assistance of the Governor General of Livonia, Jakob de la Gardie (AOB II, 5, p. 227, no. 107). De la Gardie promised to burgomaster Eke that on arrival in Riga the Chancellor would pay the remaining debt (AOB I, 2, p. 587, and II, 5, pp. 228, 243, 255), but Eke insisted in payment at once. De la Gardie then paid the remaining mortgage and requested the Chancellor to honour the debt by Christmas. Burgomaster Eke and the Chancellor had agreed that Rencēni (Ranzen, a subsidiary estate of Burtnieki) would remain in the possession of the burgomaster for five years. Eke died at the time of the final settlement, and it seems that Rencēni came into possession of the Chancellor simultaniously with Burtnieki. Only from 1625 onwards does Burtnieki appear in the accounts.

In the revision of 1638 (ARL, p. 547) it was reported that together with the major estate of Burtnieki the Chancellor had received eleven smaller estates in the Burtnieki district, which were named. By comparing the names with the list of peasants in the internal register it appears that all but two of these small estates were 1638 occupied by peasants. Three of those—Blanka (Blankenfeld), Negurska (Nougurskihof), and Viļķis—were still in existence as farms before the present Soviet collectivization. Rencēni (which burgomaster Eke requested from the Chancellor for five years) was in 1638 occupied by two peasants (ARL, p. CCLXXIX). Doctormoise was in 1638 settled by a peasant. In recent times it was the farm Kunǧēns, also Mežkunǧēns (Endzelīns, p. 89). One of the two Schmöllingshofs was held in subinfeudation from the Chancellor by Johann Stapel, and this had the Latvian name Rūte. The second Schmölligshof was listed in the internal register of 1638 and was also settled by a peasant, but it later had the Latvian name Baloži and in 1688 was an estate. The estate Landsberg was settled by a peasant. Lutermoise (Luthershof) had later the Latvian name Rentmeistera muiža and judging by this name was probably held in subinfeudation by the Chancellor's steward Behr who had assumed the title of Rentmeister. As mentioned before, Ķoņi was in 1638 settled by a peasant. Steinenhof was settled by the peasant Stene (ARL, p. 569), and the modern farm name was Stiene.

In the cash account of the Oxenstierna estates for the year 1629, a pay-ment to Buxhövden is recorded at the amount of 1300 copper dollars, equivalent to 385 Rd 16 gr. (ED 1935, p. 390). This seems to be the purchase referred to by the widow of Buxhövden, Anna Brehmen, in 1632 and 1634. The first document was dated in Stockholm (RA, TA 75, p. 228), the second at Tartu (Dorpat; *ibid.*). In the first document, Anna Brehmen states that several years ago her late husband Johan Buxhövden from Pedel had sold the estate Heiken (mis-spelt for Heideken) in the Burtnieki district to the Chancellor and she promises to deliver the proper purchase letter to the officers of the

Chancellor after her return to Livonia. According to customs she claims to be entitled to receive from the purchaser 100 riksdollars above the purchase price and acknowledges the receipt of 50 dollars copper mint from the wife of the Chancellor. The rest had been promised to be paid in Livonia at the amount of 85 riksdollars and 10 marks copper mint. The second document is a receipt acknowledging that 50 Swedish dollars had been received in Sweden and another 40 riksdollars had been paid by the steward at Valmiera. It is perplexing that this time the sold estate is named as Offerlachs in the Vecate (Ottenhof) district. There was an estate in the Burtnieki district, called Heidekenshof (Brosemoise). In the revision of 1638 (ARL, p. 587) Hans Heidtchen's widow, Anna Heidemann, was recorded as its possessor, but the steward of the Chancellor did not claim it and this estate never became the possession of Axel Oxenstierna. On the other hand, in the same revision among the Chancellor's estates in the Burtnieki district was mentioned Buxthovedens Hoff (ARL, p. 547). Further in the internal register of the bishopric for 1638 Buxthövdens Hofstelle in the Vecate district was named (ARL, p. CCLXXXV). It had been settled by a peasant who was not named in the official revision of that year. The problem remains unsolved why the widow of Buxhövden in her first receipt mentioned the estate Heideken (Latvian name: Ēķins), situated to the south of the Burtnieki Lake. Count Karl Gustav Oxenstierna's submission to the reduction commission, referred to in Chapter Nine, shows that Offerlachs and Buxhövdens Hofstelle were identical. There is no tradition of a Latvian name of this estate, but it was located between the peasant farms Ridēns and Lapis (ED 1974, p. 122) on the Salaca river, to the northwest of the Burtnieki Lake. A document dated 24 January 1634 states that the purchase price of this estate was 700 Rd (RA, TA 134, fol. 34).

In the Burtnieki district Heinrich Pfeil and Johann von Wahlen possessed jointly the estate Sauļi (Saulhof), but they had no Royal confirmation for their title of the estate (ARL, p. 599). This was discovered by the son of Axel Oxenstierna, Count Erik, and he sued in the Tartu High Court for repossession of the estate. On 12 January 1650, both possessors petitioned Count Erik to show clemency and leave them the estate as a fief from the Chancellor (RA, TA 75, p. 222). It appears that the request was granted because 1686 Heinrich Pfeil lost the estate in the great takeover of estates by the Crown, the so-called reduction of estates.

The next major estate which the Chancellor could take in possession from the Royal grant was Trikāta. The accounts start with the year 1626. On 17 September 1633 through legal intermediators the Chancellor settled with the nobleman Otto von Sacken disputed land in Trikāta (RA, TA 75, p. 224). It was only a minor acquisition, but it led to a purchase of an estate. The deal was clinched when, on 21 December 1634, 3000 riksdollars in specie were paid (*ibid.*, p. 225, and ED 1935, p. 392). In the receipt the German name of the purchased estate was Lißen, but in the revision of 1638 the estate was called Wahlenhof (ARL, p. 611). In the history of Livonian estates by Leonard von Stryk (Stryk, p. 424) the name of this estate is Alt-Sackenhof, allegedly purchased for 2000 riksdollars in specie. This price mentioned by Stryk is obviously spurious. The Latvian name of the estate is Vāle, but the name Lisa (Lißen), that was given to it in the revision of 1638, is that of a river in the Trikāta district–a tributary of the Abula which, in turn, flows into the Gauja (Aa). In the receipt, Otto von Sacken mentions that the estate was situated in the Wiggiben hundred. In 1638 this hundred consisted of 12 settled and 15 abandoned peasant homesteads. According to the internal register the settled farms held 7 unci and the abandoned farms 7 ¼ unci. In the official 1638 register, names of 2 settled and 8 abandoned farms are not mentioned. In the purchase contract (AOB I, 9, p. 194), Sacken (Sack) promised to hand over 10 peasant farms.

In the Trikāta district the Chancellor acquired the estate Brenguļi (Wrangelshof, ARL, p. 611), obviously on the strength of the Royal letter of 8 February, which granted to him all noblemen estates that had fallen to the Crown as ownerless goods (*iure caduco*) and had not yet been granted. In 1645 the Chancellor granted Brenguļi with 11 unci peasants' land and 13 unci demesne to Adam Hirtenberg and to his wife in succession. Axel Oxenstierna signed the document on 20 January 1645, his sons Erik and Johan confirmed the same on 12 October 1645 and Queen Kristina on 16 June 1646 (RA, TA 75, pp. 103–104). Consequently the revenue from this estate was received by the Chancellor from 1631 to 1645 only (ED 1935, pp. 32–39).

The revision of 1638 in the Trikāta district further mentions Landtsberghof (ARL, p. 611) which in his time the bishop had incorporated into the district and which can be identified with Vijciems.

Outside the boundaries of the bishopric was situated Ropaži (Rodenpois). This large estate had also been possessed by the Catholic bishops and Bishop Otto Schenking had it mortgaged. On 18 January 1631 Axel Oxenstierna wrote to the King and complained that the mortgagees refused to accept settlement because the King had allegedly conferred the estate to them (AOB I, 6, p. 69). In his general confirmation of 8 February 1632 the King specifically mentioned Ropaži indicating that the donation of this estate had been granted on false pretence and ordered the mortgagees to accept the repayment of the debt and to hand over the estate to the Chancellor. On 8 May 1634 a total of 5111 Rd was paid (RA, TA 70, p. 18). From 1634 onwards the Chancellor received the revenue of Ropaži, but because it was a separate entity the accounts were not always incorporated in the consolidated account. Axel Oxenstierna had also purchased an annex to Ropaži (LR, F I: 10, fol. 912).

From the year 1627 onwards the accounts recorded Cēsis (Wenden). Cēsis consisted of a town, the estate of Cēsis, and twain Lodenhofs (Latvian: Vaive; ARL, p. 453). Karl Oxenstierna reported to the reduction commission that his grandfather had acquired the both Vaive estates and Liepmuiža (Lindenhöfchen) *iure caduco.*

In the Cēsis district more of the Chancellor's possessions were intermingled with other possessions than in any other district. This created strife and differences of opinions. The notary of Riga, Hinrich Lademacher, had two tenements in the town of Cēsis and several peasants belonging to the tenements. The land of two of those peasants was intermixed with land of Oxenstierna's peasants. In the official revision of 1638, Lademacher complained (ARL, p. 474) that the Chancellor's steward and his bailiff had three peasant farms (Swikiß, Buciß, and Saback) appropriated and of those Saback settled with a new-settler, but the other two farms had been assigned to peasants of the Chancellor. In 1636 Lademacher had initiated a court case. In the revision of 1638 and the internal register of the same year there is indeed recorded, under Cēsis, a peasant Matz Sabach (*ibid.*, pp. 467 and CCLIII) which is the present farm Zābaki. As to Buciß, this homestead is not shown in the official revision of 1638 but can be found in the internal register as part of the farmstead Andres Skundrich (*ibid.*, p. CCLII), recorded in the revision as Andreß Kurich (*ibid.*, p. 467).

Axel Oxenstierna's bailiff of Trikāta, Erik Hansson, was granted by the King the estate Ieriķi (Ramotzki) in the Cēsis district. On 21 July 1646 Axel Oxenstierna granted to Hansson and his descendants (RA, TA 75, p. 242) the abandoned peasant holding Mežkrievi (ARL, pp. 460 and CCLV). This still existing farm was situated in the Cēsis district among Ieriķi peasant farms. For customary dues and services to work this farm the Chancellor assigned Lauring Allein (*ibid.*, p. CCLV) alias Alleintz (*ibid.*, p. 459)–still existing as Alaiņi–and Jahn Laetze (*ibid.*, p. 456) alias Masa Latz (*ibid.*, p. CCLIV).

Considerable difficulties had to be overcome by Axel Oxenstierna in acquiring Bānūži (Kudling). On 20 October 1630 this estate had been granted by the King to Heinrich Ledebohrn who was then captain at the Valmiera garrison but later a steward of the Oxenstierna estates. Bānūži was claimed by Johann Bogenhausen and it was granted to him by the King on 24 September 1631 while Ledebohrn received compensation with a grant of an estate in the Tartu district (*ibid.*, p. 479; Stryk, p. 313). Axel Oxenstierna regarded Bānūži as an estate belonging to his domain despite the fact that the territory only precariously adjoined his Cēsis possessions. Despite the support of the Governor

General of Livonia, Johan Skytte, Bānūži could be acquired by the Chancellor only after the death of Bogenhausen. On 23 April 1642 the steward of Axel Oxenstierna, Jakob Behr, requested the court of Cēsis to make an inventory of the estate and the peasantry. In his testament Bogenhausen had provided for his heirs 1800 riksdollars. They claimed 1000 riksdollars as compensation for the estate of Bānūži. At first Behr was willing to pay only 600 riksdollars, but in 1642 the demanded 1000 riksdollars were paid (ED 1935, p. 401).

Count Erik Oxenstierna advised steward Behr, in an instruction of 9 January 1649, that Bānūži was too remotely situated and should be leased to a reliable man (*ibid.*, p. 183). On 3 September 1650 the Chancellor confirmed the action of the steward who on the advice of Erik Oxenstierna had promised to lease the estate of Bānūži to the assistant judge, Hermann Schwembler. The original contract was for three years at a payment of 100 riksdollars. The Chancellor extended the contract to six years at a payment of 180 riksdollars (RA, TA 75, p. 223). Bānūži was managed by the Chancellor on his own account only from1646 to 1652 (ED 1935, pp. 39–41).

In the Cēsis district intermixed with the Chancellor's peasants were also the peasants of the estates Rāmuļi (Ramelshof) and Drabeži (Drobbusch or Bergenhof). The first had been the possession of the Chancellor's steward Anders Munck, the second was possessed by the nobleman Hinrich Patkul. In 1647 Rāmuļi was mortgaged by the son of the late steward, also Anders Munck, to the Governor General of Livonia, Gabriel Oxenstierna (a half brother of Axel Oxenstierna), but Patkul sold Drabeži to the same for 2000 riksdollars (Stryk, p. 241). On behalf of the Chancellor, his steward, David Reimers von Rosenfeld, on 9 October 1647 lodged a protest at the court (RA, TA 75, pp. 229– 230) against both these transactions. The reason for the protest was that these transactions allegedly prejudiced the interests of the Chancellor.

The stewards of Axel Oxenstierna kept a watchful eye on the interests of their lord. The Chancellor had instructed them to consolidate the bishopric 'by reconciliation, admonishing, by legal means, or by hand'. This was executed to the letter. As an example of an estate which was acquired 'by hand', was that possessed by a petty Polish nobleman Matthias Commerovski in the Burtnieki district (see ARL, p. 371). He was evicted by the officers of the Chancellor. It is understandable that cases of this method of acquisition of estates are not meticulously recorded.

ESTABLISHING OF NEW ESTATES

The officers of the Chancellor were not only keen to acquire existing estates but were active also in creating new manors. Because of increased peasant population, fields of existing demesne could be expanded and new manors established. Population growth was a result of fugitives returning after war hostilities had ceased, as well as a result of natural increase. In addition the Oxenstierna's estates attracted peasants from other manors. Despite attempts to enforce the major feature of serfdom, namely, prohibition to leave one's place of abode, the Livonian peasants of the seventeenth century were very mobile seeking out better conditions and less harsh masters. According to custom, new-settlers did enjoy three years' freedom from statute labour and from paying customary dues to the lord. Because of the shortage of bondsmen, every lord was keen to attract new-settlers and consequently under various pretexts refused to return runaways to their previous lord. As a rule, conditions for bondsmen were better in large estates with absentee lords and the economy directed by stewards as contrasted to small estates with the lord of the manor in personal command. The Chancellor's estates were large, administered by stewards and bailiffs and consequently an attraction to fugitive peasants.

On the other hand, these advantages to the peasantry were to some extent offset by disadvantages. On large estates with plenty of uncleared land and some excess of man-power the lord was tempted to establish new manors. For this two methods were available.Firstly, land could be cleared in the wastes or commons. Secondly, peasants could be displaced from their holdings, which were then converted into a demesne. To the displaced peasants some plots were allocated in the wilderness to establish new farms. Both methods were unpalatable to the peasants. With the first method their service obligation increased—more labour was to be rendered by the peasant with his own draught animals, implements, and food. With the second method the peasant lost his farm with fields cultivated for generations and therefore of superior quality. Both methods increased the load of statute labour of the peasantry. While thus both methods were equally burdensome for the peasantry, the method of displacing peasants from their farms created a psychological burden and hatred against the lords and their stewards. The advantage to the national economy gained by expansion of the arable fields had to be paid for by the suffering and tears of the displaced farmers. Less odious, from a modern point of view, were cases when a demesne was established on peasant land left vacant by fugitives.

In the Oxenstierna's estates, manors established by displacing peasants can be discovered from maps drawn by land surveyors. These maps show peasant farm names on the arable fields of manors, which is evidence that at some time these fields had been peasant farms. For instance, on a map (EKA, LJkA, L of M, B, 10, 41) drawn during the period of the Great Swedish Land Survey in 1681 the arable fields of Valmiera demesne have the following names: Swirste Kaln, Widdes Tyrum, Ollender Tyrum, Putne Tyrum, Silus Tyrum, Wiles Kaln.

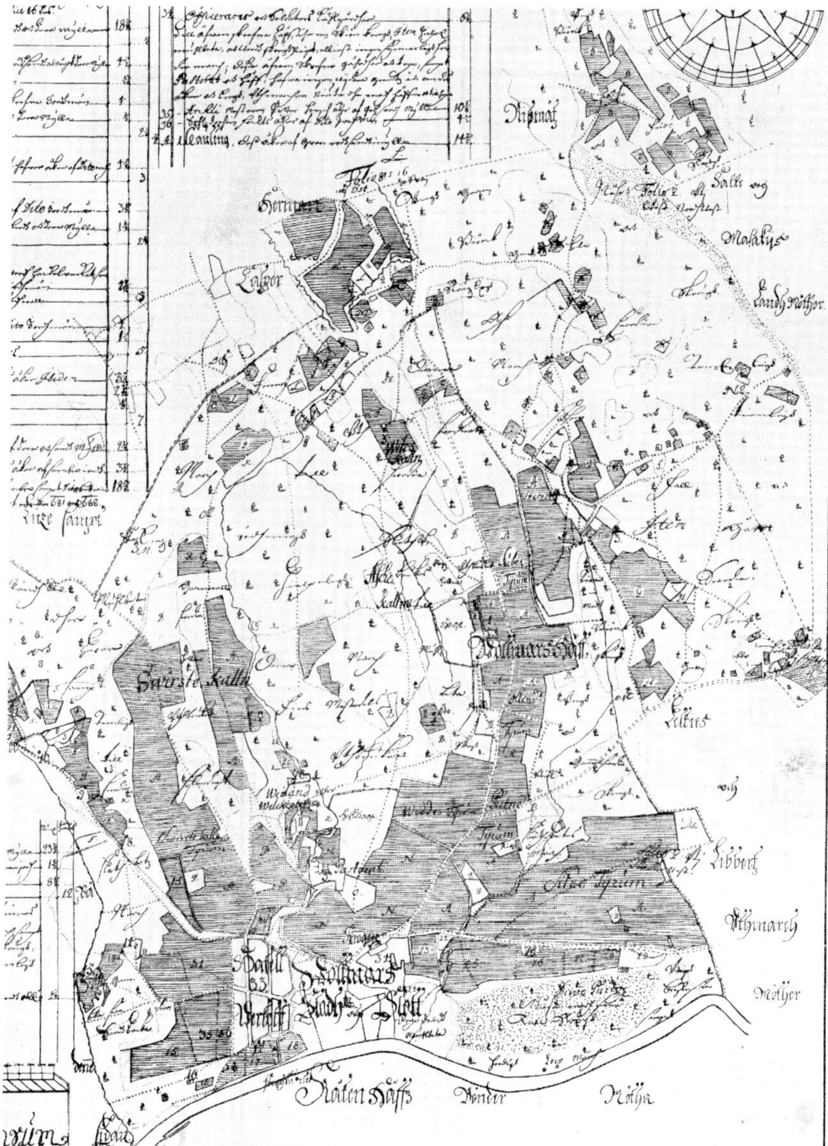

FRAGMENT OF A MAP OF THE FIELDS OF VALMIERA (1681)

(EKA, LJkA, L of M, B 10, 41)

Tyrum (in modern Latvian 'tīrums') means arable field. Kaln (in modern Latvian 'kalns') means a hill. All the names but one in the example are peasant farm names. The only exception is Widdes Tyrum (in modern Latvian 'vidus tīrums') –it means the middle field and, as shown on the map, the field is indeed situated in the middle between the other fields.

Until the recent past, before collectivization of the Latvian countryside by the Soviets, the name Silus had been preserved in Burtnieki in the modern Latvian version of Zilūzis. Very popular farm names were the various forms of Putns, Putniņš, Putnēns, and a number of these farm names have been preserved up until recent times. The popularity of this name is not surprising because, while Zilūzis has no obvious meaning, Putns etc. means a bird. Wiles Kaln was still a peasant's farm in 1624, but not any more in 1638, which would indicate that in the meantime it had been added to the demesne.

Foundations of manors are also recorded in the official land revisions which periodically were undertaken on behalf of the Crown to establish taxation obligations. In the revision of 1638 the instruction (§ 9) commanded an enquiry as to whether, since the previous land revision (in 1630), any new manor had been established or whether the possessors intended to establish the same. In Cēsis the reply was (ARL, p. 454) that a demesne had been established on Leymath Zehmat (Zehmat, in modern Latvian 'ciemats', means peasant farm). At Valmiera no new demesne had been established. At Mujāņi (*ibid.*, p. 536) the revision found that a previous demesne with the name Dūķeŗi (Ducker) was at present (1638) being tilled by a peasant (*ibid.*, p.540). The assumption obviously was that it was planned to displace him and to utilize the land as a demesne. It seems that these plans were put into effect only at the end of the seventeenth century (see Chapter Nine). At Burtnieki (*ibid.*, p. 548) four peasants had been displaced and a demesne with the German name of Baunerhof established. The name was mis-spelt Bauenhof and is the Latvian Bauņi. At Ēvele and Trikāta no new demesne had been established. In the district of Valmiera, Tarnisa, Kauguri, Kokmuiža, and Mūrmuiža were founded on land expropriated from peasants (*ibid.*, p. 500).

In the private register of the peasantry of the Axel Oxenstierna's estates there is an entry dated April 1638 for Valmiera about the foundation of Kauguri (*ibid.*, pp. CCLIX and CCLX). In the record the name Masa Tohm had been crossed out and a note attached: 'is taken for a demesne called Kaugur hoff over [the river] Aa [Latvian: Gauja] and settled on. . . [unclearly written name, possibly: Rume]'. Further on in the same document there is a crossed out note: '¼ Kaugur, ½ Bumester taken for a demesne and the peasants transferred to Anten. ½ Tohman Jurgen is also evicted (abgesetzt)'. Not crossed out is the continuation of the note 'and transferred to Mujāni estate'.

At the Tidö archives in a survey for the year 1652 of the Oxenstierna's estates is included a description of the foundation of Rencēni (Ranzen), but the date when this demesne was established is not given. In 1638 Rencēni was not a demesne, but settled by two peasants. In the official revision of 1638 Frantz Moißneck and Claeß Moeßneck both were shown as abandoned homesteads (ARL, p. 566), but in the internal register of the same year these peasants were shown as living on their homesteads.

The name 'Moisneks' was not used in the internal register (*ibid.*, p. CCLXXIX) but used in the official revision. In modern Latvian 'muižnieks' in this case means a person settled on a previous estate. It appears from this evidence that Rencēni was re-established by the officers of the Chancellor between 1638 and 1652. The record of 1652 mentioned that the demesne was founded on the following peasant farms (names modernized and put by the present author in alphabetical order): Ādams half uncus, Cēlājs half uncus, Ērķins half uncus, Kaza one uncus, Mauris a quarter uncus, Milnastis half uncus, Parķis one uncus, Piga half uncus, Tītka one uncus, Zābaks one uncus, Zīle one uncus; total 'approximately [sic] 7 ½ unci infields and some swidden'. From this list, farm names are preserved until the present times of Mauris, Tītka, and possibly Milles with the present name of Milnastis. In the official 1638 revision (*ibid.*, p. 562 f.) the names of Ādams, Ērķins, Milnastis, and Zīle can be found. Of those the only settled farm was Ādams with half an uncus, the rest were abandoned farms. It seems that the demesne was established mainly on abandoned peasant land.

In the 1638 revision among the 57 abandoned peasant farms (*ibid.*, p. 562) there were with the ending -moise: Rentze Moise ½ uncus, Suinmois 1 uncus, Wergemoise ½ uncus, Wißmoiß ½ uncus, Lukemuise ½ uncus, Langißmoise 1 uncus. 'Moise' (in modern Latvian 'muiža') means demesne. If a previous demesne was converted into a peasant farm, the peasant who settled on it usually assumed the name of the previous demesne. In 1638 these previous six manors had been abandoned by their peasant settlers. In a not very reliable history of Livonian estates (Stryk, p. 144) we read: 'In the year 1586 Ranzen with 50 peasants was mortgaged for a debt of 6000 guilders to the brothers Johann and Friedrich Büring, but the Bishop of Cēsis dislodged them in 1590'. We might conclude that there had been various attempts to establish a demesne at Rencēni and that Axel Oxenstierna was successful with his attempt somewhere between 1638 and 1652. Significantly, up until the present time there has been preserved not only the estate of Rencēni but also the peasant farm of Rencis. We could guess that Rencis was at some time displaced and on his homestead the estate Rencēni established.

About the year 1650 in the district of Burtnieki a new demesne was established with the Latvian name Jaunburtnieki (German name: Sternhof; TA, Survey of 1652). The following peasants were evicted (modern spelling of names): Stauris 1 uncus, Namcis 1 uncus, Zilūzis 1 uncus, Mūsiņš 1 uncus, Pustulis ¾ uncus, Pauzulis ¾ uncus, Pirtnieks ¼ uncus, Skujēns 1 uncus.

In order to enlarge the demesne fields of Cēsis, the following cottars were expropriated: Gruels, Kalliņš, Pricis, Bruds, and one other whose name was not recorded; a total of 1 ½ unci (TA, Survey of 1652).

Foundations of new estates proceeded also after the death of Axel Oxenstierna by his heirs, even at a larger scale than during the Chancellor's time.

GRANTS BY THE CHANCELLOR

Axel Oxenstierna not only acquired estates and founded new ones, he also granted land and peasants in subinfeudation, as mentioned already in another context. Firstly such grants went to the clergy in addition to a stipend paid by the management of the estates. At Ropaži in the revision of 1638, the clergyman complained that he had not received any stipend, but he had two peasants with a total of half an uncus land (ARL, pp. 123 and 125). The pastor at Cēsis (Bartolomeus Meyer) had at his disposal four peasants with 4 unci land and two abandoned farmsteads with 1 uncus land (*ibid.*, p. CCLIII). Four other peasants with one uncus of land had been taken away from him (*ibid.*, p. CCLVI). In the revision of 1638, the land of the four peasants the pastor retained was recorded at 2 ½ unci (*ibid.*, p. 488), and not at 4 unci as mentioned in the internal record.

At Valmiera there were two pastors–Joachim Cascheinius who was preaching to Latvians and Germans and Siegfried Georgi who was preaching to the Finns at Valmiera and Cēsis. According to the revision the former had at his disposal four peasants with 1 uncus land (*ibid.*, p. 535), but according to the internal record of the estate–only two peasants with 1 uncus (*ibid.*, p. CCLX). The revision took place later than the compilation of the internal record and consequently it can be assumed that the two peasants were granted to Pastor Cascheinius in the meantime. In the internal record (*ibid.*, p. CCLX) it is mentioned that to the Finnish preacher Georgi a half uncus peasant had been assigned. The official revision is silent on this point.

At Burtnieki the pastor was magister Hermann Ibingck. According to internal records he had at his disposal 5 peasants with 4 ½ unci of land, one peasant had fled, and the abandoned land was ½ uncus. In addition the pastor held 6 abandoned peasant farms with 2 ¾ unci (*ibid.*, p. CCLXXVIII). According to the revision of 1638 he had 5 peasants with 4 unci of land and ¼ uncus of abandoned land. (*ibid.*, p. 587). The figures of the official revision are probably spurious.

Mujāni belonged to the Rubene (Pappendorf) parish and one peasant with half of an uncus land was granted to the pastor (*ibid.*, p. 537). On 6 May 1630 the pastor of Valtenberģis (Salisburg), Jakob Holdius, received Skaņkalne (RA, Oxenst. saml., E 1069).

In a report dated 14 April 1630 (printed in *Baltische Monatschrift* 1904, p. 457) Superintendent Samson praised the Chancellor's maintenance of the clergy: 'The estates of His Grace–Burtnieki, Valmiera, Trikāta, Cēsis, Mujāni, and Rubene are well provided. His Grace has the great fame that in this case nothing is wanting.'

Secondly peasants and land were granted to retainers (see Chapter Five). Retainers were armed men on horseback, ready for warfare. Because during wartime Axel Oxenstierna kept a substantial garrison in the granted estates on his own expenses, he was freed from the obligation to keep retainers. Nevertheless, beginning in 1625 Oxenstierna maintained retainers who were remunerated in cash. Beginning in 1633 retainers in the Chancellor's estates were installed as in other Livonian estates by granting to them land and peasants. From the internal rolls of the estates for 1638 and the official revision of the same year the following picture emerges.

For Valmiera Captain Heinrich Ledebohrn (variously spelt Ledeborn, Ledebohr, and Ledebaur; first name also Hinrich) kept two horses. For this he received a grant of 4 abandoned peasant farms with 2 unci (ARL, p. CCLXIII), but according to the revision of 1638–5 peasants with 1 ⅞ unci (*ibid.*, p. 535). He was also the chief steward of Axel Oxenstierna in his Latvian estates and for this service he was granted the estate (Hoflage) of Völkersam and 8 peasants with 4 unci of land (*ibid*, p. CCLXII). Of those 8 peasant farms three were joined together (shown by a brace in the register) and from one farm the peasant had fled. In the official revision of 1638 the remaining farms were recorded among those of the peasants of Valmiera, possessed by the Chancellor, and not by Ledebohrn. In Ledebohrn's possession was temporarily Patkule (Gilsen) in the Cesvaine district (*ibid.*, p. 1171; Stryk, p. 274).

In Valmiera there were a further three retainers. Lieutenant Berend Mortenson for 4 horses had received 6 peasants with 3 unci land, and a seventh farmstead (Strīķis) had been expropriated with 1 ½ unci for construction of a demesne. He had, further, 3 abandoned peasant farmsteads with 1 ½ unci and was promised after measurement one more uncus of land (ARL, p. CCLXII). According to the revision of 1638, the six peasants had 2 ½ unci of land and the seventh 1 ½ unci. Nothing was said about the promise of further land or about the abandoned peasant homesteads (*ibid.*, p. 536). Lieutenant

Israel Andersson for 2 horses had a grant of 5 peasants with 3 unci and 4 abandoned homesteads with 1 ½ unci of land (*ibid.*, p. CCLXVII). According to the revision of 1638 he had 4 peasant homesteads with 1 ½ unci of land (*ibid.*, p. 536; these are the abandoned homesteads mentioned in the internal register). Ensign (Fähnrich) Markus (Markuß) Matzson for 3 horses had 4 peasants (*ibid.*, p. CCLXX) or 6 peasants (*ibid.*, p. 536) with 3 unci of land. The names of the peasants are different in each of the records and in the official revision the 4 peasants are mentioned among the Oxenstierna's peasant farms.

At Burtnieki sergeant-major Nils Kontinen (Continen) for 2 horses had 3 peasants with 2 unci and unsettled land of three homesteads with 2 unci subject to a survey (*ibid.*, p. CCLXXXI). In the official revision of 1638 the 3 abandoned homesteads with 2 unci are mentioned as possessed by Kontinen (*ibid.*, p. 586), but the names of the 3 peasants appear among the Oxenstierna's peasants (*ibid.*, pp. 569, 570).

According to the revision of 1638 ensign Klas Martensson for 2 horses had a demesne of 2 unci (*ibid.*, p. 586), but according to the internal register he had three peasant homesteads–one of ½ uncus and two abandoned farmsteads subject to measurement (*ibid.*, p. CCLXXXV). Matthias Weber for 3 horses had 4 peasants with 3 unci (*ibid.*, pp. 586 and CCLXXXV). The names of the peasant farms in the two records are different except of one farm (Pilath), which had been added to another (Gehne).

Finally at Mujāni Hans Lenz for 2 horses had received 4 peasants with 2 unci land (*ibid.*, p. 546), but according to internal record–3 settled farms with 2 unci and 4 abandoned homesteads with 2 unci (*ibid.*, p. CCXCVII). In the official revision the settled farms are shown among the Oxenstierna's peasants. In 1638 a total of 20 horses had to be held by the retainers. Actually at a muster in 1639 only 11 horses were present, and, as can be seen from the previous, the two extant records are not in agreement.

The third group of landholders, who did not pay the management for the land, were the reeves. In lieu of statute labour they supervised the services of the peasants. In 1638, including Ropaži, there were 22 reeves with 22 ½ unci of land. Free land was also granted to new-settlers for three years. In 1638 there were 97 ½ units of new-settlers with suspended service obligations and 57 ¼ unci of land. There were a further 12 freemen with 9 ¼ unci.

A fourth group of grants by Axel Oxenstierna was given out of charity and other reasons. The widow of the burgomaster of Cēsis had been granted one peasant (*ibid.*, p. 488), which as in further cases means a grant of services and dues and not a grant of the peasant himself. The widow of Johann von Wahlen, who was the heiress, was granted the estate of Braslava (Breslau) with

12 settled peasants and 8 abandoned peasant farms (*ibid.*, p. 589). Johann Stapel was granted the estate Rūte (Groß Schmöllingshof; see p. 15) with 4 peasant farms (*ibid.*, p. 591). The widow of Judge Jonas Traneus was granted two peasants and one abandoned peasant holding. Against this grant the possessor of Dūre (Duhrenhof), Wilhelm Möller, lodged a protest in 1638 (*ibid.*, p. 592). The land surveyor had been granted 2 peasants with 1 uncus land (*ibid.*, p. 586). The Chancellor had also issued a *salva guardia* to the peasant Janis Jörgen of Valmiera (AOB I, 6, pp. 399–400). No reason was mentioned in the letter. There was no peasant of this name at Valmiera. It is possible that the freeman and weaver Jurgen Mißweber (ARL, pp. 530 and CCLX) had been meant.

GROWTH

The growth of Axel Oxenstierna's Livonian estates is best characterized by the records of annual payment unci (about this term see Appendix). In the year 1623 the Chancellor received revenue from his Latvian estates from 72 unci. At his death in 1654 this had increased to 713 unci. The comparison does not include Ropaži. Around the growing trend there are fluctuations caused by bad years, but nevertheless the growth was remarkable. (See graph.)

PAYMENT UNCI 1623–1654 (IN BRACKETS INTERPOLATED FIGURES)

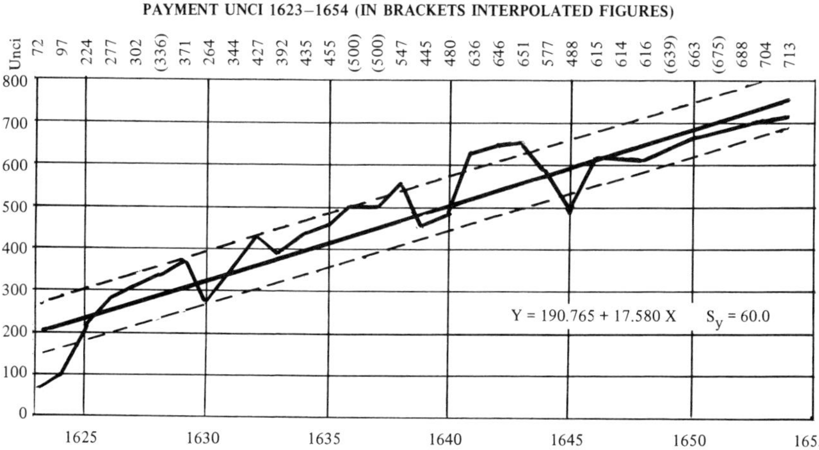

The linear trend value increased from 208 unci in 1623 to 753 unci in 1654, which is a 4.1 % increase per annum (compound interest rate). Regarding actual payment unci, we can compare the situation in 1638 with that in 1652. As to payment unci the year 1638 is above the linear trend and the year 1652 below the trend, but because of the comprehensive data it is suitable for comparison. In 1638 settled land (without Ropaži) was 668 ½ unci and 966 farms. After deduction of the land of the reeves, peasants granted to the clergy, new-settlers, peasants granted in subinfeudation, and grants to retainers, payment unci were 546 ½ and 800 farmsteads. Regrettably there are no data for 1638 about the land of the demesne.

For 1652 there is a most comprehensive survey of the Oxenstierna's Livonian estates at the Tidö archives (ED 1935, pp. 46–48). The following is a summary of the survey. At Valmiera the fields of the demesne were estimated at 3 ½ unci of which two unci were tilled. Peasant land amounted to a total of 103 ½ unci and of those 78 unci were paying customary dues to the lord. This estimate does not include the fields of the Finnish colonists, which were 7 ¼ unci and 5 morgen. It further does not include the fields of the burgesses of Valmiera town and the fields of the officers, a total of approximately 10 unci, although all was not taken up (see RA, TA 342, no. 28). In the final sum of 1143 ⅛ unci these lands are not included.

Half a mile from Valmiera were the two manors – Kokmuiža and Tarnisa, separated by the river Mellupe. The fields of each of these estates consisted of 2 ½ unci, but abandoned peasant land was also in use. Thus good and bad land in each estate could be estimated at 4 unci. The total of peasant land of both estates was 68 ¾ unci and of this 43 payment unci. On the other side of the Gauja river was situated Kauguri with 2 ½ unci demesne land and Mūrmuiža with the same amount of land; the total of peasant land was 57 ¾ unci and of this 42 ½ payment unci.

At Burtnieki there were in the demesne 6 unci land and in addition an abandoned peasant farm of one uncus. Peasant land was 62 ½ unci, of this 53 ½ payment unci. At Jaunburtnieki there were in the demesne fields 7 unci expropriated from peasant land. Peasant land was 26 ¾ unci, of this 22 ¾ payment unci. Bauņi was established by Heinrich Ledebohrn on 1 ½ unci. After adding peasant land to the demesne there were approx. 4 unci. Peasant land was 51 ¾ unci, of this 48 ¾ payment unci. Vecate was established by Bishop Schenking at the river Salaca. There were in the demesne 5 unci fields, but because the land was suffering from excess of water all was not usable. Peasant land was 57 ¾ unci, of this 47 ¼ payment unci. Rencēni was established on peasant land and had approx. 7 ¾ infields and some swidden. Peasant land was 91 ½ unci, of this 49 ¼ payment unci. There were a number of abandoned peasant farms, but the majority of them had been appropriated by other peasants and without a survey this could not be put in order. The abandoned lands were mainly sandy and swidden. Ēvele with added (peasant) land had approx. 6 unci, not including the swidden. Peasant land was 62 unci, of this 45 ¼ payment unci. This was according to the old land registers, but judging by evidence there was less peasant land. Several years ago a land survey had been started and, when it was found that there was less land than recorded in the terriers, all the peasants demanded the measurement. In order to avoid losses the lord (Axel Oxenstierna) would suffer, the land survey was stopped.

At Mujāni the infields of the demesne consisted of approx. 4 unci, swidden and abandoned land of 2 unci. Peasant land was 56 unci, of this 54 ¾ payment unci.

Trikāta was surveyed by a land-surveyor. Good and bad land, including the wood, which could be converted into arable land, and three peasant farms (Ķevētis, Kosaks, and Altīte), was 11 unci and 50 ½ morgen. At Vijciems there were approx. 2 unci of ploughland, at Vāle together with expropriated peasant land there were approx. 2 ½ unci. Peasant land in Trikāta was 150 ½ unci, of this 107 payment unci.

Brenguļi had been granted to Adam Hirtenberg. In the year 1643 it was surveyed and the land of the demesne together with peasant land was 24 unci. The peasants paid for 11 unci.

At Cēsis castle there were in the demesne approx. 4 unci. At the twain Vaive estates there were further 4 unci. Expropriated peasant land was 1 ½ unci. All this land could not be utilized for want of manure. Peasant land was 120 ¾ unci, of this 96 payment unci.

Bānūži, since Easter 1649, had been leased to Hermann Schwembler. In the demesne were some 1 ½ unci of infields and in addition swidden adjacent at a distance. In the year 1643 the land was surveyed and together with peasant land found to be 15 unci. Payment was received from seven half uncus peasants and from three ¾ uncus peasants.

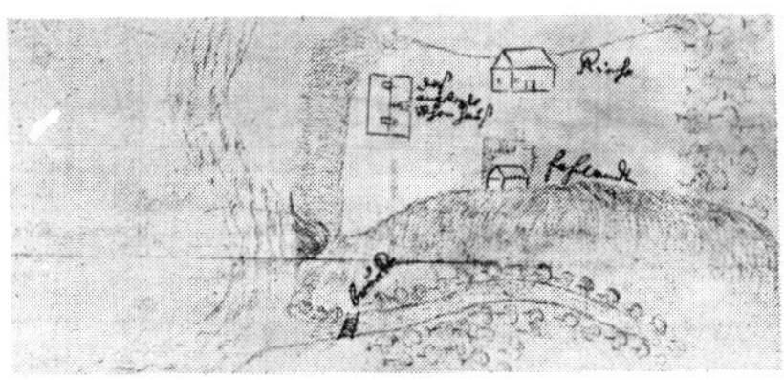

JAKOB SPRENGPORT'S SKETCH OF A NEW DEMESNE AT ROPAŽI (1653)

Source: RA, TA 271

SUMMARY OF UNCI OF THE BISHOPRIC IN 1652

	Unci	%
In the fields of the estates	71 ¼	6.2
Payments from peasants was received from	688 ¼	60.2
Abandoned land and impoverished peasants	177 ¼	15.5
Reeves and freemen	23 ¾	5.0
New-settlers since 1637	34 –	
At Bānūži leased land [to Hermann Schwembler] (settled 4 ¾, abandoned 1)	5 ¾	13.1
Veļķi (Welckenhof) [leased to Christoph Völkersam]	9 –	
Brenguļi (Wrangelshof) [leased to Adam Hirtenberg]	32 ½	
Rentmeistera muiža (Luthershof)	8 ½	
Granted to retainers and others: settled 39 ½, abandoned 30 ¼	69 ¾	
To the clergy: settled 22 ⅛, abandoned 1	23 ⅛	
Total	1143 ⅛	100.0

In comparison with 1638 the index of payment unci had increased from 100 to 126. The uncus is a cadastral measure and consequently subject to change in its value. Therefore a more suitable yardstick for comparisons is the mantal—the unit from which statute labour was presented. In 1639 the mantal of the Chancellor's estates was 652, but in 1652 it had increased to 857, or from 100 to 131. Abandoned peasant land and that of impoverished peasants had decreased from 288 ¼ unci in 1639 to 177 ¼ unci in 1652, or from 100 to 61. Reeves' and freemen's land had decreased from 31 ¾ unci in 1639 to 23 ¾ unci in 1652 (from 100 to 75), mainly because the manorial officers of Axel Oxenstierna endeavoured to liquidate the category of freemen. An example of this is the freeman Šķibusts. This farm was still in existence before the collectivization in recent times. In the year 1615, Bishop Otto Schenking had granted to Šķibusts freedom from statute labour and customary dues (ED 1935, p. 115). In the revision of 1638 (ARL, p. 506) he told the commissioners that he had been a freeman even before the Bishop's time. Because he had refused to accept the Roman Catholic faith, the Bishop had demanded annual payment of 80 marks. After the Swedish conquest the Chancellor had read his privilege and the steward of Valmiera, Munck, had not demanded any more payment from him. Also the new steward, Ledebohrn, at first demanded nothing more, but four years previously (i.e., 1634) he had demanded 20 riksdollars. Because Šķibusts could not pay this amount the steward had taken from him 5 cows and 2 oxen. He was now paying 200 marks. A copy of the freedom charter of Mārtiņš Šķibusts in Latin has been preserved in the Tidö archives. The charter states that Šķibusts had been emancipated because of his impoverishment during the war. There was nothing mentioned in the Bishop's letter that Šķibusts had been a freeman before his time. If Šķibusts had no other claim to freedom than impoverishment then after recuperation the steward of Valmiera was justified in demanding payment from him. In other cases where the stewards took away liberty from the freemen, there was less justification in a society where tradition played such a significant part.

The comparison of land granted to retainers shows a significant increase from 20 unci to 69 ¾ unci (or from 100 to 349). Also the clergy had received more land and their share had increased from 14 ½ unci to 23 ⅛ unci, or from 100 to 159.

On the whole, despite setbacks, the growth all round the bishopric had been remarkable, which is reflected in the increased revenue to the lord.

CHAPTER TWO

MANAGEMENT

PERSONAL MANAGEMENT

From the cash accounts of the Axel Oxenstierna's estates and the expenditure on fish, due to the Chancellor's preference for the latter, it is evident that he personally was in his Latvian estates from 18 November 1625 to 20 January 1626 (ED 1935, p. 388; RA, TA 342; see the charter for Cēsis, signed 12 January 1626, and letters: AOB I, 3, pp. 233–303). From his correspondence with the King, Gustav Adolf (AOB, *passim*), it emerges that he was busy organizing support and provisions for the King who was engaged in battles of the war with Poland. After Axel Oxenstierna left his Livonian estates about the 20 January 1626, he never visited them again, but directed the management by correspondence.

On the other hand, his son Count Erik Axelsson on several occasions visited the estates. At the age of 22 he was in 1646 appointed Governor of Estonia and resided in Tallinn (former Reval). In January of that year he visited his father's domains in Livonia as can be seen from signatures and expenditures in the accounts (ED 1935, p. 135). From these accounts and signatures on documents, we learn that Count Erik visited his father's Livonian estates also in January (he spent there Christmas–see Fries, p. 116) and May 1649, 1650, 1651, May 1652, and February 1653 (ED 1935, *passim*). The instructions Count Erik issued show substantial knowledge and skill of management. Father and son cooperated closely. Count Erik in his commands always mentioned that the instructions were subject to approval by his father, but the Chancellor also frequently in his instructions to the steward referred to his son. Despite this personal involvement in the management of the bishopric by Axel and Erik Oxenstierna, the main directions of everyday affairs were entrusted to the steward and his assistants. Nevertheless, a vast correspondence (RA, TA 269 ff) with the stewards, and also instructions, testify to the personal interest of Count Erik in the management of the bishopric.

The first extant instruction of Axel Oxenstierna was not directed to a steward. It was an instruction for the accountant Per Bengtsson (Benchttsson). The instruction was written in Swedish, while the following extant instructions

ERIK OXENSTIERNA
(Adapted from Ellen Fries, *op. cit.*)

until the First Northern War were written in German. Per Bengtsson was ordered to go to Livonia and take over the accounts for 1627 and 1628 from Erik Hansson (ED 1935, pp. 163–167). Together with the steward (Anders Munck) he had to prepare a correct roll of each district and hundred with detailed information about the demesne and peasants. The names of the manors were mentioned in the instruction. Bengtsson was commanded to acquire a specified number of cattle, sheep, and pigs, for each manor, if necessary from Kurzeme (Courland) or Finland. The amount of grain and other crops to be sown was specified. Reorganization of several manors was recommended. The peasants had to be put to labour or the service had to be commuted. Fishing rights were to be leased. To save on military expenses agricultural pursuits of the military had to be encouraged. Specified amounts of provision and salt were to be stored at Valmiera.

The accountant was further instructed to prepare a wacka-book (roll of peasants) with details about customary dues to be paid and service to be performed. Each hundred had to be inspected together with Traneus and one or two trustworthy men. All unnecessary expenses had to be avoided. All cash was to be taken in custody by the steward and at first opportunity transferred by bill of exchange to the Chancellor. All produce was to be sold to reliable merchants in Riga, in the first place, to Meyer, the friend of the Chancellor. What had to be sent to the Chancellor over the sea should be sent at seasons when the risk was minimal. If riksdollars were available they had to be sent in preference to Swedish or Polnish money, either in cash or by bill of exchange. Detailed instructions followed on how to collect the dues, about Otepää (the estate in the Estonian speaking part of Livonia), about the stud, necessary buildings, and public-houses.

THE STEWARDS

Up until 1631 the steward was a Finnish nobleman, Captain Anders Munck, who died in 1634. He was held in high regard by the Chancellor. Munck was succeeded by Captain Heinrich Ledebohrn. Next in command from 1643/1644 was Heinrich Rautenstein and from 12 September 1646 Captain David Reimers (nobleman's name: von Rosenfeld). From 1649 the steward was Jakob Behr (appointed on 20 November 1649; RA, TA 273), who was in the Chancellor's service from 1624 (ARL, p. 475). After Behr's death in 1652, Axel Oxenstierna temporarily appointed Adam Hirtenberg. He was a physician and surgeon of the Swedish army. After retirement he had served as advisor and chief inspector of the bishopric from 1646. As steward and commandant was appointed Captain Jakob Sprengport (whose name before ennoblement was Roland). Sprengport was the last steward during Axel Oxenstierna's lifetime. After the Chancellor's death the guardians of the heirs and trustees of the estates instigated court proceedings against Sprengport because of his activities during the First Northern War, when the garrison and the strongholds of the Oxenstierna's estates were taken over by the Crown and Sprengport was confronted with demands of dual loyalty.

The steward was assisted by an accountant. As mentioned above, the first accountant was Per Bengtsson. He was followed by Bengt Arvedsson who died in 1635. For a short time the accountant was Sverker Josephsson, succeeded in 1636 by Jakob Behr, who in turn was succeeded by Christian Bierbauch. The title of accountant was changed by Jakob Behr to the title of treasurer (Rentmeister). The treasurer was assisted by a secretary, who in 1652 was Heinrich Weber.

To the top management belonged also the clergy, a judge, a land-surveyor, and teachers. Last but not least there was also an executioner, but, it seems, not a permanent officer. There is evidence that hangings, and punishments of witches, were performed by executioners invited from other places.

GUIDLINES TO STEWARDS

Count Erik appointed Jakob Behr to the office of a steward and signed the relevant instruction at Burtnieki on 9 January 1649 (RA, TA 75, pp. 50–76, printed ED 1935, pp. 169–185). This instruction detailed the obligations and duties of a steward. Jakob Behr was appointed by Count Erik subject to confirmation by the lord (Axel Oxenstierna). He was no new-comer to a responsible office. As mentioned, since 1636 he had been accountant of the Oxenstierna's Livonian estates. The preamble of the instruction referred to his previous service. The instruction started with the time hallowed command to be found already in the thirteenth century instruction of Walter de Henle: 'Estentendez vos terres e vos tenemens par vos gens iurey'. The previous steward, Captain David Reimers von Rosenfeld, and the accountant Christian Bierbauch were ordered to prepare a list of all documents and to make inventories of the castles, estates, buildings, storage of grain, live-stock, and means of transport. With the assistance of the artillery specialists an inventory of the artillery had to be made. After the inventory the steward had to assume actual management and to introduce proper order in everything.

The details of the instruction started with church affairs. The steward had to promote the dignity of the clergy and to support the clergy with his own example. He had to pay attention that the peasants were not aggravated with statute labour on holy days and in the night before a holy day because that would prevent them attending the church service. In the estates morning and evening prayers were to be introduced. The steward had to support the church jurisdiction and assist the clergy in receiving customary dues (tithe) from the peasantry. He had to help in the upkeep of church buildings and ornaments within the bounds of his usual obligations. He had to support the subconsistory (church court) by appointing representatives from the peasantry and others from each parish. These together with the pastors had to look after the buildings and the incomes and expenditures. Proper accounts were to be kept. If special expenses were needed, the steward had to request, at first, Count Erik's, then the lord's acceptance. In cases of recalcitrance the assistance of the governor general or the superintendent had to be sought. A paragraph of the instruction dealt then with the conflict about the Rubene parish with councillor Patkul.

In the Oxenstierna's estates Swedish law and a court in the first instance had been introduced. Regarding this court the instruction commanded the steward to follow the Chancellor's and Count Erik's regulations. The steward had to assist the court. He had to attempt to induce the nobility living within the precincts of the Oxenstierna estates to obey the court. If this could not be achieved by voluntary means, the steward had to seek the general's or the governor's assistance. The steward was prohibited from interfering in the jurisdiction of the court and had to be on good terms with the court without permitting intrusion into his own affairs.

The following three paragraphs of the instruction dealt with affairs of the two towns–Cēsis and Valmiera. These towns had received special charters from Count Erik. The steward had to promote observance of these charters. He had to prevent peasants or others trading outside the towns and had to watch that communication with the city of Riga was directed through Cēsis or Valmiera.

The steward had to assist new-settlers in Valmiera by alloting the fields without infringing on the fields of the Valmiera manor. A burgomaster for Valmiera was needed and if a suitable person could be found Count Erik was to be consulted before the appointment. The erecting of panelled and stone buildings had to be promoted. If the burgesses wanted to hire a worker for construction work, the steward was permitted to allocate to them statute labourers but without a horse. The duty of officers of the garrison was to guard the gates of the town, and they should not interfere in other matters. The Finnish colonists had to live on their plots of land and should not be permitted to live in the town, except as a special favour. The outline of the streets had to be observed according to the chart. Buildings not conforming to the chart could be temporarily left, but changes had to be encouraged.

CHURCH OF VALMIERA

CHURCH OF BURTNIEKI

Drawn by surveyor Johann Abraham Ulrich (17th century)
Collection of J.G.Herder-Institute Marburg, Germany

BURTNIEKI

Engraving from the Paulucci-Album in the Municipal Library of Riga

Several following articles of the instruction dealt with military affairs. The construction of the rampart of Valmiera was to be regarded as a very important task. To this work 60 statute labourers on foot and 22 with horses had to be assigned, but at such times that did not interfere with tilling of the fields. The instruction detailed the construction of a barracks and specified which sections of the rampart had to be constructed first and in which way, as well as decided on the employment of labour of the soldiers in the construction work. Traffic over the rampart was punishable, the only way into and out of the town was through the gates. Gates and bastions had to be guarded by the Finnish colonists.

In the garrison proper, order had to be established. The Finnish colonists had to live in the huts on their fields. They had to deliver each tenth sheaf from their fields to the manor and had to serve as guards, but they were free from other obligations, except the building of bridges, construction of the gates and the rampart, and other accessary work. Half of the colonists had to be drilled every fortnight. Their young sons who were suitable had to be apprenticed to artisans. If colonists were enlisted as soldiers their land was to be disposed to benefit the lord.

The present number of 80 soldiers had to be maintained and the aged and invalids were to be replaced. The labour of all soldiers had to be utilized exclusively for the benefit of Axel Oxenstierna, except invalids and those allocated to other obligations. The steward was assigned two soldiers in the summer and three in the winter, the lieutenant had been allocated two, the sergeant-major one. Except for guard duties, all soldiers had to serve in the lord's tasks four days a week, but the remaining time they could spend as they please. Every fortnight they had to be drilled. Old soldiers had to be provided for, but only in kind, without payment of cash.

The retainers had to be kept according to the lord's orders. They could be used by the steward to carry out executions. In cases of death of a retainer Count Erik had to be notified and he would then request his father's instructions. The artillery master had to be concerned with making arms and keeping the artillery in good shape. He had to order as needed iron and other supplies from Sweden and was to be allocated three handy-men.

From paragraph 14 to 45 the instruction was devoted to what Count Erik called the most prominent part of the office of the steward–the economy of the estates. Referring to personal discussions and the previous experiences of the steward, the Count pointed out that agriculture fundamentally rested on the availability of manure and consequently on live-stock. Pilfering, negligence in tending and feeding of cattle leading to poor quality of animals were the main defects to be corrected. In future the wives of the bailiffs had to more frequently inspect the pastures and feeding of cattle. To purchase the needed live-stock of high quality the lord had allocated, for 1648, one thousand riks-dollars. Pigs, goats, and poultry had to be kept at suitable estates but no more grain than allocated should be fed to them. The stud was to be liquidated, the mares and stallions had to be sold or distributed among the estates (the stud had been established by the Chancellor's special order dated 4 August 1646 –see RA, TA 75, p. 142).

For the upkeep of live-stock meadows were essential. The clearing of the meadows was an urgent task. This had to be achieved by the ordinary statute labourers on foot, and an additional 20 statute labourers from Burtnieki were to be employed. The stables had to be lavishly littered with straw to provide sufficient manure so that every fifth, sixth, or at least seventh, year all infields could be manured. What could not be manured was to be fallowed in order not to squander seed. The steward had to calculate how much grain to sow in the infields and in which way to make swidden and water-meadows.

Next in attention were the workers performing statute labour. As a guidance Count Erik wrote that a weekly worker should work in (plough and sow) 6 leaps (the Riga leap was 66–68 litres) of rye and 8–10 leaps of summer crop. The steward had to allocate to each estate the necessary number of workers and prepare a written list of the same. Excessive labour was to be commuted and paid for in cash. Care had to be taken to select for payment of cash those peasants who were able to pay. Workers on foot could be leased but not horse teams. The bailiffs had to observe the work registers. The *otrinieki* (second workers from each peasant's houshold) had to be put to work from St. George's day (23 April) to Michaelmas (29 September). As a rule this was commuted, but David Reimers had initiated that in addition to commutation payment second workers should perform work for six weeks. If *kārtnieki* (third workers demanded in turn) were needed to tend the cattle, the steward had to proceed according to custom.

Regarding spinning and weaving attention had to be paid that this should be advantageous for the lord. All spinning and weaving had to be properly recorded. In the work registers notes had to be made of how many weavers were in each farm and whether they worked during working hours. As to sowing, attention had to be paid that no misappropriation happened. The nature of the land had to be taken into account as to the kind of grain and mode of sowing. The quantity sown had to be recorded and the corresponding notched tallies had to be added to the accounts. The same had to be observed with harvesting and threshing. More barns and granges (granaries) were to be constructed. The grange-tenders had to keep proper tallies and these had to be handed in with the accounts.

The erection of buildings in the estates had to be carefully planned at a minimum of expenses. Expenses out of the ordinary needed prior confirmation by the lord.

Fishing and hunting were to be conducted to benefit the lord. Corn-mills had to be constructed at suitable places and the millers were to be properly supervised to prevent any pilfering of the dues. Nobody was permitted to grind corn on the mills without proper payment in kind, but those with an exemption had to document this by dropping a note into the box; this referred especially to the grain of the estates. As to taverns, the lord's interests were to be observed. In principle, taverns should not be leased and had to be supplied with good products, such as ale, mead, bread, brandy, herring, etc. Only the lord was entitled to keep taverns and for those who infringed this privilege the minimum penalty was confiscation. Malt had to be guarded against pilfering and nobody should engage in malting without a proper permission.

Peasant dues had to be demanded in proper time and no debts were permitted. In the opinion of Count Erik, everything had to be taken from the peasants except what was needed for sustenance of people and live-stock. If the peasant was in need, a loan of seed and grain for bread could be granted. Those who were impoverished and not able to pay their customary dues were to be issued with a note about their debt. Payments had then to be receipted on the same note and the peasant had to present this note at the wacka (the annual meeting of peasants).

The next paragraphs of the instruction regulated the size of the measures and the weight, and also the amounts the bailiffs were permitted to overcharge for possible losses (at one per cent). The granaries had to be protected against fire and only the lord's grain could be stored in the lord's granaries. About the transport of grain, proper records had to be kept.

Special care was to be taken that the bailiffs conducted their office in a proper manner, that they did not pilfer, booze, trade with peasants, use workers for their own benefit, or keep their own cattle or poultry. Only two horses were permitted to each bailiff and for those feed could be accounted for. Bailiffs had to be content with their remuneration and not demand anything additional from the peasants. Each bailiff was allocated two peasants on foot and a good German servant provided a reeve was subtracted from the account. This meant that in such cases the customary dues from an additional peasant were paid to the lord. The next paragraph listed the names of the bailiffs and established the procedure of their appointment and dismissal.

Regarding the annual inspection of the peasants (the wacka) the instruction pointed out that this was a means to check on the bailiffs. The steward had to listen to the complaints of the peasants. Proper registers of the unci had to be kept with records of payments and debts. Abandoned unci were to be adequately recorded. Good land-surveyors had to be engaged and the unci properly measured. Abandoned holdings had to be settled. Count Erik had discussed with the steward the manors to be abandoned (Vāle, Vijciems, and Vaive), but he had not made up his mind yet. Because Bānūži was situated too far from other estates it was to be leased to a safe man with proper guarantees.

The produce of the estates was to be sold to the widow of the Riga merchant, Mrs Meyer, at a price foreigners would pay. Care had to be taken as to the kind of money at which the sales were settled. All accounts had to be finalized at St. John's day and in the autumn a budget was to be prepared and sent to the lord in Sweden. For the next year the personnel of the estates remained the same.

The steward had to maintain existing boundaries. At Valmiera a proper office had to be established and all the paperwork concentrated there. Adam Hirtenberg would serve as an advisor to the steward, especially on questions of sales of the produce.

The title of the steward had been changed from Hauptmann (captain) to Rentmeister for good reasons, but he would receive the full remuneration of the Hauptmann. The steward would in future have the service of a secretary instead of an accountant. The instruction finished with an admonition to the steward to be a faithful servant.

The reason for the change of the title of the steward was obviously because Behr was the first civilian officer appointed to the office. All previous stewards were military men combining the office of a steward with the office of commander of the garrison and the rank of captain.

During Behr's stewardship in 1649, Klas Eriksson Tors was sent by Axel Oxenstierna on an auditing and inspection tour to Finland and the bishopric (his report, dated 1 March 1649, see RA, TA 271).

Late in 1652 Behr died and Axel Oxenstierna himself appointed again a captain in charge of the bishopric–Captain Jakob Sprengport. The management of the economy the Chancellor entrusted to Adam Hirtenberg, probably on a temporary basis, because Hirtenberg was on the spot but Sprengport was in Stockholm.

The Chancellor issued to Sprengport two instructions, both dated Stockholm 20 September 1652 (RA, TA 75, pp. 38–49). The first dealt with the economy, the second with military matters (see Chapter Five). Sprengport was ordered as soon as possible to travel to Livonia. In the first instruction regarding cartage (the transport of commodities by peasant statute labour) the Chancellor gave orders to save the peasants and not send them in seasons when roads were in bad shape. He mentioned also that his son Erik would arrive in the bishopric in the winter and make further dispositions as to the management of the economy. Count Erik indeed arrived in the bishopric in February 1653 and issued a written instruction to Captain Sprengport.

The instruction of Count Erik to Behr was very much put in general terms. His instruction to Captain Jakob Sprengport of 8 February 1653, signed at Valmiera (RA, TA 75, pp. 77–94; RA, Oxenst. saml., Ser. D II, 1; printed ED 1935, p. 185 ff.), devoted more attention to details. After dealing with the offices of the bailiffs he adressed himself to the new steward.

The fields of the estates had to be divided into three parts (for winter corn, summer corn, and fallow) and the parts had to be paled (fenced in). In this way labour of field-guards and herdsmen could be put to better use. Because the three-field system was already in use on the infields, the emphasis is to be placed on Count Erik's desire for better use of the labour of field-guards and herdsmen. He further recommended the introduction of ox-teams in the estates. For a start every manor had to acquire five or more pairs of oxen. In Latvia the exclusive draught animal was the horse but Count Erik had obviously observed the use of ox-teams on his Estonian estates. It seems that this instruction was not carried out because statute labour was performed by peasants with their own draught animals and not the animals of the estate.

Imitating the Curonian model, he recommended to put suitable fields for a year under water and convert them to fishponds. The repeated emphasis was in the following on animal husbandry. At Valmiera an animal farm was to be established. He suggested as an experiment to employ permanent dairymaids who would receive sustenance and remuneration from the manor. The work of the statute labourers who previously had performed this task had to be commuted to money payment. Cattle of better quality had to be purchased at Riga or anywhere it could be found. At Valmiera, Cēsis, and Ropaži, sheepfolds had to be established starting with one hundred sheep in each place. Rams, ewes, and a manager were to be imported from Prussia. Four years earlier in his previous instruction, Count Erik had ordered disbanding the stud. Now he commanded that a stud be established at Burtnieki. Necessary buildings had to be erected. Stallions and mares would be brought over from Sweden. No reason was given for this reversal of the previous order, but there is evidence that this was the wish of the Chancellor.

Pigs of good quality had to be introduced instead of poor quality animals. At suitable places fishponds had to be constructed and the fish sold in the city. At each estate a hop-garden, kitchen-gardens, and orchards had to be planted. Bee hives had to be put up in suitable places.

Various types of mills were to be constructed. For the corn-mills of Valmiera and Cēsis new Rheinish millstones had to be purchased. Because several

German millers had applied for a job, Count Erik stipulated conditions of remuneration. The burning of ashes and cooking of saltpetre was recommended. Roofing of the castles of Trikāta and Cēsis was a necessary task. A mason could be employed.

As the bailiffs of Ropaži, Ledebohrn and Ackerfeld, intended to leave their jobs, a considerable section of the instruction was devoted to Ropaži. The bailiff to be appointed had to prepare a map to be sent to Sweden for the information of the Chancellor. In future, Ropaži was to be managed under the supervision of the steward at Valmiera and Cēsis. Further sections of the instruction dealt with military affairs, the local court and the ecclesiastical court, the clergy, and the schools.

Above an allusion was made to the thirteenth century instruction of Walter of Henley. The similarity of this medieval document and the seventeenth century Erik Oxenstierna's instructions is remarkable. Both authors, Walter of Henley and Erik Oxenstierna, are motivated by the fear of God and both admonish guarding against the wicked world. Both instructions are directed to survey land and tenements, instruct how much corn to be sown, how much live-stock to have on the manors, how to choose bailiffs and servants, how to keep proper records. Even the instructions regarding manure are similar (see Lamond, pp. 18–23). The similarity can be explained in two ways. Firstly Livonia of the seventeenth century was still in the Middle Ages and secondly both authors were guided by common sense.

There was a fundamental difference between the Chancellor's manors and other manors in Livonia at his time. The common character of all manors was that the economy had to render profit to the lord, but the difference was that the Swedish Chancellor had taken upon himself the obligation to keep a garrison on his own account and to erect fortifications. This makes the Chancellor's manors more medieval than the rest of contemporary manors.

The obligation to keep military installations not only created economic problems of a peculiar kind, but also led to complications when war broke out and the garrison and fortifications passed into the management of the Crown, to be discussed later.

THE BAILIFFS

The bailiff (Swedish: amtman, contemporary spelling; amptman; German: Amtmann, Vogt; Latvian: muižkungs) was the manager of an individual manor or estate. Assuming office he swore (ED 1935, p. 146) to carry out faithfully his obligations and to ensure that statute labour was rendered only for the lord's tasks, except when directed otherwise by the steward. He promised not to take gifts from the peasants in lieu of work. He would ensure that abandoned holdings were not used by their neighbours but be tilled for the lord's benefit. Swidden could be made only with the steward's permission. The bailiff swore to look together with the reeves after the grain in the fields and the granges and to prevent pilfering. All threshed grain had to be measured and put into the grange. The tallies of the granges had to be delivered without forgery to be entered into the accounts. All customary dues from peasants were to be demanded in time and no debts permitted. The bailiff further swore that in the rolls he would not enter wealthy peasants pretending that they were destitute. He would deliver monthly reports to the accountant and in sum do everything that would benefit the manorial lord and prevent his losses.

The obligations and duties of bailiffs were laid down in an ordinance by steward Heinrich Rautenstein at Stockholm on 19 July 1643 (RA, TA 270). The ordinance consisted of 24 paragraphs and dealt with the attitude of bailiffs toward reeves, cultivation of fields, the meadows, sowing, harvesting, the wacka, the granges, live-stock of the manor and that of the bailiff himself, the monthly accounts, the peasantry, refugees, and the utilization of abandoned land.

On 8 February 1653 Count Erik issued a memorial to the steward Jakob Sprengport, which dealt also with the bailiffs (RA, TA 75; RA, Oxenst. saml., Ser. D II, 1; printed ED 1935, pp. 185–195, see §§ 1–8). The memorial repeated the relevant section of the 1649 instruction. It started with an admonition to fear God, to be faithful and avoid all wrongdoings, not to squander, not to be dissolute and to be content with their salaries, not engage in commerce, and not to utilize statute labour for their own benefit. The bailiffs had to assist the steward in his annual muster of the peasantry (the wacka) in order to plan the economy for the next year.

The instruction further emphasized that an important task of the bailiff was to conserve the peasantry. Abandoned farms should be settled, destitute peasants who had lost their draught animals should be helped.

THE REEVES

At the lowest level of management were the reeves. The estates were divided into hundreds (hundred in Latvian: pagasts; Estonian: wacka; both these terms were used in Swedish and in German). Administratively in charge of the hundred was the reeve (Latvian: vagaris, Estonian: kubias, Polish: starost; both the latter terms were used also in Swedish and in German). The reeve did not pay customary dues (except at the end of the century, when a quantity of wax was demanded) and his main obligation was to assist the bailiff in supervising and directing statute labour of the peasants of his hundred. Being free from the payment of customary dues, reeves, as a rule, were the wealthiest peasants in the hundred and therefore also honoured. On the other hand, there are folksongs speaking about the reeve in derogatory terms. While the stewards and bailiffs were either Germans, Finns, or Swedes, the reeves in the Latvian districts were Latvians and in the Estonian districts–Estonians. Very often the bailiffs had no great experience in management and relied heavily on the reeves. In order to remain in office the latter were eager to serve the interests of the lord. The stewards relied on the reeves to check the activities of the bailiffs. Once a year an assembly of the householders was called–the wacka. The spokesmen at these assamblies were the reeves. At the wacka the account of the bailiff was checked and next year's statute labour and customary dues fixed according to the changed capacity of the peasant households. In some estates the century old custom prevailed that after the business session a feast at the expenses of the manor was given. At the Oxenstierna's estates in 1624 seven barrels of ale at the wacka were consumed. In the following years this increased to 12 barrels per annum. From 1640 to 1646 only one to three barrels, 1650–9 ½, 1652 to 1654–8 to 11 barrels of ale were served (ED 1935, pp. 354–357).

The government in its turn used the reeves for gathering information about the manors in the land revisions. The reeves had to take an oath: 'I (name) swear by the almighty God that to all questions asked by the commissioners I will reply and tell the complete truth nobody to favour or to harm and I will nothing hide. So help me God, my wife and children, my fields, animals, and everything which belongs to me.' The reeves were then asked to state the wealth of the peasants in the hundred, the amount of live-stock, the size of the man-power and other economic questions. The purpose of these inquiries was to fix the uncus number of each peasant and then to add up the unci for each manor and to allocate taxation according to the aggregate. Taxes had to be paid exclusively by the peasants, the manorial government only acting as collectors.

Taxation is a touchy question and, notwithstanding that the evidence was given under oath, in cases of perjury calling disaster upon the person giving the oath by loss of his family, live-stock, fields, and all what he owned, the reeves often claimed ignorance. For instance, at the revision of 1638 the reeve of the Āraiši hundred in the Cēsis district, Matz Jaube, had replied when asked about the size of man-power of peasants in the hundred: 'He does not know how many sons every peasant has because it is impossible for him to crawl through every hut' (ARL, p. 455). On the other hand, he displayed an amazing memory when asked about the quantity of customary dues in previous times and at present and about statute labour. Other reeves when asked about the names of abandoned holdings could recite long lists of names, but could not remember the names of the farmers of the hundred. There was no tax on abandoned holdings. The commissioners could ferret out from the reeves only the number of the settled farms. For detailed information about each farm replies could be obtained only from each individual landholder and these answers were not given under oath. A characteristics of the reeves was given by steward Heinrich Rautenstein on 16 December 1642 (RA, TA 270): 'The reeves are related to the subjects and they turn a blind eye to their shortcomings' (Die Cubiaßen oder Eltesten sein mit den Unterthanen vorwandt und sehen durch die Finger).

THE TOWNS

Together with the landed estates of the Valmiera district the Chancellor was granted the town of Valmiera. According to a list of citizens, in 1619 there were 25 families in Valmiera (ED 1935, pp. 56–57). A great number of the names were Polish and it is possible that, before the town was taken by the Swedes, those fled and thus Valmiera was nothing more than a name. This is evidenced from the Chancellor's confirmation of Valmiera's 'old privileges' on 12 January 1626 inviting the citizens of Cēsis to settle at Valmiera (AOB I, 3, pp. 300–301, no. 152). To establish the garrison at Valmiera, which was the obligation of the Chancellor, 142 families from Finland were settled in Valmiera, in 1626. They were granted live-stock and seed as a loan and they did not pay taxes up to 1644 when the management started to require every tenth sheaf from the harvest.

Valmiera was in fact an agricultural village. The occupation of the citizens was agriculture and soldiering, helping to construct the rampart, and guarding it. Not much trade or craftmanship was practised there except when, at a later stage, the Chancellor introduced spinning and weaving for the children of the citizens.

The town of Cēsis, which together with the Cēsis starosty was granted to the Chancellor on 7 July 1627, had quite a different character. Before this grant the town of Cēsis had received a privilege from the King on 15 February 1626 (RA, LTR). The fact that Cēsis had received a Royal charter immensely enhanced the self-esteem of its citizens and they looked upon neighbouring Valmiera (29 km to the north) with contempt.

Probably to counteract this, Count Erik by granting a charter to Valmiera (RA, Livonica 257) on 18 May 1642 (?) stated in the first paragraph that, subject to ratification by his father, the town of Valmiera had the same rights, liberties, and privileges as the town of Cēsis. The charter stated that the town of Valmiera was entitled to a council of five persons and for the commune an

CĒSIS: MARKET-PLACE 1842

Lithograph by Georg Friedrich Schlater after drawing by Hermann Eduard Hartmann
Collection of J.G.Herder-Institute

alderman was to be appointed to represent the citizens at the council. Prospective citizens had to approach the council about their planned trade. Brewing and baking was reserved to brewers and bakers, but everybody was entitled to brew and bake bread on his own behalf. A market would be established on Wednesdays and Fridays and forestalling and regrating was prohibited. The Count had handed over to the council a map of the town showing 24 houses with 24 leapsteads (each 0.371 ha) of fields and necessary meadows. These 24 houses had to be built from stone or in a panelled construction according to plans confirmed by the Count. Those who were prepared to build according to the plans would be freed for two years from paying rates and five years from giving a tenth from their fields. In contrast to these 24 houses the other allotments could receive from the town only a garden-plot. Owners of those could build according to a pattern confirmed by the council either in stone or timber, but the roof had to be tiles or other fireproof material. Those citizens would be freed from payment of rent for one year. The 24 houses could be alloted only with the consent of the steward but the other houses could be alloted by the council subject to the disposition of the Chancellor or his heirs, and six lots had to be reserved for them. Rates were to be paid as in Cēsis. A quarter of the rates at present and a half in future had to be paid to the management of the bishopric. All settlers be obligated not to leave before four years. The Finnish colonists had to leave the town and settle on land to be alloted to them except those who would be granted special permission to remain in the town.

On 8 January 1646 Count Erik amended the privileges of Valmiera (ED 1935, pp. 132–135). The preamble stated that the Chancellor with great expenses had started to fortify the town and that it was necessary to establish a definite order in the settlement. The 36 big houses (not any longer 24 houses!) should receive land a total of 30 leapsteads, half tillage and half woodland (to burn clearings, i. e. swidden), and each lot should receive a garden-plot near the Riga gates. The smaller houses should receive from 14 to 20 leapsteads.

Those who desired to settle at Valmiera had to report to the council and testify about their origin and what they intended to do for subsistence. Then with the consent of the council they had to approach the steward who would allocate the building lot. The next paragraph stipulated the years the new-settler was free from rates and dues. Members of the nobility were also entitled to build in the town, but only on the same conditions as others. In the interest of cleanliness all Finnish colonists should live on their land outside the town and the soldiers should be billeted in barracks along the rampart. Inside the walls, the town should have its own jurisdiction and for this purpose a burgomaster and five councillors had to keep law and order. The citizens were freed from cartage and statute labour. During attacks by an enemy they would not be obliged to guard the town, but when their number increased they had to divide themselves into units and from every house a good churl was to be provided with weapons, who at wartime would defend the town and during peacetime would serve on occasions as guard of honour. The peasants of the bishopric would be advised to take their produce for sale to the town. On the 29 December 1673 these privileges were confirmed by Karl Gustav Oxenstierna and he issued a new privilege at the same date.

Despite the building regulations providing that all houses must have a roof of fireproof material, Valmiera suffered repeatedly from fire. In 1639 half of Valmiera burnt down–a total of 37 houses. In a conflagration in 1640 only five or six houses were saved (RA, Oxenst. saml.).

In the meantime, the town of Cēsis had substantial disagreements with the officers of the Chancellor. To its several petitions the Chancellor replied on the 5 May 1630 (AOB I, 5, no. 229; see the complaints RA, Oxenst. saml., Ser. B: III, B 2). He promised to order his servants to advise the peasants to sell their produce to the citizens of Cēsis and not to trade preferably in Riga. He rejected the complaint that a garrison had been stationed at Cēsis. This was not to prejudice the town, but on the contrary–it could only enhance economic activities. All citizens had to take part in the construction of fortifications because this was in the interests of the citizens themselves. On the complaint that the town had not received the promised six years relief from payments the Chancellor replied that this would be compensated by increased economic activities. It was not in the Chancellor's power to prohibit Russians trading in Cēsis. The Chancellor advised the town not to remind him so much about their old privileges, because they had acquired a mill from the King by false pretences. The town would flourish if instead of complaining it would pay more attention to handicrafts, trade, and agriculture. He rejected the request of the town to grant it an estate because near the town there was sufficient abandoned land which could be tilled. With careful management the town would prosper and the Chancellor was willing to leave to it its old rights.

The council of the town was not satisfied and complained to the Crown. In a Royal resolution of 6 September 1636 forestalling and regrating was prohibited and ale from the country was not permitted to be imported into the city. Artisans were not permitted to change their trade or to brew ale. Noblemen's servants could settle in the town, but they had to obey the jurisdiction established there. Those, who within three years had not started building, would lose their lot.

Disagreement between the Chancellor and the town of Cēsis became with time more pronounced. In 1636, steward Ledebohrn wrote to the Chancellor (RA, Oxenst. saml.) that the troublemaker was a certain Dr Frost who had instigated the town to complain in Sweden. On the 26 May 1640 the burgomaster and the council of Cēsis complained to the Chancellor that the officers of the castle instigated citizens not to obey and that they allocated houses of the town without consent of the council. The council complained further that the servants of the Chancellor were taking away citizens' meadows, that they took over churches and dismantled the walls of the city and the gates of the churchyard. They summoned before the court of the bishopric people who were under the jurisdiction of the town. They permitted brewing and the sale of ale but from the peasants, whom the town had permitted to brew against payment for the benefit of the school and the infirmery, they confiscated ale and smashed the casks. Citizens who according to the late King's privilege cut timber were prosecuted and their axes confiscated. The peasants of the citizens were exploited for the benefit of the castle. The officers of the Chancellor did not permit the use of the tavern near the Rauna gate. The servants of the Chancellor had the keys of the gates and they closed the gates too early which impaired the life of the city. At Sundays they closed the gates in order to force peasants to go to the Chancellor's taverns after divine service and to become intoxicated.

At Tidö archives there is extant a list of the citizens of Cēsis, dated 14 January 1647 (printed ED 1935, pp. 154–157). The summary listed a total of 86 persons (males and widows) and of those 9 were of the town government including two burgomasters, five councillors, and one secretary (the nominal list gave only 8 names). Three were clerics (the pastor, the teacher, and the organ player). 29 were merchants including 8 widows. These belonged to the merchants guild. The 37 artisans had their own alderman and regarded themselves to be of a craftmen guild. Among the artisans were 9 weavers and two tailors, who were listed as Latvians (Unteutschen), and Latvian names can be found also among the other artisans.

In 1668 a list of the houses and building lots at Cēsis was prepared. It contained 34 former cleric houses at the disposition of the estate government and 87 houses at the disposition of the municipal government, or a total of 121 houses (RA, TA 83, pp. 485–489).

The economic significance of the two towns–Cēsis and Valmiera–was of no great importance within Livonia. The scene was dominated by Riga which attracted commerce from a wide perimeter and where artisanship and craftmanship was flourishing. Nevertheless, for the Chancellor, the towns of Cēsis and Valmiera were important as defence posts which he had to maintain as a condition of his Livonian fief.

CHAPTER THREE

THE ECONOMY

THE ACCOUNTS

Accounts of the Oxenstierna's estates in Livonia had been preserved at the Tidö castle in Sweden (now in the Riksarkiv in Stockholm) and they are a unique source for a detailed insight into the working of this large county in Swedish Livonia in particular and for the economic history of the seventeenth century in general. Axel Oxenstierna and his son Count Erik had adopted an ingenious scheme for book-keeping in order to check on the manorial officers and to prevent embezzlement. The aim of the elaborate book-keeping scheme was not to draw up a balance-sheet and a profit and loss account. Such a system of accountancy would be useless in an economy based on statute labour and customary dues and bound by tradition.

We learn about the system of accountancy used from the instructions given to the stewards and other officers of the bishopric and from the results of the book-keeping itself. Information about practical questions of agriculture can be gleaned from the accounts and contemporary books published for the benefit of manorial officers, namely, Salomon Gubert, *Stratagema Oeconomicum* Oder Ackerstudent, Denen jungen vngeübten Ackerleuten in Lieffland zum nöhtigem Vnterricht [. . .] dargestellet, Riga 1645 (two copies of this book were purchased by Erik Oxenstierna in 1646 for the bishopric—see ED 1935, p. 407), Johann Herrmann (von Neydenburg), *Liefflädischer Landmann*, Riga 1662, and others.

The most important document on which the book-keeping of the Chancellor's estates was based was the roll he had demanded to be prepared by Per Bengtsson and which was later regularly revised. In this terrier or, as it was called, the Wackenbuch were entered by name all peasants and unoccupied holdings. The capacity of the peasants to work and to pay was expressed in the fractions of uncus of land and in the mantal. In addition, the size of the demesne fields was also noted in the same document. The terrier or landbook was supplemented by rolls recording the grain and other produce in storage and the inventory of animals. On the basis of the terrier, statute work journals, and tallies, the debt registers of the peasants were compiled.

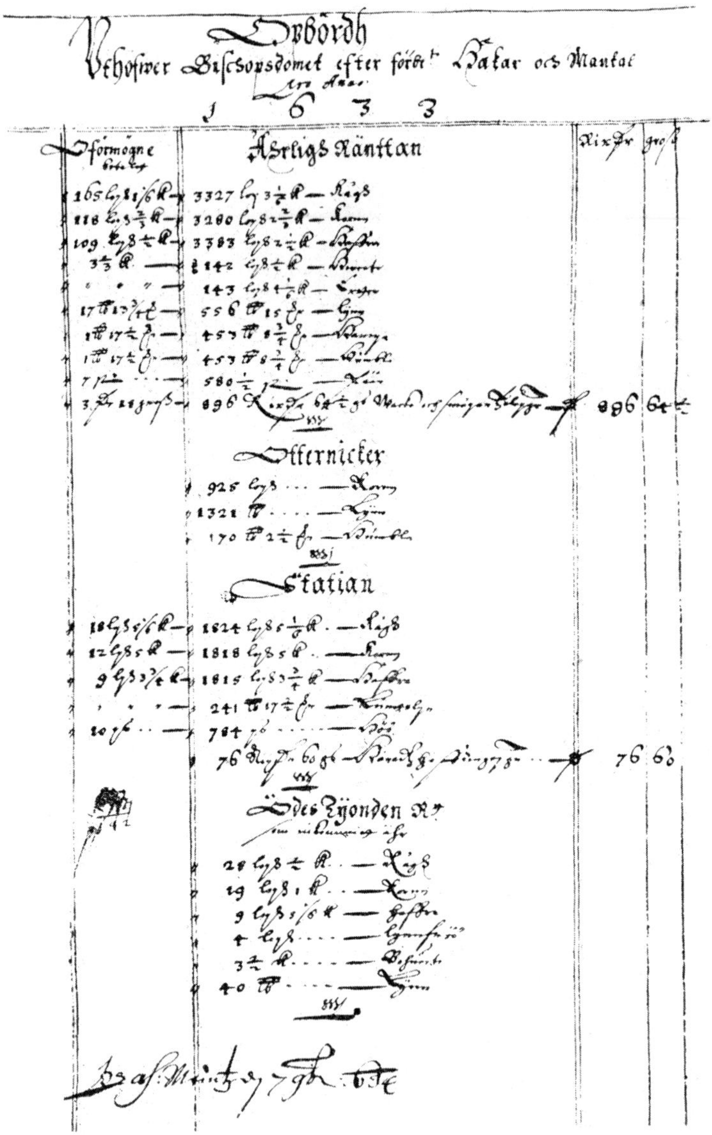

Upbördh
Uthofwer Biscopsdömet efter förbe:t Talar och Mantal
Åhr Anno
1633

Åhrligs Ränttan
Offernicker
Statian
Odes Tijonden

FACSIMILE OF A PAGE FROM THE ANNUAL ACCOUNT FOR 1633

Stratagema Oeconomicum

Oder

Ackerstudent/

Denen jungen vngeübten Ackerleuten in Lieffland zum nöhtigem Vnterricht / vermittelst vieljährigen Observationibus, auch fürnehmer Philosophorum Placitis dargestellet

von

SALOMONE GUBERTO, der Gemeine Gottes zu Sonsel Pastore.

Cum Grat. & Privil. S. R. M. Suec.

Riga / Gedruckt vnd verlegt durch Gerhard Schrödern / 1645.

TITLE PAGE OF SALOMON GUBERT'S AGRICULTURAL HANDBOOK

The obligation of the bailiff was to prepare monthly accounts of all income and expenditure in money and in kind, which had to be handed in to the accountant or secretary. He then summarized these accounts, added those of the central management, and sent these monthly accounts to the Chancellor. On the 1 August each year the accountant prepared a summary account for the whole year. After auditing this was also sent to the Chancellor. How long it took to prepare the general account can be seen from a note on the general account for the year 1633. The Chancellor received it in Mainz, Germany, on 7 November 1634–only three months after closing the books, a remarkably speedy result.

With the expansion of the economy and more paperwork it took longer to collect the data and to prepare the accounts. For instance, the accounts of Jakob Gutrich for the year 1676/1677, closing with July, arrived in Stockholm on 17 June 1678 and the accountant Lars Gulbrandsson finally entered them into the books on 1 April 1679 (RA, TA 171 and 172).

To check on the accounts, as mentioned previously, the peasants were assembled annually at a meeting for each hundred and publicly queried about their dues and services. The granges were entrusted to grange-wards from the ranks of the peasantry. Being illiterate they had to record incoming and outgoing produce on tallies of which the receiver had one half and the deliverer the corresponding half of the lengthwise split stick. The quantities were notched simultaneously on both halves pressed together. On such tallies were also recorded the customary dues of the peasants. At the meetings of the hundred these tallies were compared and the half of the manorial officers collated with the written documents and added to the accounts. In addition, praxis had developed several questions to be asked to check the accounts.

RECALCULATING THE ACCOUNTS IN MONEY TERMS

On the basis of the general annual accounts for the years 1624 up to 1654, the author of this volume had prepared tables bringing together in separate accounts the various items of the produce and the turnover of cash. These tables were published by the author in 1935. See *Uksenšernas Vidzemes muižu saimniecības grāmatas 1624–1654*, Riga 1935, in Latvian with a German key to the tables. In the present volume these tables have been recast. Firstly physical measurements of the approximately sixty products have been expressed in money terms. Secondly the results have been summarized into seven accounts (cash, produce, manors, peasants, the Crown, possessor's account, balance) and crosswise into nine items (balance, sales, customary dues, transfers, demesne, remunerations, produce refined, gains and losses, and totals) and entered into a double-entry scheme. To achieve this the following calculations had to be performed. From the year 1630 onwards the cash account of our source was written in riksdollars. This currency was chosen and prices given in various other currencies were recalculated into riksdollars. Before 1630 the cash accounts were not written in riksdollars but in various different currencies and these had to be recalculated to put all the accounts on an even footing. The riksdollar was the most stable currency of the seventeenth century, despite the fact that there were various types of riksdollars; to make the accounts uniform the riksdollar specie was selected.

In our sources the cash account for the first year (1624) was written in Riga dollars, but some items were written in Swedish silver öre. The rate of exchange was mentioned in the cash account for a bill of exchange. 2166 Riga dollars and 4 marks were the equivalent of 1000 riksdollars at 13 marks each. The riksdollar was valued at 78 groschen, but the Riga dollar was valued at 36 groschen.

In 1625 the cash account was written in Riga dollars and Swedish dollars. Prices were in marks and öre. The rate of exchange was 13 marks for 1 riksdollar at 78 groschen. The Riga dollar was 27 öre, the Swedish dollar 32 öre. In 1626 the cash account was in Riga dollars and Swedish dollars, prices in marks, öre, and riksdollars. One riksdollar was 15 marks or 90 groschen. In 1627 the cash account was written in Swedish dollars. The rate of exchange was that of 1626. In 1629 (for 1628 the account is missing) the cash account was written in Swedish copper dollars but in some cases also in Riga marks. Prices were in copper currency, but for flax, hemp, and hops, in riksdollars. One Swedish dollar was 108 öre. One riksdollar was taken to be equivalent of 3.375 copper dollars. In some cases the riksdollar in the accounts had been valued differently.

For the most important commodities prices were obtainable from the Oxenstierna records of sales. That different prices were recorded for the same commodity did not matter because, for our calculation, prices are weighted with quantities. Some difficulties were experienced when products of the same kind were not only sold but also bought. If bought from merchants, they were usually products of higher quality, for instance, grain for seed to improve the strain, higher quality live-stock, and similar cases. If products were purchased from peasants, as a rule they were paid lower prices. Because the quantities purchased in comparison with sales were small, these products have been calculated at the sales prices and the difference reflects itself in the gains and losses item.

For some products there were either no prices available in the account for the year in question or there were no prices in the entire series of accounts. The missing prices had to be estimated on the basis of similarity in the relative price movements. For instance, for some years prices of peas were missing. Because prices of peas roughly equalled prices of rye, the latter prices were taken also for peas. Similarly prices for malt and hops were estimated on the basis of price movements for ale. The possible error of these estimates is not very large because these products did not play a significant role.

Of greater importance are gaps resulting from the fact that in some cases data were missing about the number of horses, oxen, and pigs. These gaps could not be filled. On the other hand, it was possible to estimate missing data about woven linen cloth representing a considerable value. There were no data for the years 1636, 1641, 1644, and 1654. For the year 1654 missing data about linen cloth could be supplemented without difficulties. For years with data it was established that a significant correlation existed between the quantity of spun flax and the quantity of woven linen cloth. The regression was as follows:

$$\log(\text{flax in stones}) = 0.77138 \log(\text{linen cloth in ells}) + 1.78363.$$

The calculated quantity of linen cloth was divided into low quality and superior quality cloth in proportion to the quality recorded for the previous years. Because usually the bulk of linen cloth was sent to the Chancellor's household in Sweden, it was assumed that, for the years where the quantities had to be calculated, the entire production was sent to Sweden. Missing data for tow were calculated in a similar way.

There is one peculiarity of the accounts, dictated by the technique of accounting in the Oxenstierna's estates. All items were accounted for in gross and the net item was entered on the opposite side of the ledger. For instance, peasants' customary dues were shown as what ought to have been paid and on the other side of the ledger—what had been actually received. In our summary this has been preserved because the difference shows the amounts of the debts of the peasants.

EXPLANATION OF THE ACCOUNTS

In the cash account the first item—balance—on the debit side shows the balance in hand at the beginning of the year, on the credit side—at the end of the year. Sales is selfexplanatory. Peasants' customary dues: debit—their obligation to pay cash, credit—actually paid amounts. Transfer: debit—received amounts, credit—paid amounts. From which account received and to which paid is shown on the adjoining accounts on the opposite side as required by double-entry book-keeping. Remunerations: the actually paid amount is credit minus debit. Debit and credit of the cash account balance in the totals. Where a discrepancy arose which could not be explained, the opening balance of the cash account of the following year is different from the closing balance of the previous year.

The second account (Produce) in conditions of a predominantly natural economy is the dominating one if calculated in money terms. Balance on the debit side is the amount in storage at the beginning of the year, on the credit side is the amount in storage at the closing of the year. While the closing balance of the cash account save for discrepancies must equal the opening balance of the next year, this is not the case with the produce account. The produce of each balance is valued at prices of the corresponding year and the differences of closing and opening balances show the changes in prices. The item Sales shows purchases (in debit) and sales (in credit) from the granary. The amounts do not necessary correspond to the amounts in the cash account because there have been also purchases and sales directly from the individual manors and not only from the central granary. Received customary dues are in the debit but on the credit side are entered either debts or cancelled deliveries. Transfers: debit–purchases, credit–deliveries, payments, and deliveries to the Crown (taxes, upkeep of the garrison) and to the possessor's account, usually to the household of the Chancellor in Sweden. Demesne–see next account. Remuneration: payments in kind to the officials of the manors and the central management. Produce refined: on the credit side–malt, hops, flax, etc., on the debit side–ale, linen cloth, and other finished products. Neither the cash account nor the produce account is balanced by gains and losses, only by transferring to the next year at prices of the current year.

The account labelled Manors shows transaction of the individual manors. Direct sales are recorded in the credit but corrections are inserted in the debit. Transfers are shown in the debit and credit. Demesne: seed for the manorial fields is entered on the debit side, harvested crop plus the natural increase of animals–on the credit side. The balancing item is gains and losses–gains in the debit, losses in the credit.

Peasants account. Customary dues are the sum of dues in cash and in kind entered on the credit side. Debts are on the debit side. The gains from this account are in the debit as balancing item.

The Crown's account sums up in the debit payments in cash and in kind: taxes and amounts spent on the garrison. Counterbalancing items are on the credit side. The balance is in gains and losses on the credit side.

Possessor's account shows on the debit side appropriations in cash and in kind, on the credit side–counterbalancing items. The net revenue drawn by the possessor is in gains and losses on the credit side. Balance account sums up the balances of the cash account and the produce account and balances the differences between opening and closing balances in gains and losses.

	CASH		PRODUCE		MANORS	
1624	Dr	Cr	Dr	Cr	Dr	Cr
Balance	–	–	327	2252	–	–
Sales	2141	–	–	2118	–	23
Customary dues	338	–	6934	23	–	–
Transfer	–	2264	321	4512	378	–
Demesne	–	–	4171	2335	2335	4171
Remuneration	–	215	–	1280	1495	–
Produce refined	–	–	2410	1643	1643	2410
Gains & losses	–	–	–	–	753	–
Totals	2479	2479	14163	14163	6604	6604
1625	Dr	Cr	Dr	Cr	Dr	Cr
Balance	–	114	2180	2508	–	–
Sales	6564	–	–	6227	–	337
Customary dues	576	–	8671	822	–	–
Transfer	–	6552	1600	5192	1195	–
Demesne	–	–	6959	2363	2363	6959
Remuneration	–	474	–	2171	2645	–
Produce refined	–	–	2630	2757	2757	2630
Gains & losses	–	–	–	–	966	–
Totals	7140	7140	22040	22040	9926	9926
1626	Dr	Cr	Dr	Cr	Dr	Cr
Balance	99	1268	2346	2663	–	–
Sales	4199	–	–	4045	–	154
Customary dues	2037	5	9655	600	–	–
Transfer	2845	7488	–	4762	725	–
Demesne	–	–	2409	701	701	2409
Remuneration	–	419	–	1425	1844	–
Produce refined	–	–	2074	2288	2288	2074
Gains & losses	–	–	–	–	–	921
Totals	9180	9180	16484	16484	5558	5558

PEASANTS		THE CROWN		POSSESSOR		BALANCE	
Dr	Cr	Dr	Cr	Dr	Cr	Dr	Cr
–	–	–	–	–	–	2252	327
–	–	–	–	–	–	–	–
23	7272	–	–	–	–	–	–
–	–	3850	-	2542	315	–	–
–	–	–	–	–	–	–	–
–	–	–	–	–	–	–	–
–	–	–	–	–	–	–	–
7249	–	–	3850	–	2227	–	1925
7272	7272	3850	3850	2542	2542	2252	2252
Dr	Cr	Dr	Cr	Dr	Cr	Dr	Cr
–	–	–	–	–	–	2622	2180
–	–	–	–	–	–	–	–
822	9247	–	–	–	–	–	–
25	–	6357	1444	4011	–	–	–
–	–	–	–	–	–	–	–
–	–	–	–	–	–	–	–
–	–	–	–	–	–	–	–
8400	–	–	4913	–	4011	–	442
9247	9247	6357	6357	4011	4011	2622	2622
Dr	Cr	Dr	Cr	Dr	Cr	Dr	Cr
–	–	–	–	–	–	3931	2445
–	–	–	–	–	–	–	–
605	11692	–	–	–	–	–	–
–	–	5969	–	5556	2845	–	–
–	–	–	–	–	–	–	–
–	–	–	–	–	–	–	–
–	–	–	–	–	–	–	–
11087	–	–	5969	–	2711	–	1486
11692	11692	5969	5969	5556	5556	3931	3931

	CASH		PRODUCE		MANORS	
1629	Dr	Cr	Dr	Cr	Dr	Cr
Balance	–	343	1058	252	–	–
Sales	6819	–	–	6814	–	5
Customary dues	2048	580	12155	2719	–	–
Transfer	150	7772	–	3587	1005	150
Demesne	–	–	1795	811	811	1795
Remuneration	–	322	–	1181	1503	–
Produce refined	–	–	1195	839	839	1195
Gains & losses	–	–	–	–	–	1013
Totals	9017	9017	16203	16203	4158	4158
1630	Dr	Cr	Dr	Cr	Dr	Cr
Balance	343	49	305	993	–	–
Sales	6660	–	–	6634	–	26
Customary dues	1558	288	14302	4521	–	–
Transfer	2154	9779	818	5783	1149	5
Demesne	–	–	4301	1530	1530	4301
Remuneration	–	599	–	685	1284	–
Produce refined	–	–	704	284	284	704
Gains & losses	–	–	–	–	789	–
Totals	10715	10715	20430	20430	5036	5036
1631	Dr	Cr	Dr	Cr	Dr	Cr
Balance	49	154	981	1280	–	–
Sales	2872	195	195	2872	–	–
Customary dues	1542	326	12309	3247	–	–
Transfer	699	3974	–	6310	810	159
Demesne	–	–	2336	1475	1475	2336
Remuneration	–	513	–	1048	1561	–
Produce refined	–	–	694	283	283	694
Gains & losses	–	–	–	–	–	940
Totals	5162	5162	16515	16515	4129	4129

PEASANTS		THE CROWN		POSSESSOR		BALANCE	
Dr	Cr	Dr	Cr	Dr	Cr	Dr	Cr
–	–	–	–	–	–	595	1058
–	–	–	–	–	–	–	–
3299	14203	–	–	–	–	–	–
–	–	2356	–	7998	–	–	–
–	–	–	–	–	–	–	–
–	–	–	–	–	–	–	–
–	–	–	–	–	–	–	–
10904	–	–	2356	–	7998	463	–
14203	14203	2356	2356	7998	7998	1058	1058
Dr	Cr	Dr	Cr	Dr	Cr	Dr	Cr
–	–	–	–	–	–	1042	648
–	–	–	–	–	–	–	–
4809	15860	–	–	–	–	–	–
–	–	6344	–	8069	2967	–	–
–	–	–	–	–	–	–	–
–	–	–	–	–	–	–	–
–	–	–	–	–	–	–	–
11051	–	–	6344	–	5102	–	394
15860	15860	6344	6344	8069	8069	1042	1042
Dr	Cr	Dr	Cr	Dr	Cr	Dr	Cr
–	–	–	–	–	–	1434	1030
–	–	–	–	–	–	–	–
3573	13851	–	–	–	–	–	–
–	–	4082	196	5396	344	–	–
–	–	–	–	–	–	–	–
–	–	–	–	–	–	–	–
–	–	–	–	–	–	–	–
10278	–	–	3886	–	5052	–	404
13851	13851	4082	4082	5396	5396	1434	1434

	CASH		PRODUCE		MANORS	
1632	Dr	Cr	Dr	Cr	Dr	Cr
Balance	154	14	1133	1425	–	–
Sales	7834	3	3	7834	–	–
Customary dues	2083	701	12405	3712	–	–
Transfer	654	9394	–	2916	983	198
Demesne	–	–	4574	1165	1165	4574
Remuneration	–	613	192	1300	1913	192
Produce refined	–	–	237	192	192	237
Gains & losses	–	–	–	–	948	–
Totals	10725	10725	18544	18544	5201	5201
1633	Dr	Cr	Dr	Cr	Dr	Cr
Balance	14	285	1362	1198	–	–
Sales	8144	–	–	7890	–	254
Customary dues	2964	819	12964	4890	–	–
Transfer	894	10165	18	2528	1856	447
Demesne	–	–	4616	1553	1553	4616
Remuneration	–	747	559	1879	2626	559
Produce refined	–	–	564	145	145	564
Gains & losses	–	–	–	–	260	–
Totals	12016	12016	20083	20083	6440	6440
1634	Dr	Cr	Dr	Cr	Dr	Cr
Balance	424	5064	1444	2186	–	–
Sales	11400	1313	–	11017	1313	383
Customary dues	2241	641	16726	2305	–	–
Transfer	271	6754	–	5459	2787	–
Demesne	–	–	5977	1914	1914	5977
Remuneration	828	1392	822	2568	3960	1650
Produce refined	–	–	734	254	254	734
Gains & losses	–	–	–	–	–	1484
Totals	15164	15164	25703	25703	10228	10228

PEASANTS		THE CROWN		POSSESSOR		BALANCE	
Dr	Cr	Dr	Cr	Dr	Cr	Dr	Cr
–	–	–	–	–	–	1439	1287
–	–	–	–	–	–	–	–
4413	14488	–	–	–	–	–	–
–	–	3166	–	8161	456	–	–
–	–	–	–	–	–	–	–
–	–	–	–	–	–	–	–
–	–	–	–	–	–	–	–
10075	–	–	3166	–	7705	–	152
14488	14488	3166	3166	8161	8161	1439	1439
Dr	Cr	Dr	Cr	Dr	Cr	Dr	Cr
–	–	–	–	–	–	1483	1376
–	–	–	–	–	–	–	–
5709	15928	–	–	–	–	–	–
–	–	2736	–	8101	465	–	–
–	–	–	–	–	–	–	–
–	–	–	–	–	–	–	–
–	–	–	–	–	–	–	–
10219	–	–	2736	–	7636	–	107
15928	15928	2736	2736	8101	8101	1483	1483
Dr	Cr	Dr	Cr	Dr	Cr	Dr	Cr
–	–	–	–	–	–	7250	1868
–	–	–	–	–	–	–	–
2946	18967	–	–	–	–	–	–
–	–	425	271	11788	2787	–	–
–	–	–	–	–	–	–	–
–	–	–	–	–	–	–	–
–	–	–	–	–	–	–	–
16021	–	–	154	–	9001	–	5382
18967	18967	425	425	11788	11788	7250	7250

	CASH		PRODUCE		MANORS	
1635	Dr	Cr	Dr	Cr	Dr	Cr
Balance	5064	1830	2524	3373	–	–
Sales	8949	143	143	8885	–	64
Customary dues	3843	1328	28839	8961	–	–
Transfer	1035	15155	–	14063	1789	705
Demesne	–	–	8659	3549	3549	8659
Remuneration	–	435	1551	3401	3836	1551
Produce refined	–	–	689	173	173	689
Gains & losses	–	–	–	–	2321	–
Totals	18891	18891	42405	42405	11668	11668

	CASH		PRODUCE		MANORS	
1636	Dr	Cr	Dr	Cr	Dr	Cr
Balance	1830	148	2690	2432	–	–
Sales	10128	101	101	10128	–	–
Customary dues	2810	932	15488	4842	–	–
Transfer	2776	13692	249	3391	–	1896
Demesne	–	–	4903	2086	2086	4903
Remuneration	–	2671	532	1520	4191	532
Produce refined	–	–	684	248	248	684
Gains & losses	–	–	–	–	1490	–
Totals	17544	17544	24647	24647	8015	8015

	CASH		PRODUCE		MANORS	
1637	Dr	Cr	Dr	Cr	Dr	Cr
Balance	148	–	2613	2547	–	–
Sales	757	344	344	691	–	66
Customary dues	2682	102	15136	1139	–	–
Transfer	10	2803	465	16645	475	270
Demesne	–	–	8355	2517	2517	8355
Remuneration	–	348	–	4051	4399	–
Produce refined	–	–	858	181	181	858
Gains & losses	–	–	–	–	1977	–
Totals	3597	3597	27771	27771	9549	9549

PEASANTS		THE CROWN		POSSESSOR		BALANCE	
Dr	Cr	Dr	Cr	Dr	Cr	Dr	Cr
–	–	–	–	–	–	5203	7588
–	–	–	–	–	–	–	–
10289	32682	–	–	–	–	–	–
–	–	8352	330	19077	–	–	–
–	–	–	–	–	–	–	–
–	–	–	–	–	–	–	–
–	–	–	–	–	–	–	–
22393	–	–	8022	–	19077	2385	–
32682	32682	8352	8352	19077	19077	7588	7588

Dr	Cr	Dr	Cr	Dr	Cr	Dr	Cr
–	–	–	–	–	–	2580	4520
–	–	–	–	–	–	–	–
5774	18298	–	–	–	–	–	–
–	–	2530	–	14509	1085	–	–
–	–	–	–	–	–	–	–
–	–	–	–	–	–	–	–
–	–	–	–	–	–	–	–
12524	–	–	2530	–	13424	1940	–
18298	18298	2530	2530	14509	14509	4520	4520

Dr	Cr	Dr	Cr	Dr	Cr	Dr	Cr
–	–	–	–	–	–	2547	2761
–	–	–	–	–	–	–	–
1241	17818	–	–	–	–	–	–
–	–	1961	–	17012	205	–	–
–	–	–	–	–	–	–	–
–	–	–	–	–	–	–	–
–	–	–	–	–	–	–	–
16577	–	–	1961	–	16807	214	–
17818	17818	1961	1961	17012	17012	2761	2761

	CASH		PRODUCE		MANORS	
1639	Dr	Cr	Dr	Cr	Dr	Cr
Balance	5371	26	4368	3536	–	–
Sales	12199	62	62	12199	–	–
Customary dues	4600	435	12483	1711	–	–
Transfer	1208	21214	600	4209	12	763
Demesne	–	–	6780	1795	1795	6780
Remuneration	–	1641	–	1695	3336	–
Produce refined	–	–	1070	218	218	1070
Gains & losses	–	–	–	–	3252	–
Totals	23378	23378	25363	25363	8613	8613

	CASH		PRODUCE		MANORS	
1640	Dr	Cr	Dr	Cr	Dr	Cr
Balance	26	164	3438	3735	–	–
Sales	12848	53	53	12519	–	329
Customary dues	4356	613	11702	2084	–	–
Transfer	561	14973	490	2208	–	–
Demesne	–	–	7519	2028	2028	7519
Remuneration	–	1988	103	1699	3687	103
Produce refined	–	–	1827	859	859	1827
Gains & losses	–	–	–	–	3204	–
Totals	17791	17791	25132	25132	9778	9778

	CASH		PRODUCE		MANORS	
1641	Dr	Cr	Dr	Cr	Dr	Cr
Balance	164	3001	4112	4614	–	–
Sales	10330	107	107	10306	–	24
Customary dues	4044	1335	14848	6768	–	–
Transfer	1273	9485	156	2136	10	383
Demesne	–	–	7314	1787	1787	7314
Remuneration	–	1883	92	1903	3786	92
Produce refined	–	–	1914	1029	1029	1914
Gains & losses	–	–	–	–	3115	–
Totals	15811	15811	28543	28543	9727	9727

PEASANTS		THE CROWN		POSSESSOR		BALANCE	
Dr	Cr	Dr	Cr	Dr	Cr	Dr	Cr
–	–	–	–	–	–	3562	9739
–	–	–	–	–	–	–	–
2146	17083	–	–	–	–	–	–
–	–	3230	–	22181	1045	–	–
–	–	–	–	–	–	–	–
–	–	–	–	–	–	–	–
–	–	–	–	–	–	–	–
14937	–	–	3230	–	21136	6177	–
17083	17083	3230	3230	22181	22181	9739	9739

Dr	Cr	Dr	Cr	Dr	Cr	Dr	Cr
–	–	–	–	–	–	3899	3464
–	–	–	–	–	–	–	–
2697	16058	–	–	–	–	–	–
–	–	550	–	16631	1051	–	–
–	–	–	–	–	–	–	–
–	–	–	–	–	–	–	–
–	–	–	–	–	–	–	–
13361	–	–	550	–	15580	–	435
16058	16058	550	550	16631	16631	3899	3899

Dr	Cr	Dr	Cr	Dr	Cr	Dr	Cr
–	–	–	–	–	–	7615	4276
–	–	–	–	–	–	–	–
8103	18892	–	–	–	–	–	–
–	–	3691	–	7920	1046	–	–
–	–	–	–	–	–	–	–
–	–	–	–	–	–	–	–
–	–	–	–	–	–	–	–
10789	–	–	3691	–	6874	–	3339
18892	18892	3691	3691	7920	7920	7615	7615

1642	CASH Dr	CASH Cr	PRODUCE Dr	PRODUCE Cr	MANORS Dr	MANORS Cr
Balance	3001	1279	4870	5115	–	–
Sales	14446	–	–	13238	–	1208
Customary dues	4735	2484	23474	11593	–	–
Transfer	–	15908	461	3061	18	–
Demesne	–	–	7170	1944	1944	7170
Remuneration	–	2511	25	2209	4720	25
Produce refined	–	–	2220	1060	1060	2220
Gains & losses	–	–	–	–	2881	–
Totals	22182	22182	38220	38220	10623	10623

1643	CASH Dr	CASH Cr	PRODUCE Dr	PRODUCE Cr	MANORS Dr	MANORS Cr
Balance	1280	5034	4771	6009	–	–
Sales	13359	102	102	12836	–	523
Customary dues	5512	2154	22988	11568	–	–
Transfer	3065	15926	123	3112	2596	–
Demesne	–	–	9203	1893	1893	9203
Remuneration	–	–	–	2666	2666	–
Produce refined	–	–	1643	746	746	1643
Gains & losses	–	–	–	–	3468	–
Totals	23216	23216	38830	38830	11369	11369

1644	CASH Dr	CASH Cr	PRODUCE Dr	PRODUCE Cr	MANORS Dr	MANORS Cr
Balance	5034	4287	6168	5824	–	–
Sales	14298	65	65	13950	–	348
Customary dues	5641	2148	23952	11795	–	–
Transfer	605	16197	471	3384	–	212
Demesne	–	–	7682	2099	2099	7682
Remuneration	–	2881	–	2112	4993	–
Produce refined	–	–	1608	782	782	1608
Gains & losses	–	–	–	–	1976	–
Totals	25578	25578	39946	39946	9850	9850

PEASANTS		THE CROWN		POSSESSOR		BALANCE	
Dr	Cr	Dr	Cr	Dr	Cr	Dr	Cr
–	–	–	–	–	–	6394	7871
–	–	–	–	–	–	–	–
14077	28209	–	–	–	–	–	–
–	–	748	–	17892	150	–	–
–	–	–	–	–	–	–	–
–	–	–	–	–	–	–	–
–	–	–	–	–	–	–	–
14132	–	–	748	–	17742	1477	–
28209	28209	748	748	17892	17892	7871	7871
Dr	Cr	Dr	Cr	Dr	Cr	Dr	Cr
–	–	–	–	–	–	11043	6051
–	–	–	–	–	–	–	–
13722	28500	–	–	–	–	–	–
–	–	1344	65	15098	3123	–	–
–	–	–	–	–	–	–	–
–	–	–	–	–	–	–	–
–	–	–	–	–	–	–	–
14778	–	–	1279	–	11975	–	4992
28500	28500	1344	1344	15098	15098	11043	11043
Dr	Cr	Dr	Cr	Dr	Cr	Dr	Cr
–	–	–	–	–	–	10111	11202
–	–	–	–	–	–	–	–
13943	29593	–	–	–	–	–	–
–	–	1147	–	18434	864	–	–
–	–	–	–	–	–	–	–
–	–	–	–	–	–	–	–
–	–	–	–	–	–	–	–
15650	–	–	1147	–	17570	1091	–
29593	29593	1147	1147	18434	18434	11202	11202

	CASH		PRODUCE		MANORS	
1645	Dr	Cr	Dr	Cr	Dr	Cr
Balance	4287	3990	5718	5969	–	–
Sales	4108	87	87	3781	–	327
Customary dues	4701	290	14034	1799	–	–
Transfer	522	6654	652	14157	–	–
Demesne	–	–	8732	1913	1913	8732
Remuneration	–	2597	–	2433	5030	–
Produce refined	–	–	1744	915	915	1744
Gains & losses	–	–	–	–	2945	–
Totals	13618	13618	30967	30967	10803	10803
1646	Dr	Cr	Dr	Cr	Dr	Cr
Balance	1405	751	6276	5413	–	–
Sales	12242	136	136	11949	–	293
Customary dues	4767	204	11622	1650	–	–
Transfer	–	14473	–	3229	382	–
Demesne	–	–	7316	1997	1997	7316
Remuneration	–	2850	–	2325	5175	–
Produce refined	–	–	2256	1043	1043	2256
Gains & losses	–	–	–	–	1268	–
Totals	18414	18414	27606	27606	9865	9865
1647	Dr	Cr	Dr	Cr	Dr	Cr
Balance	751	1607	4444	4342	–	–
Sales	9842	65	65	9611	–	231
Customary dues	5538	1951	14337	4586	–	–
Transfer	4053	13738	1337	3969	–	–
Demesne	–	–	7119	3081	3081	7119
Remuneration	–	2823	9	2872	5695	9
Produce refined	–	–	2330	1180	1180	2330
Gains & losses	-	–	–	–	–	267
Totals	20184	20184	29641	29641	9956	9956

PEASANTS		THE CROWN		POSSESSOR		BALANCE	
Dr	Cr	Dr	Cr	Dr	Cr	Dr	Cr
–	–	–	–	–	–	9959	10005
–	–	–	–	–	–	–	–
2089	18735	–	–	–	–	–	–
–	–	5145	–	15666	1174	–	–
–	–	–	–	–	–	–	–
–	–	–	–	–	–	–	–
–	–	–	–	–	–	–	–
16646	–	–	5145	–	14492	46	–
18735	18735	5145	5145	15666	15666	10005	10005
Dr	Cr	Dr	Cr	Dr	Cr	Dr	Cr
–	–	–	–	–	–	6164	7681
–	–	–	–	–	–	–	–
1854	16389	–	–	–	–	–	–
–	–	1921	–	15399	–	–	–
–	–	–	–	–	–	–	–
–	–	–	–	–	–	–	–
–	–	–	–	–	–	–	–
14535	–	–	1921	–	15399	1517	–
16389	16389	1921	1921	15399	15399	7681	7681
Dr	Cr	Dr	Cr	Dr	Cr	Dr	Cr
–	–	–	–	–	–	5949	5195
–	–	–	–	–	–	–	–
6537	19875	–	–	–	–	–	–
–	–	2151	–	15556	5390	–	–
–	–	–	–	–	–	–	–
–	–	–	–	–	–	–	–
–	–	–	–	–	–	–	–
13338	–	–	2151	–	10166	–	754
19875	19875	2151	2151	15556	15556	5949	5949

	CASH		PRODUCE		MANORS	
1650	Dr	Cr	Dr	Cr	Dr	Cr
Balance	2993	2485	6234	8283	–	–
Sales	41252	1075	584	40300	491	952
Customary dues	7437	1673	33142	8294	–	–
Transfer	180	44940	1496	6123	–	–
Demesne	–	–	28166	5583	5583	28166
Remuneration	404	2093	–	2719	4812	404
Produce refined	–	–	4678	2998	2998	4678
Gains & losses	–	–	–	–	20316	–
Totals	52266	52266	74300	74300	34200	34200

	CASH		PRODUCE		MANORS	
1652	Dr	Cr	Dr	Cr	Dr	Cr
Balance	1076	3635	7140	9064	–	–
Sales	19636	570	570	18755	–	881
Customary dues	8329	2058	29474	7235	–	–
Transfer	1882	21354	–	21648	908	–
Demesne	–	–	29019	5137	5137	29019
Remuneration	–	3306	–	3878	7184	–
Produce refined	–	–	3310	3796	3796	3310
Gains & losses	–	–	–	–	16185	–
Totals	30923	30923	69513	69513	33210	33210

	CASH		PRODUCE		MANORS	
1653	Dr	Cr	Dr	Cr	Dr	Cr
Balance	3635	7518	6722	7818	–	–
Sales	15615	860	302	11581	860	4336
Customary dues	9376	2915	17881	4919	–	–
Tranfer	1718	17169	618	9315	–	595
Demesne	–	–	12757	2424	2424	12757
Remuneration	1266	3148	–	3628	6776	1266
Produce refined	–	–	3342	1937	1937	3342
Gains & losses	–	–	–	–	10299	–
Totals	31610	31610	41622	41622	22296	22296

PEASANTS		THE CROWN		POSSESSOR		BALANCE	
Dr	Cr	Dr	Cr	Dr	Cr	Dr	Cr
–	–	–	–	–	–	10778	9227
–	–	–	–	–	–	–	–
9967	40579	–	–	–	–	–	–
–	–	2331	–	48732	1676	–	–
–	–	–	–	–	–	–	–
–	–	–	–	–	–	–	–
–	–	–	–	–	–	–	–
30612	–	–	2331	–	47056	–	1541
40579	40579	2331	2331	48732	48732	10768	10768

Dr	Cr	Dr	Cr	Dr	Cr	Dr	Cr
–	–	–	–	–	–	12699	8216
–	–	–	–	–	–	–	–
9293	37803	–	–	–	–	–	–
–	–	5010	–	37084	1882	–	–
–	–	–	–	–	–	–	–
–	–	–	–	–	–	–	–
–	–	–	–	–	–	–	–
28510	–	–	5010	–	35202	–	4483
37803	37803	5010	5010	37084	37084	12699	12699

Dr	Cr	Dr	Cr	Dr	Cr	Dr	Cr
–	–	–	–	–	–	15336	10357
–	–	–	–	–	–	–	–
7834	27257	–	–	–	–	–	–
–	–	1302	–	25182	1741	–	–
–	–	–	–	–	–	–	–
–	–	–	–	–	–	–	–
–	–	–	–	–	–	–	–
19423	–	–	1302	–	23441	–	4979
27257	27257	1302	1302	25182	25182	15336	15336

1654	CASH Dr	CASH Cr	PRODUCE Dr	PRODUCE Cr	MANORS Dr	MANORS Cr
Balance	7518	1835	6781	6061	–	–
Sales	16268	542	196	15707	542	757
Customary dues	8664	949	17548	4532	–	–
Transfer	20969	47073	6	4977	–	18421
Demesne	–	–	12118	2413	2413	12118
Remuneration	719	3739	–	4805	8544	719
Produce refined	–	–	4047	2201	2201	4047
Gains & losses	–	–	–	–	22362	–
Totals	54138	54138	40696	40696	36062	36062

SIGNIFICANCE OF THE PEASANTRY IN THE ECONOMY

A cursory glance at the results of the accounts shows that from the two sources of revenue–the manors and the peasants–the most important were the peasants. If we consider that the peasants were the nearly exclusive workers on the manors and at that worked free of charge, the division of the revenue into these two sources seems to be superflous because everything can be attributed to peasants. On the other hand, the economy of the manors was directed by the manorial officials, while the economy of the peasant farms was exclusively managed by the peasants themselves. The management of the Oxenstierna estates did not directly interfere with the economy of the peasant households except by establishing new demesne, when in some cases peasant farms were appropriated and expelled peasants were forced to cultivate new farms in the wilderness. Indirectly the manor influenced the peasant economy by the demands of statute labour, which forced the peasants to keep an excessive number of horses and more farmhands than needed to manage the farms; these had to be supported from the produce of the peasant farms. On the other hand, the demand to pay customary dues did not much, if at all, influence cultivation of crops and breeding of animals because the demand of the manor adopted itself to what was available–debts were cancelled and substitutions accepted.

To compare the revenue of the Oxenstierna estates from its manors and the peasantry–if the revenue from the manors is taken as 100, the revenue from the peasants was 389. This refers to the whole period from 1624 to 1654. The relationship changed considerably over time. During the six years from

PEASANTS		THE CROWN		POSSESSOR		BALANCE	
Dr	Cr	Dr	Cr	Dr	Cr	Dr	Cr
–	–	–	–	–	–	7896	14299
–	–	–	–	–	–	–	–
5481	26212	–	–	–	–	–	–
–	–	7715	–	44335	2554	–	–
–	–	–	–	–	–	–	–
–	–	–	–	–	–	–	–
–	–	–	–	–	–	–	–
20731	–	–	7715	–	41781	6403	–
26212	26212	7715	7715	44335	44335	14299	14299

1624 to 1631 when Munck was the steward, three years were bad years occasioned by poor and bad crops (1625/1626, 1629/1630, 1631/1632) and consequently the manorial general account shows losses for these years. As a result, on balance for the period 1624 to 1631 manors show losses and income came exclusively from the peasants' account. During the following period of eleven years, with the steward Ledebohrn at the helm there was only one year with losses on the manorial account (1634). Despite three poor years (1636, 1639, 1642) the manorial account gave a gain to total revenue. If the manorial gain is put at 100, the peasants contributed 726. During the two subsequent years of Rautenstein's stewardship the proportion declined and was 100 to 656. During Reimers' two years the second (1646/1647) was a year of bad crops and therefore the manors suffered losses, with the result that the peasants gave 2785 as against 100 from the manors. Jakob Behr was steward from 1649 to 1652, but only for the two years 1650 and 1652 records are extant. During his and the following Sprengport's period there was an unprecedented increase in total revenue and the manors improved more than the peasants. The two years of Behr's management show 162 for the peasants account as against 100 for the manorial account. During Sprengport's regime the proportion was 123 as to 100.

MONEY ECONOMY AND NATURAL ECONOMY

Another important question is about the relationship of money economy to natural economy. If the totals of the cash account are regarded as representing money economy and the totals of the produce account representing natural economy, the relationship was 100: 165 in favour of natural economy. During the six subsequent periods under the six stewards the situation was as follows. Under Munck the relationship was 100: 242, Ledebohrn's period 100: 175, Rautenstein's period 100: 181, Reimers' period 100: 182, Behr's period 100: 173, but during Sprengport's period in the second year money economy overtook natural economy and for both years the average was 100: 90 in favour of money economy. There had occurred a structural change in the economy.

It is evident that, as far as the manorial economy goes, the development shows a growing trend in favour of money economy. It seems that the same tendency was developing as to the peasant economy. This is evident from a report by the steward Behr to Count Erik (RA, TA 269, 10 September 1650). He wrote that he had ordered ordinances to be published in all churches of the bishopric against regrating of live-stock or other commodities by the merchants of Riga. As a penalty the steward intended to confiscate the cash received by the peasants and had regrets that the relevant information could be received only after a lapse of time. The steward informed Count Erik about this measure he had taken because he expected complaints by the peasants to the Chancellor.

YIELD RATIOS

In the previous discussion, poor and bad years of crops were mentioned. These can only with difficulties be gauged from the tables presented because in the item Demesne, in the credit, to the value of the crop is also added the natural increase of live-stock and the comparison with the value of seed in the debit does not represent the yield. Therefore this is singled out for a separate discussion.

Slicher van Bath has drawn attention to the significance of calculations of yield ratios to evaluate the crop (Slicher van Bath 1963). Yield ratio describes the proportion of seed to yield. To calculate the yield ratios for the Oxenstierna estates the harvest recorded for a certain year was divided by the seed of the previous year. This had to be done even for rye which is harvested before the summer crop, because threshing proceeded after the closing of accounts in mid year and continued even during the following winter. Thus the yield was known only the following economic year.

Our graph shows the yield ratios for rye and barley on the Chancellor's Livonian estates. For both crops there is a discernible growing trend of the period. The trend has been calculated by iterating trend values for the missing years. The trend line (regression) obtained for rye was $Y = 2.670 + 0.046\ X$. The trend value for the year 1624 is 2.72 and for the year 1653 it is 4.06. The standard error of estimate is 0.9. Slicher van Bath regards as normal crops 85 %

YIELD OF RYE 1624–1654

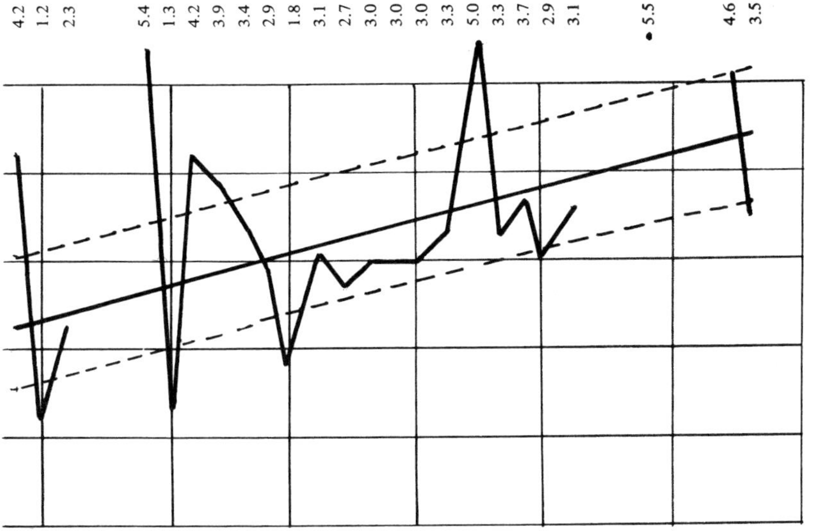

YIELD OF BARLEY 1624–1654

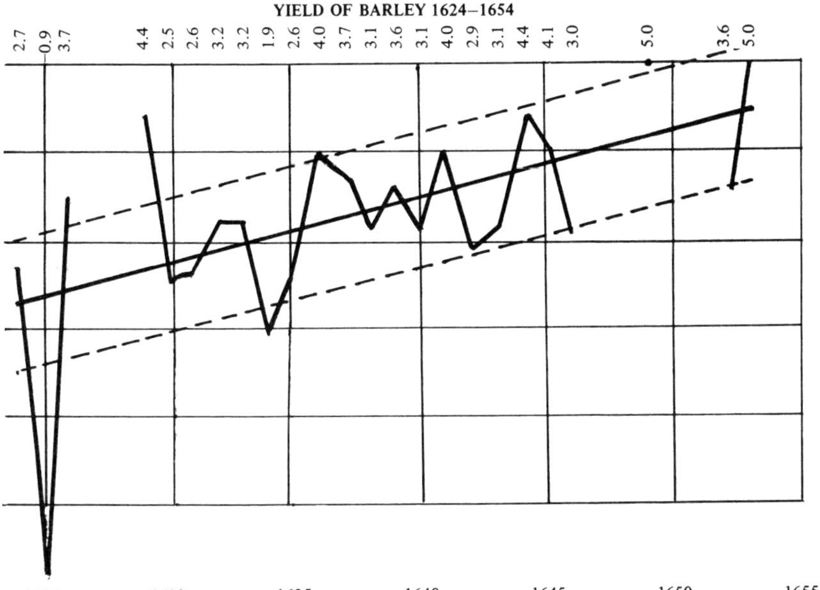

to 115 % from the average, i.e. ± 15 %. In our case it is more meaningful to take, instead of the average, the trend line. In our calculation one standard error of estimate includes his plus minus 15 %. Thus the really bad years were 1625, 1630, and 1635, and poor years were from 1636 to 1640, and 1645. Excellent winter crop years were 1624, 1629, 1642, and 1649.

For barley the trend was Y = 2.670 + 0.046 X. The trend increased from 2.29 in 1624 to 4.44 in 1653. One standard error of estimate was 0.76 which as in the case of rye also covers the plus minus limit of 15 % around the trend. Bad years were 1625, 1634, 1635, and 1642, also 1646. Outstanding years were 1629, 1636, 1641, 1644, 1645, 1649, and 1653.

The question is how to explain the increase in the yield ratio. One explanation could be that the increased yield ratio was only fictitious, not occurring in reality but only because the more efficient management prevented pilfering. The second possibility is that the increase of the trend was really reflecting improvements in field husbandry.

The instructions given to the stewards always stressed the need for more live-stock in order to provide more manure. The same was emphasized in the contemporary literature on agriculture. The constant reminder bore fruits—after Munck's time live-stock started to increase and, despite setbacks because of cattle diseases, continued so until the end of the period. To calculate the increase of manure from live-stock it was arbitrarily assumed that the unit is the quantity of manure from one cow, bull, ox, or steer, and that a calf yields 0.5 and a sheep or pig—0.25. The index of manure (obtained by multiplying these units by the quantity of animals) increased from 134 in the first year of Ledebohrn's stewardship (1632) to 1513 in the final year of our records (1654). The equation of the linear trend is Y = −135.4 + 44.4 X. There were setbacks in the growth of the number of live-stock in the late thirties and in the disastrous year of 1647, but accumulated fertility of the soil cannot be exhausted because of temporary setback. Being able to explain the growth of the trend of the yield by a growing trend of availability of manure is reason to assume that the increase of the yield was real.

If, for the year 1664, we compare the yield of rye with manure units calculated as above on eleven manors (data from RA, TA 311), the correlation coefficient between these two variables works out at r = 0.622, which is significant at P = 0.05. This confirms the validity of the method used.

According to contemporary agricultural literature, the following norms for a satisfactory yield were recommended. Gubert writes that to manure the equivalent of one tonstead (= two leapsteads) 160 loads of dung of one-horse carts were needed. In *Der getreue Amt-Mann* oder Unterricht eines guten Haus-Halters (Riga 1696) it is stated that for the equivalent of 100 tonsteads one hundred head of cattle were needed. The handbook of R.Broocman, *En Fulständig Swensk Hus-Hålds-Bok* I–II (Norrköping 1736, 1739) stated that in Livonia for a tonstead two head of horned cattle were needed. (He describes in detail how manure was provided for in Livonia–see Chapter XX, pp. 191–197.) It is difficult to reconcile these norms. There are also calculations of optimal numbers of cattle needed for the manuring of fields in the records of the bishopric. A submission to the Chancellor of 1642 (RA, Oxenstierna af Södermöre, Ser. D II, 2, printed ED 1935, p. 161) stated that the then available number of live-stock was sufficient only for manuring of 80 to 100 tonsteads.

UNITS OF MANURE OF THE BISHOPRIC

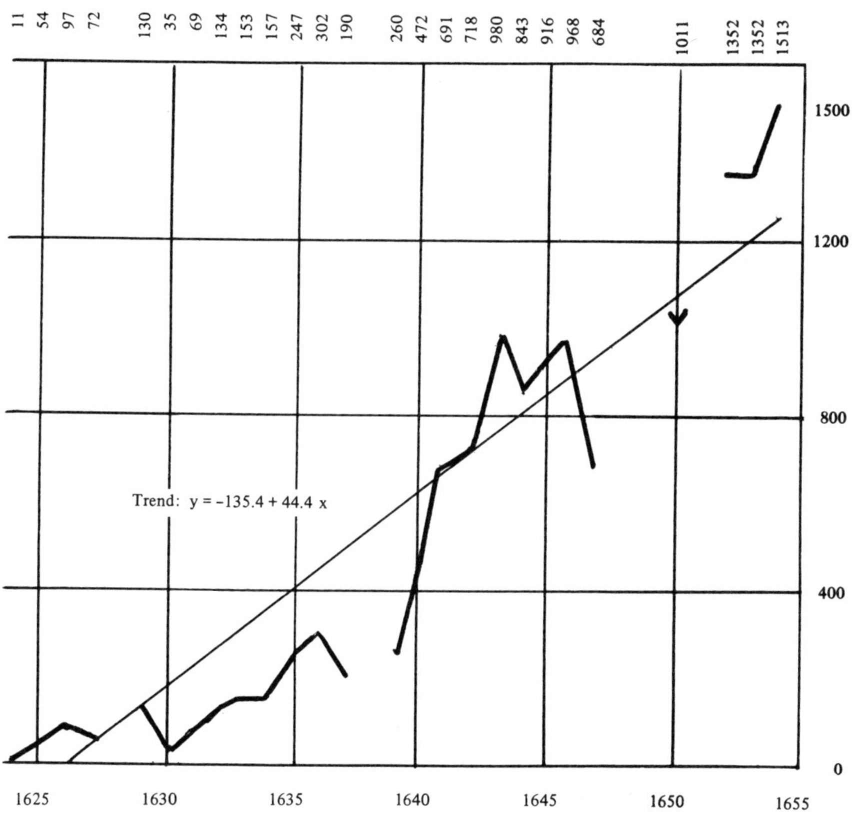

YIELD OF RYE DEPENDENT ON UNITS OF MANURE (1664)

r = 0.622

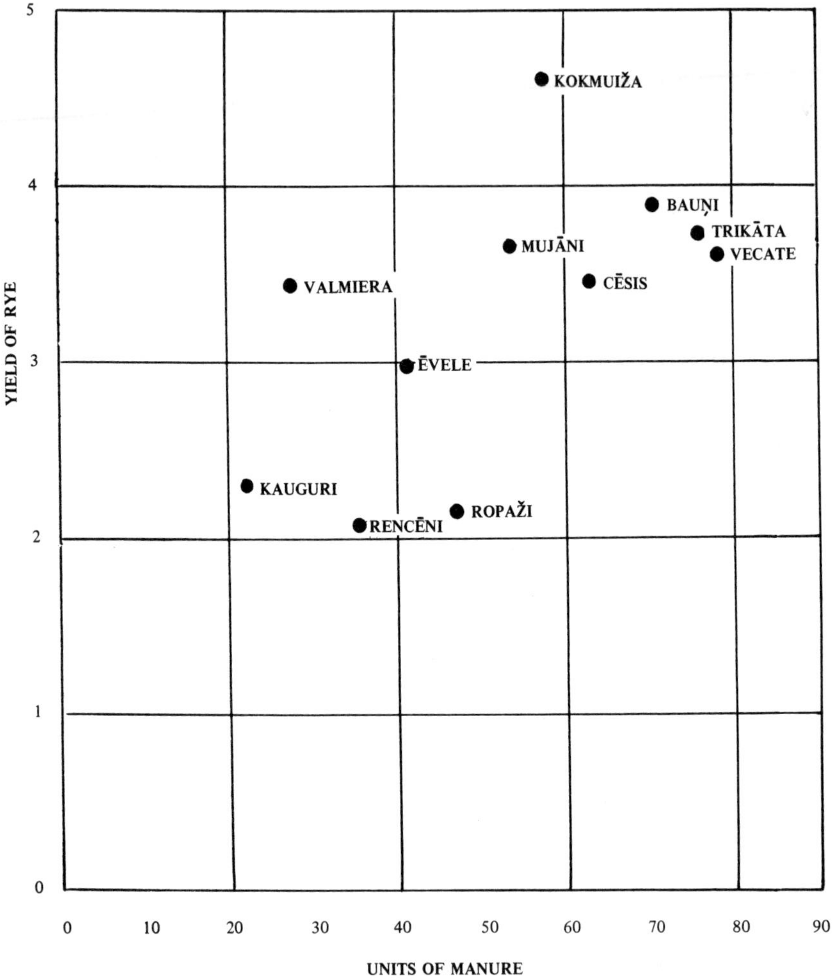

The submission further pointed out that a yield ratio of 6 to 8 was regarded as sufficient. According to our calculation, the number of cow-units in terms of manure in 1642 was 718. For 80 tonsteads this gives 9.0 units manure per tonstead, but for 100 tonsteads–7.2 units. In the year 1654 the area of various crops sown was 2586 tonsteads, but the number of horned cattle at the beginning of the year was 1049 heads. This means 0.4 head of horned cattle per tonstead while the recommendation in contemporary literature was one or two head per tonstead. A calculation with the norms mentioned in 1642 for the bishopric to obtain a yield ratio of 6 to 8, gives even worse figures. In the year 1652 the sown area in the bishopric was in round figures 2600 tonsteads. To achieve a yield ratio of 6 to 8, some 18,700 cow-units of manure would be necessary. Actually there were only 1352 cow-units or 7.2 % of the needed. The actual yield ratio of rye in 1652 was 4.6 which was well above the trend line. The yield ratio of barley was 3.6 and improved to 5.0 in 1653. The average of both years was approximately on the trend line. The management of the Oxenstierna estates had achieved over the years an improvement of the yield ratio, but obviously to achieve the target of the yield ratio of 6 to 8 was impossible with the available live-stock producing manure.

Manure collected in the stables where animals were kept during the long winter was the most important fertilizers of the fields. Of minor significance were the water-meadows. For the peasants, more important was the swidden (see Webster's *Third New International Dictionary* Swidden: 'An impermanent agricultural plot produced by cutting back and burning off vegetative cover [. . .]'). The seventeenth century practice was to cutwood-land trees and shrubs and to remove the taller timber leaving the cut off branches of the trees. Shrubs and the tree branches were collected in regularly arranged heaps and burned. The ashes were then ploughed in and seed sown. In two or three years the soil was exhausted and the swidden abandoned for some twenty years for the growth of shrubs and trees, and then the process was repeated. It is clear that for swidden a great area was needed and also a great amount of man-power. These were the reasons that the manorial economy did not often practise this sort of agriculture while the peasants had a substantial amount of swidden in addition to their permanent fields (infields) which were tilled on the three-field system (winter corn, summer corn, fallow).

In imitation of the method used on the swidden, sometimes the manors also manured the permanent fields by putting cut shrubs on the fields in regular rows, letting them dry, covering the heaps with turf–with some openings left for access of air–and then burning the heaps and finally ploughing in the ashes. Nevertheless, for the manors the main manure of the fields came from live-stock which was mainly kept for this purpose. The amount of live-stock in its turn was limited by want of pastures and by cattle diseases. This was also the experience in the Oxenstierna's estates.

The submission to the Chancellor of 1642 referred to above, was unsigned and can be dated from the context. In 1642 the accountant Jakob Behr travelled to Sweden and was paid 20 riksdollars travelling expenses (ED 1935, p. 400), and it can be assumed that he was the author of the submission. The document was written in Swedish, but it is irrelevant whether or not the Riga-born Behr had mastered the Swedish language, because it could be a translation. That the document was unsigned could point to a translation. The memorandum certainly showed familiarity with local conditions and was the work of an expert.

It started with an exposition about the extent of the manors, mentioning a total of 3120 tonsteads on 16 estates and giving a total of 615 mantal of statute labourers. The possibilities of enlarging the demesne on four estates and establishing a new one were mentioned, which could enlarge the total acreage to 4200 tonsteads. Organized on the Livonian manner (there was no explanation how the Livonian manner differed from general practice) this would mean winter corn, summer corn, and fallow, each 1400 tonsteads. This could be managed with existing man-power.

Then the author was coming to the crux of the matter. Because some of the fields had been annually used for fifty years without manuring, at some places they were not worth while tilling. The yield of those fields was only the second grain and on other fields only seed was recovered. Since the author's arrival at the bishopric some progress had been made in providing live-stock, nevertheless it was sufficient only to manure 80 and at the most 100 tonsteads of land. On the average only the third or fourth grain was obtained instead of the possible sixth to eighth grain.

For a higher yield more live-stock would be necessary, but, as this was not possible to achieve, the author suggested to reduce temporarily the acreage leaving the surplus in fallow. In doing so there would be a surplus of statute labour and this should be used to clear overgrown meadows and pastures. This was the best means of providing feed for live-stock and consequently obtaining more manure. Mentioning Burtnieki, Vecate and Ēvele, as the most suitable estates for clearing meadows and pastures, the author thought that from these estates the whole bishopric in future could be supplied with live-stock.

He then suggested to till only a third of the arable leaving two thirds in fallow. The 1400 tonsteads of land to be tilled should be divided according to the three-field system: a third for winter corn, a third for summer corn, and a third fallow. To these reduced fields the necessary statute labourers would be allocated, the rest used for clearing meadows and pastures, erection and repair of buildings, and the surplus had to be commuted. If put into effect, the reduced winter corn fields would yield 2760 tons at the sixth grain, the summer corn fields would yield 3220 tons at the seventh grain. With increased live-stock, after six years the prospective harvest would be 4600 tons rye at the fifth grain or 5520 tons at the sixth grain and barley 5520 tons at the sixth grain or 6440 tons at the seventh grain. With the old method only 2400 tons of rye and 3200 tons of summer crop could be achieved (converting into modern measures—a ton was 132 to 136 litres; a Swedish ton was 126 litres).

The memorandum concluded that, by adopting the plan outlined, His Excellency, after six years, would have regained initial losses, the fields would be improved, meadows and pastures cleared, more live-stock acquired, and buildings improved. The memorandum closed with a statement that for the year 1642 cash from commutation of week-work had been reduced because of failure of crops.

The plan was aborted and nothing came of it. Obviously the Chancellor was not inclined to reduce his revenue even with a prospect to regain the loss later and to reap the large benefit from the suggested improvements. Instead the Chancellor's policy was gradually to increase the number of live-stock and thus to achieve a higher yield over time and not to suffer losses for six years as suggested by the memorandum. Probably the Chancellor doubted whether after the six years anticipated higher yields would be achieved. Nevertheless, if the author of the memorandum was indeed Jakob Behr, as our guess is, then at his visit in Stockholm he established a firm reputation with the Chancellor and after several years became the first and the only civilian steward appointed by the Chancellor interrupting a succession of military men in this office.

SIDELINES

In addition to the major pursuit of the economy in the bishopric—agriculture—some sidelines were gradually introduced. The most important was spinning and weaving and the Oxenstierna's textile industry has been called an example of industrial production of the pre-capitalistic period (Soom 1954, p. 149). Work was done by skilled statute workers and professional weavers. In the revision of 1638, for instance, at Trikāta a peasant was mentioned who did not do other statute work but only weaving. He held an eighth of an uncus of land from the castle and was weaving in a room at the castle. In 1640 a salaried Latvian weaver was engaged from Riga. He lived at Cēsis and worked for the bishopric. In 1648 at Valmiera a special ten by eighteen fathom house was erected where a school and a weaving manufacture was installed for children of the Finnish colonists and soldiers. In 1651 a total of 33 Finnish boys was registered, ranging from one year to 18 years of age (RA, TA 342).

In 1653 there were 16 children working (RA, Oxenst. saml.). Production by the Finnish children and Latvian peasants increased (ED 1935, pp. 349,351) from 2538 ells (each ell approx. 52 cm) in 1631 to 10,611 ells in 1653, but declined to 10,016 ells the following year. At the beginning coarse fabrics dominated, gradually replaced by finer ones. The bulk of linen and also of the coarse fabrics went to Sweden. In 1653 the Latvian peasants of the bishopric produced 6196 ells of linen and 1521 ells of tow fabric, but the Finnish children with the help of peasants 2754 ells of linen and 140 ells of tow fabric. The expenses in cash were 241 riksdollars paid to weavers, 6 and a half Rd spent on the Finnish boys for shoes, clothing, and milk, and 9 and a half Rd paid to the guardian of the Finnish children and to his wife. For repairs of spinning-wheels was paid 3.51 Rd. Total cash expenditure was 260.51 Rd. The value of the fabrics was 1612.65 Rd. In 1654 the peasants produced 4813 ells of linen and 1640 ells of tow fabric, the Finnish children 2772 ells of linen and 116 of tow fabric, the professional weavers 675 ells of finest linen. Expenses in cash: to the professional weavers 190.83 Rd, on the Finnish children was spent 2.75 Rd, for spinning-wheels was paid 12.23 Rd. Total cash expenses: 205.81 riksdollars. The value of the product was 1502.40 Rd. In both years feeding of the children had not been included in the calculation except expenditure for milk in 1653. There is an estimate extant that feeding and clothing cost 21 Rd 3 groschen per child per annum (RA, TA 342). The profitability of the weaving industry is obvious.

Other industrial enterprises in the bishopric were mills, in the first place corn-mills and secondly saw-mills. For grinding corn customers paid in kind. Part of this payment kept the miller, part was delivered to the granary of the bishopric. The obligation of the miller was also to repair the mill. In 1662 on an inspection tour Jakob Schnack, who was one of the guardians of the minor heirs of the bishopric, found that at Ropaži there was an excellent corn-mill (RA, TA 75, 1660–1663). Because it was near Riga he ordered the milling of all the grain available at Ropaži. The flour was to be sold in Riga before the council of Riga found this out and ordered all grain to be milled in the municipal mills of Riga. He also ordered the establishment of a saw-mill at Ropaži and was convinced that because of high prices of boards this would give a handsome profit. It took the agile mind of a university trained outsider to see opportunities not sensed by the officers of the bishopric engaged in their daily routine.

Burning of quicklime and making of bricks was another industrial enterprise. At the start the burning of quicklime was done by Finnish soldiers. In 1624 a total of only 85 bags was produced. It was used for building works of the bishopric and with expansion of production partly sold. In 1654 a total of 5 loads and 11 barrels of quicklime was sold for 14 Rd 18 groschen. In 1625 a bricklayer was invited from Birži. He trained six soldiers (LR, Del 2, 22, F 8: B). In 1639 for the construction of a brickworks 104 Rd was spent and in the following year 96 Rd. Two soldiers from Valmiera were sent to Jelgava (Mitau) in the Duchy of Kurzeme to learn the craft. They were paid 3 Rd for travelling expenses and the master who taught them also received 3 Rd. In addition, from Kurzeme, a brickmaker was invited who received 60 Rd per annum. Bricks were mainly used for the building needs of the bishopric but some were sold for the building of churches and other needs. 4000 bricks were sold for 24 Rd in 1641 and 7000 bricks and 5300 tiles in 1643. In subsequent years the number of bricks sold was 2000 to 3000.

Another industrial enterprise was the brewing of ale. For home use brewing was permitted to peasants and citizens of towns. Peasants were also allowed to sell ale against a payment of excise. At an early stage the estates established public-houses and taverns and took over previously established ones. At first ale brewed by the publicans was sold. Then the estates started to brew using statute labour. In 1640 the estates purchased brewing implements and brewing started at a larger scale. At the same time there appear in the cash accounts fines received for illegal trade with ale, and, in the ale accounts, incomes of confiscated ale are registered. While in the earlier years peasants who sold ale paid fixed amounts to the bishopric, in later years, starting with 1652, the bishopric paid the innkeepers for the selling of ale in the taverns and public-houses.

Ale was sold not only in the taverns but also by the clergy at fairs near churches. In 1638 the steward Behr suggested to the Chancellor to take over the sale of ale at fairs (ED 1935, p. 17).

After the First Northern War a new industrial enterprise was introduced in the bishopric. On 12 July 1665 the guardians of the Oxenstiernas af Södermöre concluded an agreement with Wilhelm Breitenstein to establish in the bishopric a glass manufacture (RA, TA 75, p. 257). In the agreement the quantities of pane glass and other glass products were specified and also the remuneration to be paid to Breitenstein. Three years later—on 6 August 1668— the guardians, in a resolution, stated that the sales of glass had been disappointingly small and instructed the steward to bargain with the glass-maker about his remuneration (*ibid.*, p. 269). A map on the scale of 1: 10,400 of the Tarnisa estate, drawn between 1681 to 1684 (EKA), shows *Glasschyn* which means glass manufacture. Very likely another glass manufacture was established in the wide Ropaži forests, where peasants burnt ashes to sell in Riga and the Crown burnt charcoal for its artillery. In the Ropaži hundred until recent times a farm with the name Glāžušķūnis (meaning glass-shed) has been in existence (Endzelīns, p. 57).

SALE OF PRODUCE

The major produce sold by the bishopric was grain. The bulk was sold in Riga to Heinrich Meyer and after his death (1645) to his widow. From 1631 Heinrich Meyer was an alderman of the city of Riga and from 1642 a member of the council of Riga. Axel Oxenstierna described him in one of his instructions as his friend. Meyer also purchased commodities for the Chancellor to be sent to Prussia and later to Sweden and was executing monetary transactions on his behalf. Other merchants to whom grain was sold were Konrad Zobel (1644), Kord Struckman, Adrian von Friberg (1653), Heinrich Wulfenschild (1654), and the burgomaster of Pärnu, Arend Eckhof (1635). After the First Northern War grain of the Oxenstierna's estates was mainly sold to the Riga merchant Johan Nagel.

In the early years, with the shortage of grain, Meyer was advancing cash without interest for future sales. At the next stage grain was sold against payment at delivery. Before the First Northern War grain had to be kept in storage, for which the merchants charged, and interest had to be paid for advances on the stored grain. Even after the war merchants took grain only on consignment, paying after the grain was sold.

CAPITAL VALUE OF THE ESTATES

The graph shows the growth of the capitalized value of the Oxenstierna's Livonian estates. Calculation was performed with the net revenue shown in the tables (pp. 58–75) and the prevailing interest rate of 8 %. The linear trend of the capital value increased from 72,000 Rd in 1624 to 330,000 Rd in 1654. Eli F. Heckscher mentions that the capitalized value of Axel Oxenstierna's Swedish and Finnish estates (for 1653) had been 610,000 dollars silver mint (Heckscher, I, 2, p. 316). He has applied for the calculation the interest rate of 4.5 %. If we calculate at 8 %, we scale down the capitalized value to 343,000 dollars silver mint or the equivalent of 172,000 riksdollars. The capitalized value of Oxenstierna's Livonian estates on the trend value calculated above for 1653 is 321,000 Rd, but the actual capitalized value for 1653 was 293,000 Rd. The average for four years–1650, 1652, 1653, and 1654–was 461,000 Rd. The conclusion is that the Livonian estates of the Chancellor were of larger value than his Swedish and Finnish estates.

Indirect evidence about the great significance of the revenue derived from the bishopric is provided by the testament of Axel Oxenstierna (AOB, I, 1, p. 640–testament dated 10 February 1650). In his testament he stated that his debts should be paid from the revenue of the bishopric save the expenses of the

CAPITAL VALUE OF THE BISHOPRIC 1624–1654

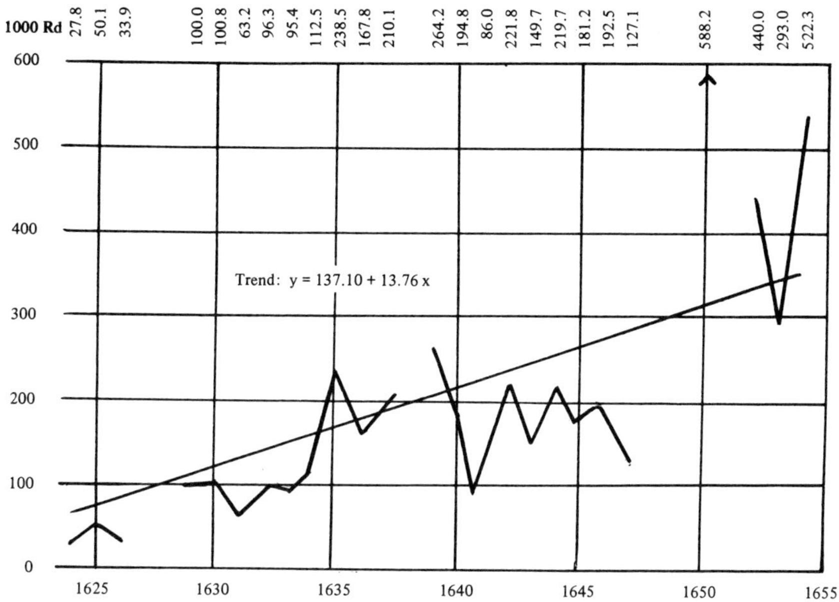

garrison. The amount of the debts was not mentioned and space had been only left to enter it. Only in the supplement to the testament (*ibid.*, p. 660), dated 31 January 1652, the amount of debts was mentioned, namely, 4000 Rd to his daughter and 8000 Rd to the heirs of Isak and Arend Spiering. In the same supplement a valuation of live-stock was given, as well as the value of the debts of the peasants. Regrettably the figure mentioned was only the total for all estates in Sweden, Finland, Estonia, and Livonia (*ibid.*, p. 661). Live-stock was valued at 6000 Rd and peasant debts at 12,000 Rd.

At the beginning of the economic year 1652, live-stock in the bishopric was at a value of 4336 Rd and the peasant debts amounted to 9293 Rd. We do not know the principles of valuation of the live-stock and the peasant debts used by Axel Oxenstierna's accountant and consequently whether the two sets of figures are comparable or not. Nevertheless, the great significance of the Livonian estates of Axel Oxenstierna becomes evident even from this incomplete comparison. That the valuation of the accountant of the Oxenstierna estates and our valuation on the basis of contemporary data cannot be very different shows from the following comparison. The value of total live-stock was 6000 Rd, that of the bishopric in round figures 4000 Rd which is 66.6 % of the total. The total value of the Oxenstierna estates can be estimated at

AVERAGE VALUE OF ONE UNCUS 1624–1654

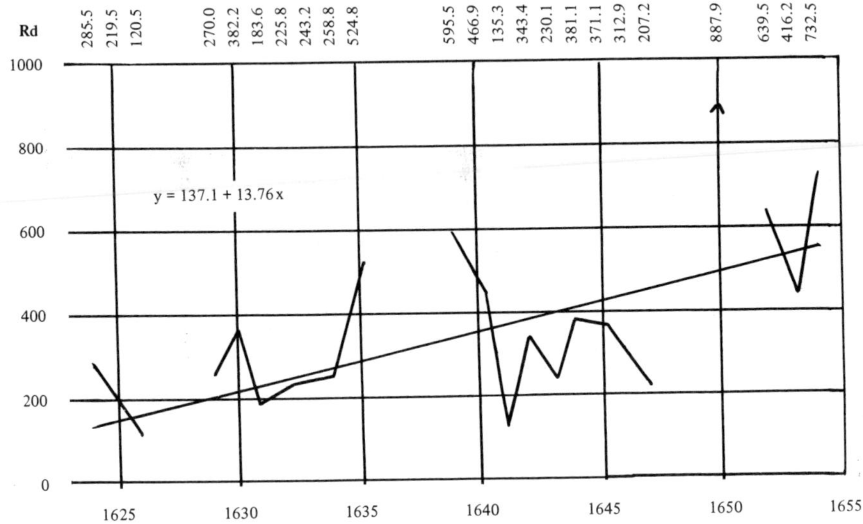

500,000 Rd (Sweden and Finland 172,000 Rd, Livonia 320,000 Rd, leaving 8000 Rd for Estonia). Of this Livonia constituted 60 %. On the basis of these approximate figures we can say that live-stock constituted from the total value in all Oxenstierna estates 12.5 %, but in the Livonian estates 12.0 %. It is significant that Axel Oxenstierna regarded live-stock as the most representative part of his wealth by singling it out in his testament. That both sets of percentages calculated above are so near, scarcely could be accidental and therefore it is possible to accept the absolute estimates as being near the truth.

Annual growth of capitalized value of the Livonian estates from 1624 to 1654 was nearly 5.2 % (compound interest) which means doubling of the capitalized value approximately every fourteen years. In evaluating this growth of the capital value, attention must be drawn to the fact that there was a growth of unci from which revenue was derived and at the same time the value of each uncus also increased. The linear trend of the value of each uncus was $Y = 137.1 + 13.76\ X$. In 1624 the value on the trend of one uncus was 150.9 Rd, which till 1654 had increased to 440.4 Rd. The value of the bishopric per uncus permits us to judge to a certain extent about the certainly infrequent purchases of land for the bishopric. In 1629 the Chancellor purchased land probably containing one uncus and paid for it 386 Rd (ED 1935, p. 390). According to our calculation the uncus was worth only 270 Rd, but we do not know whether with the one settled uncus were not purchased unsettled unci too. In 1634 the Chancellor bought Vāle consisting of 7 settled and 7.5 unsettled unci for 3000 Rd (see page 17). The value per settled uncus according to our calculation was 258.8 Rd, which amounts to 1812 Rd for the settled unci and works out at 158.4 Rd per unsettled uncus. In 1648 Bānūži was purchased for 1000 Rd (see page 19). It contained 4.5 unci, which works out at 222.2 Rd per uncus. The value according to our calculation was 343 Rd per uncus or 1540 for the estate. This was then a cheap purchase, but the justification is that it was an estate remote from the centre of management. For this reason Bānūži was leased in 1650 for 30 Rd per annum. This is only 3 % from the purchase price compared with 8 % at the current rate.

Certainly the market price of estates varied with the locality, the fertility of the particular soil, and the availability of man-power. Thus a comparison with average prices is only a rough yardstick for evaluation whether a purchase was cheap or dear. On the other hand, it can be said that the purchase of Bānūži was cheap as far as compared to average value per uncus, but dear judging from the rental.

OVERALL RESULTS

During the lifetime of Axel Oxenstierna, all the time series of the bishopric register growth, that is, until the setback in the 1640's. The stagnation was caused by failure of crops and by cattle diseases.

Regrettably for the years 1648, 1649, and 1651, data are missing; these could have helped in gaining a full explanation of the amazing growth shown by the data for 1650 and 1652–1654. Partly this growth could be explained by the increase of live-stock and the resulting improvement in the manuring of the fields and partly by the fact that, during the years of poor crops, the soil had recuperated. In addition, a reason, and probably the main reason for the record income, was the increase of the market prices for commodities. For instance, the market price of rye in 1645 was 0.54 Rd per leap, 1647–0.74 Rd, 1650–1.46 Rd, 1651–1.44 Rd, 1652–1.00 Rd. Only in 1653 and 1654 did the price drop to 0.53 Rd because of unsatisfactory sales arrangement of the manorial government. Prices, which more than doubled from the late 1640's to the early 1650's, explain to a great extent the increase of income from the bishopric and also the increase of the income from the manors in comparison with increase of income from customary dues.

CHAPTER FOUR

THE PEASANTRY DURING AXEL OXENSTIERNA'S TIME

THE UNCUS REVISIONS

In the Tidö archives there are lists for several years of the peasants in each manor. These lists give the names of the peasants and their obligations to pay customary dues. They do not provide information about the man-power, the extent of fields, the chattel of the peasants, because this information is represented in the number of unci or rather the fraction of uncus each peasant holds. For more detailed information we have to turn to official inquiries executed on the order of the government, called Uncus Revision or Land Revision. During the first half of the Swedish period in Livonia land revisions were held in 1601, 1617/1618, 1624, 1627, 1630, and 1638 (ED 1938).

The first two revisions are outside the scope of the present investigation. It is only of some interest to note that in 1601, in the later Oxenstierna estates, there were 1390 settled peasant farms and 42 cottars (ED 1938, pp. 19–24). Because of the ravages of war, only 61.5 % of the peasant farms had remained in 1638.

The revision of 1624 was the first after Axel Oxenstierna had acquired estates in Livonia. In 1624 he had taken possession of only seven Valmiera and two Mujāni hundreds (pagasts) with a total of 228 peasant farms. These were completely registered in the revision (*ibid.*, p. 108). From the revision of 1630 the minutes are missing for the regions where the Oxenstierna estates were located, except for Ropaži. A comparison with the extant summaries (Almquist 1930, III, 4) shows that the revision for Cēsis, Trikāta, Valmiera, Mujāni, and Burtnieki had listed 368 farms, while in Oxenstierna's peasant rolls in these estates there were 384 settled and paying peasant farms (ED 1938, p. 108). At Ropaži the 1630 revision listed 31 peasant farms (*ibid.*, p. 228). The most comprehensive of the revisions was that of 1638. The previous land revisions had either covered only part of the province or reflected devastations of war. In 1638 these ravages to a great extent had been healed.

The full text of the revision of 1638 with commentaries and indexes has been published by the author (ARL). The following is a summary from the text of the revision about the peasantry of the Oxenstierna's estates in Livonia regarding Cēsis, Valmiera, Mujāni, Burtnieki, Ēvele, and Trikāta districts and, separately, Ropaži.

In the bishopric proper, i.e. the first six districts mentioned, there were 881 peasant holdings. Males of the farmers' families were a total of 1380 at the age of 15 years and older, and 358 below that age. Servants in the farms (farm-hands), not belonging to the family of the farmer, were 407 of 15 years of age and older, and below that age limit 24. The total man-power over 15 years of age thus was 1787. The total of men folk was 2169. It could be assumed that females were, at a minimum, the same number, and the total population on the Oxenstierna estates in 1638 is to be estimated over 4300, except the Finnish colonists, soldiers, and town dwellers.

The total of animals of the peasantry was 1400 horses, 87 oxen and bulls, 1331 cows, and 174 calves. Data about the quantity of grain sown on the fields of the peasants had not been recorded for 62 farms out of the 881. Adding these in proportion to the rest and converting the peasant leap into smaller Riga measures, the total works out (in Riga leaps): rye 2838, barley 2537, oats 2295, wheat 135.9, linseed 339.6, peas 379.3, and buckwheat 83.

For Ropaži, the adding up of the record results in 68 farms with a total of 151 men, including 123 above the age of 15 years. The total population can be estimated about 300. The farmers had 140 horses and 179 cows and bulls. Data about calves are not recorded. From the total of 68 farms 19 were cottars and, while data about sown grain were missing for one of the fullfledged farms, those data were missing for 15 cottars. Taking this into account, the total amount sown can be estimated (in Riga leaps): rye 663, barley 351, oats 402, linseed 19.2, peas 42.3, and buckwheat 29.

The commissioners estimated the number of unci for each farm. In summing up for the bishopric (except Ropaži) we obtain 450 and one eighth unci, which eventually, for the year 1641, was reduced to 402 and one quarter unci. For the latter year in Ropaži the commissioners estimated a total of 23 unci including the peasants of the pastor. The entire purpose of the exercise was to establish the unci for each estate because on unci figures the government levied taxes and calculated the number of retainers to be kept.

About the forthcoming revision, the steward Ledebohrn requested the Chancellor for instruction on how to behave (RA, Oxenst. saml., letter of 6 July 1638). He wrote that, by reporting everything correctly, the Chancellor would suffer a loss of 1000 leaps of rye, the same quantity of barley, 500 leaps of oats, and 250 riksdollars to be paid in additional taxes. A reply to this letter could not be found, possibly the Chancellor did not answer such a contentious question. Later Ledebohrn wrote to the Chancellor (RA, Oxenst. saml., 29 September 1638) informing him that the revision had taken place and everything had been recorded according to testimony of the reeves given under oath (which is not quite correct–the main evidence was given by each peasant individually). He continued: 'Nevertheless, I was able to improve things in such a way that the peasants could remain on their own and the Crown will receive its share without loss for Your Lordship if no changes would occur'.

By comparing the revision results with the internal peasant register of the same year (ARL, pp. CLXX–CLXXVI) the following discrepancies could be discovered. Of the settled holdings there were 143 listed in the internal peasant registers, which were not listed in the official revision. On the other hand, in the official revision were listed 34 which were not listed in the internal registers. The difference is 109 holdings or 11 % from the total of 990 holdings (881 + 109). Of vacant holdings 208 which were listed in the internal register were not listed in the official revision roll. In the revision roll, in turn, there were listed 90 holdings which were not listed in the internal register.

By comparing the names of the settled holdings, which were missing in the official revision, it appears that the majority were new-settlers who had the benefit of three free years, during which time they did not pay customary dues and did not perform statute work. Among the missing holdings were impoverished ones whose holders did not pay customary dues; some were ill and could not perform statute work. Among the missing holdings were also corn-mills and taverns, despite the fact that the commissioners were specially instructed to register them. The excuse one could advance for the missing mills and taverns is, that they were not mentioned in the revision by name but included in a common figure in reply to the question. There is a further possibility that those holdings, which were registered in the official revision but could not be found in the internal register, were listed in the two documents with different names. A further discrepancy could occur because there were several months' difference between the compilation of the internal register and the official revision. The internal register was prepared in April 1638, but the revision was conducted from 11 September to 4 October, starting at Cēsis and finishing at Trikāta.

Because the majority of the settled holdings which were registered in the internal rolls of the estates, but did not appear in the revision, were new-settlers, not yet paying customary dues, the steward had obviously a legitimate excuse in not presenting them to the commissioners. This probably is what he meant by his remark that the Crown would receive its share without a loss for the lord. Actually the Crown suffered losses because the next revision after 1638 followed only fifty years later and showed an increase of settlements.

PEASANT HOLDINGS

From a letter of steward Behr to Count Erik (RA, TA 269: 17 June 1649) the situation of peasant holdings can be gauged. Behr wrote that it would be an advantage if the surveyor could allocate each peasant land according to his uncus. Because there were wide areas of morass, wilderness, and poor land, the surveyor would need several years to achieve an equal distribution of land among the peasants provided he could train two students from Tartu university for the job as his assistants.

The impression we gain from this letter and other evidence is that the land of the peasants was intermixed with that of neighbouring peasants and that its quality was unequal. The peasants of the bishopric were living in single farms, not in villages (see map: ED 1964, p. 348).

CUSTOMARY DUES OF PEASANTS

For customary dues the Swedish name is *årlig räntan,* German: *Gerechtigkeit*, Latvian: *kunga tiesa*, Russian: оброк. The English term 'rent' has not been used because it is a payment of a tenant to the owner of an estate, but in our case the peasants were not tenants possessing their farms on a temporary basis. The majority held their farms on a hereditary basis. In Swedish the term *räntan* has a different meaning–compare the term *årsväxten räntan* for crop from the manorial fields. The English term 'quitrent' used by some scholars for what we call customary dues means a small annual payment by a copyholder in commutation of services formerly paid to the lord of the manor. Therefore this term is not applicable here.

Customary dues were paid in money and in kind. The amounts to be paid were established by custom and only varied slightly from year to year depending on the prosperity or meagreness of the harvest. In 1638 in the Oxenstierna estates payments in cash were 9 marks from one uncus of peasant holding and 15 marks from one mantal. This meant that peasant holdings, smaller than one uncus, paid less than 9 marks but every holding regardless of its size had to pay in addition 15 marks. In the larger estates payments in kind from one uncus were fixed at 5 leaps each of rye, barley, and oats, one lispound (20 pounds) of flax, hemp, and honey and in addition from each mantal one sixth of a leap of wheat and peas and one sheep. To replace the obligation of sending for six weeks during the summer a second statute labourer (the *otrinieks*) produce was paid from each mantal: 1 leap of barley, 5 pounds of hops, and 2 lispounds of flax. In the smaller estates the amounts to be paid were fixed at a different level.

The payment of grain in kind had to be delivered in peasant leaps (Swedish: *lop*, German: *Lof*, Latvian: *pūrs*). Peasant leap was larger than the leap used in Riga. The peasant leap was different in each manor and according to customs had to be measured either with a heap or stroked flash. In the majority of cases manorial 3 stroked peasant leaps were equivalent to 5 stroked Riga leaps. The Oxenstierna accounts record all the different leaps recalculated into Riga leaps (Riga leap was approx. 66 to 68 litres in modern terms). Similarly there was a difference with the weights at each manor. These different pounds and lispounds were also recalculated by the accountant into Riga pounds (in modern terms, a Riga pound was 420 g; a lispound was 8.4 kg and a peasant lispound of 25 pounds was 10.5 kg).

Complications into the accounts were introduced by the facts of life that the peasants often had not the specific commodity to be delivered at fixed dates–grain, flax, and hemp by St. Simon's day (28 October), sheep and cash payments at St. John's day (24 June), taxes at Easter, and other payments on New Year's day. Or, the peasants were clever enough to calculate and to compare the arbitrarily fixed substitution prices for the various commodities with market prices and either deliver commodities in kind or pay in cash. All these changes were recorded in the accounts under the captions: 'Tillbytt och i wederlagh tagitt' and 'Förbytt den eena partzelen emot den andra' (exchanged and bartered; exchanged one commodity against another).

PEASANT DEBTS

Problems for the management were created by peasants not being able to pay customary dues. The debts created mix-ups in accounting. Thus at 12 August 1633 the steward reported to the Chancellor that peasant debts had been put on peasant accounts twice and the peasants were complaining (RA, Oxenst. saml.). On 15 July 1637 the steward asked the Chancellor for advice on what to do if peasants were unable to settle their debts. The Chancellor replied that, in order not to impoverish the peasants, debts could be cancelled but without informing the debtors (RA, TA 75, pp. 246 and 247, § 16). The idea was obviously not to instigate a run of debtors with requests to cancel their debts.

The form of accounting for debts was as follows: the customary dues were accounted as to be received in full under the title 'Årlig Räntan' and later on in the general account the debts were summarized under the title 'Böndernes Restantier'. The actual receivals were the totals to be received less the debts. The debts were carried over to the next year unless they were partially or totally cancelled.

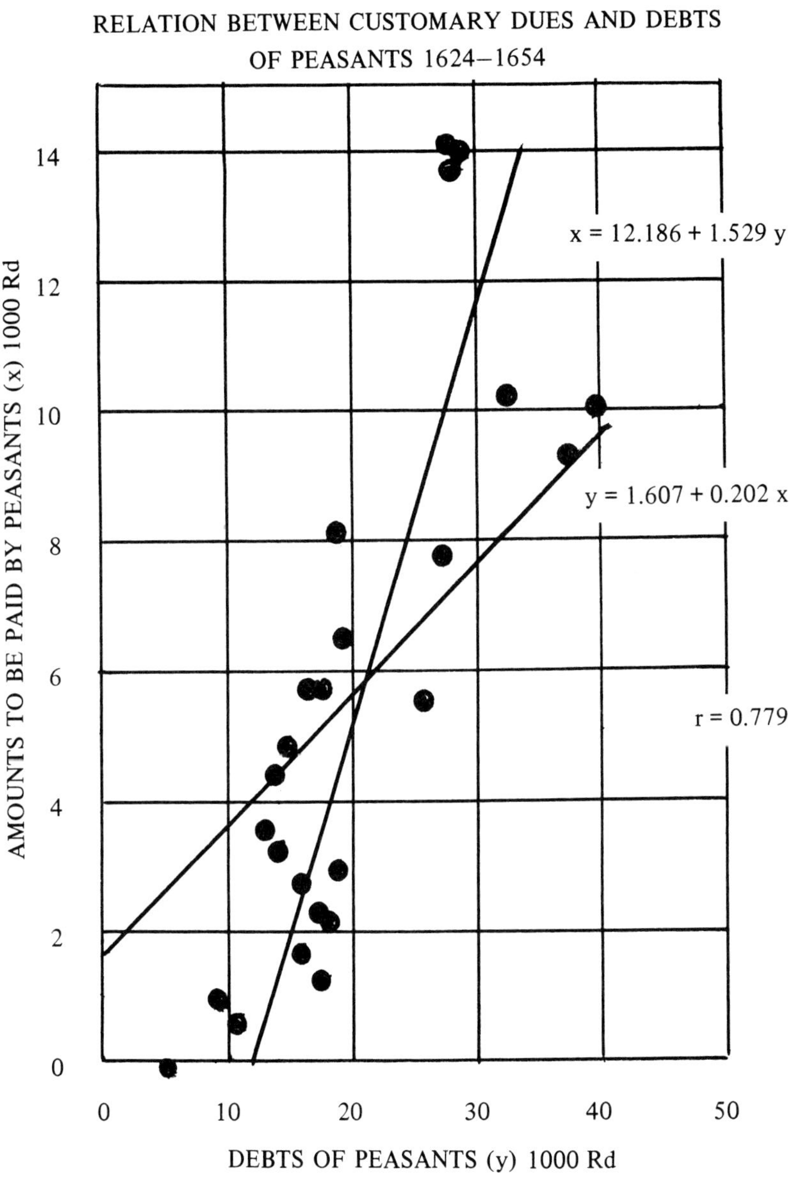
RELATION BETWEEN CUSTOMARY DUES AND DEBTS
OF PEASANTS 1624–1654
AMOUNTS TO BE PAID BY PEASANTS (x) 1000 Rd
DEBTS OF PEASANTS (y) 1000 Rd
x = 12.186 + 1.529 y
y = 1.607 + 0.202 x
r = 0.779
0
2
4
6
8
10
12
14
0
10
20
30
40
50

There is a high correlation between the annual amounts of debts and the total amount allocated for payments of customary dues (r = 0.779). The problem is – which is the dependent variable and which the independent one? Amounts allocated for payments were certainly influenced by the amounts of accumulated debts and debts were obviously dependent on the allocated amounts. Denoting the amounts to be paid by X and the amounts of accumulated debts not yet cancelled by Y, the two regression lines are:

$$Y = 1.607 + 0.202\,X \quad \text{and} \quad X = 12.186 + 1.529\,Y.$$

The reasons for the debts are evident even from the raw figures. During years of poor yield the percentage of debts was higher than in other years. Apart from the gaps in the series from 1625 to 1654, the average percentage of debts to amounts to be paid was 28 %. With poor yields of rye in 1630 it was 30 %, in 1635–31 %. In 1642 and 1643 there was a general failure of crops on the fields of the peasant farms and the percentage of debts was 50 % in 1642 and 48 % in 1643, and even 47 % in 1644 when the yield had improved.

From 1624 to 1653 there were 21 years for which data are available about peasant debts and the yield ratio for barley on manorial fields. Of those 21 years, peasant debts were above the trend for 11 years, below the trend for 10 years. The latter were years when debts were cancelled, and therefore it would not be meaningful to look for a relationship between yield ratios and peasant debts for these years.

For the relationship of the debts (Y) and the yield ratios of barley on the demesne fields (X) in the 11 years with debts above the trend, the regression equation, calculated in percentages of the trends, is $Y = 264.480 - 0.946\,X$. The correlation coefficient $r = -0.563$, which is significant at $P = 0.1$. (On the other hand, for the same relationship in years with the debts below the trend, the regression equation is $Y_1 = 69.755 - 0.109\,X_1$ and $r = -0.326$, which is not significant.)

The reader will note that this modestly significant correlation for years above the trend was achieved by comparing peasant debts with yield ratios of one of the summer crops on the demesne fields and not on peasant fields, for which data were not available. This means that fluctuations of yields on manorial fields were the same as on peasant fields even if one can expect that the level of the yield was different. A test with the yield ratio of rye on peasant debts (above the trend) resulted in a correlation coefficient of $r = -0.390$, which is not significant. For a tentative explanation of this result see later on.

NOTCHED TALLY STICKS

RELATION BETWEEN PEASANT DEBTS AND YIELD OF BARLEY

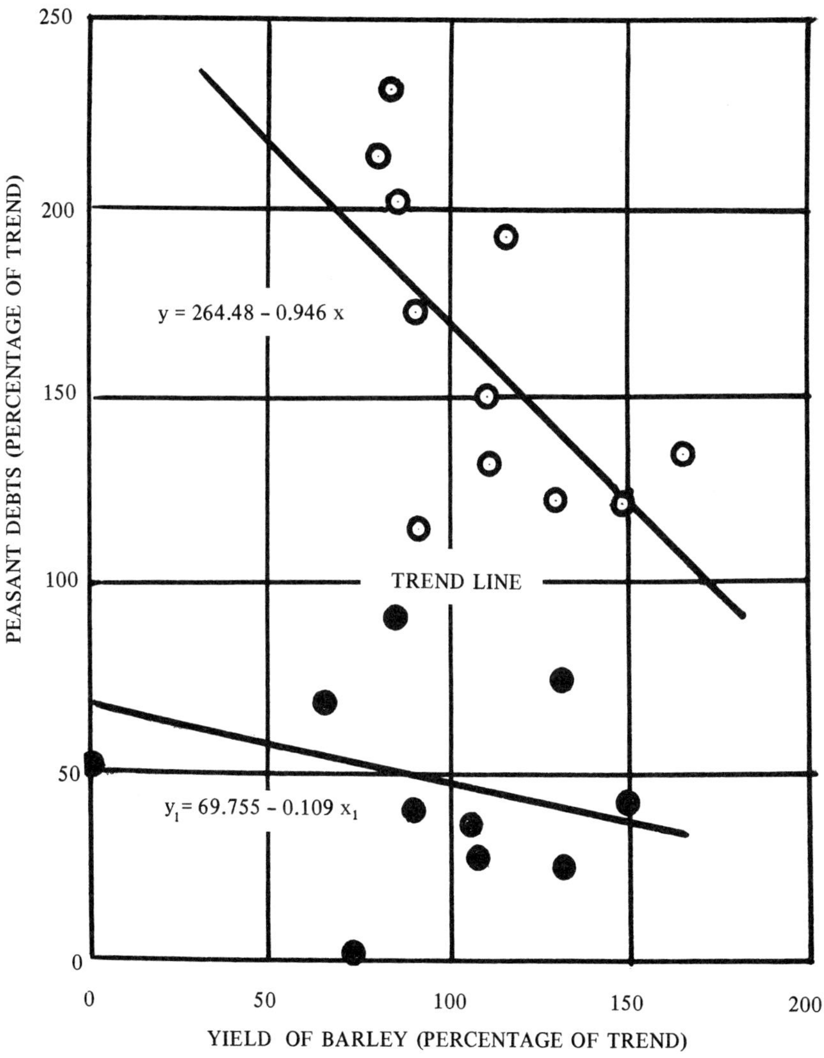

YIELD OF PEASANT CROPS

Too many data are missing for a reliable estimate of the level of yield on the peasant fields. According to the official revision of 1638, the amount of all crops sown on peasant fields in the bishopric was 8600 leaps. Manure obtained from horned cattle was 1500 units. If 14 % are added to include the manure from pigs and sheep in proportion to the number of these animals on the estates, the total of manure units is 1700 which is certainly a minimum, because peasants had in proportion more of these animals than kept by the manors. On each manure unit the peasants were sowing a minimum of 5.06 leaps as compared with 8.54 leaps on fields of demesnes. A safe conclusion from this comparison is that the yield on peasant farms was higher compared with demesne fields. With more manure available one can expect a higher yield.

There is some direct evidence to support this conclusion. At the meeting of the Chamber College on 10 March 1684 (RA, Kammarkollegium Protokoll) Michael Strokirk observed that the peasants of the bishopric worked with greater enthusiasm on their own farms than on the fields of the demesne. He noted that, as a result, the peasant farms were in a better condition than the field productivity of the demesne.

On 14 December 1689, Governor General Hastfer, together with officers handling the reduction of Livonian estates, wrote (RA, former KA, Cameralia [. . .] Livland 1690: skrivelser till Kongl. M:t, § 5) that, on land of the same quality and quantity, the yield on the peasant farms was higher than the yield on the demesne. They explained this by arguing that (1) the arable land of each peasant farm was smaller than that of the demesne; (2) on their own land the peasants worked for themselves and reaped the fruits of their labour, while from the harvest of the demesne they did not benefit and consequently worked slovenly.

In order to get some idea about the possible yield on the peasant farms, we can estimate the probable usage of the crop for the year 1638. From the estate accounts we know the amounts to be paid as customary dues, and the debts. After subtracting the latter from the former, it appears that a total of 19,000 leaps was paid. From the official revision we know that seed was 8600 leaps. The consumption of grain can be estimated as 10 to 14 leaps per capita. This gives a total of grain used of 70,600 to 87,600 leaps. From these data the yield ratio works out 8.2 to 10.2. Peasants also sold grain on the market, but we have no indication about the possible amounts to include in the above calculation, and thus the estimated yield ratio is a minimum. On the other hand, the calculated yield ratio of 8.2 to 10.2 depends on the reliability of the data about the amount sown as recorded in the official revision of 1638.

If peasants attempted to hide or underestimate the sown quantities then the calculated ratios are exaggerated. Another uncertainty is introduced by the different size of the leap as used for various purposes.

The above estimate depends also very much on the estimate of the consumption of grain per capita. In the agricultural handbook written by Herrmann (Neydenburg), the consumption figures for an estate farmhand were given as follows (Neydenburg, p. 143): 7 leaps rye, 1 leap grouts, 1 leap peas, 5 leaps malt to brew 4 tuns of ale, 10 pounds of hops, one pig, 2 milch cows and in addition 8 riksdollars. The amounts give 3812 Calories daily plus 500 Calories from ale. At the bishopric there was a farmhand in 1665 who received per annum 5 leaps rye, 5 leaps barley, one and a half lispound butter, 2 lispounds salt and 6 riksdollars 45 groschen. The calorie content of the products is 3758 C. The estimate of 10 to 14 leaps of grain is derived from these data, and it seems to be reasonable judging from the calorie content.

Our estimate certainly refers only to so-called good years. During the catastrophy in the 1640's, external help for the peasants was needed. Disaster started in the summer of 1641 when because of exceptional night frosts the blossoms of rye were damaged and because of unfavourable weather hay could not be gathered (RA, Oxenst. saml., 10 November 1641, 9 March 1642, etc.). In 1642 famine struck. The steward Ledebohrn advised the bailiffs to distribute corn for seed and grain for bread to the peasants. To the destitute peasants seed and bread-corn had to be given as a loan, to the wealthy ones it had to be sold. The bailiffs were instructed to watch out that this assistance was not granted to foreign peasants. The steward pointed out, that the assistance was necessary to prevent the peasants becoming fugitives. 1643 was a poor year, but in 1645 and 1646 cattle diseases and failure of crops were again experienced. Consumption by peasants during these years dropped dramatically and their debts rose.

The literary evidence about the disastrous years which struck the peasant farms is confirmed by the evidence from the manorial ledgers. There was a dramatic increase of peasant debts in non-delivered grain on account of customary dues.

In 1640 the debts of rye were only 74 leaps, but in 1641 the amount jumped to 1189 leaps and that of cancelled debts during the same year was 1072 leaps. For barley the debts jumped from 64 leaps to 1914 leaps and cancelled debts were 2144 leaps. For oats the debts increased from 108 to 1185 leaps. The high amounts of debts continued until 1644. The exceptionally high yield of rye in 1642 gathered from the fields of the demesne does not fit into the general picture and it is partly responsible for the fact that the relationship of peasant debts and yield of rye on the demesne resulted in an insignificant correlation coefficient.

The correlation coefficient of the yield ratio of rye and peasant debts, though insignificant, is negative as could be expected. An experiment of calculating the yield ratio on the basis of the current economic year from 1 August to 31 July to the current economic year's harvest and correlating it with peasants' debts gave not only an insignificant correlation coefficient but also one with a positive sign. This is evidence that the correct procedure is to relate current year's seed to next year's harvest, because this at least results in the negative correlation to be expected.

STATUTE LABOUR

Statute labour (Swedish: *dagsverk*, German: *Gehorch,* modern German: *Frone*, Latvian: *klaušas*, French: *corvée seigneuriale*, Russian: барщина) was of two kinds: ordinary and extraordinary. Common to both kinds was that it had to be performed by the peasant without remuneration and with his own draught animals and implements. Ordinary statute labour was to provide a worker with a horse from each farm for five working days of the week the year round or, dependent on the fraction of unci, a worker on foot for the same period. In addition each farm had to provide a second worker on foot during the summer, the so-called *otrinieks*, which usually was commuted.

Farms with excess man-power had to provide extraordinary statute labour sending a third worker on foot or with a horse the year round. Another form of extraordinary statute labour was that each peasant houshold from the hundred in turn had to send a worker to tend manorial animals, or send a night-watchman, or perform cartage service. For specially urgent seasonal work, for instance, at harvesting times boon work on occasions was called by the manor. In contrast to statute labour boon workers occasionally received food during meal times and feed for their horses, but always a modest feast was arranged after the task was finished.

Statute work was recorded in a special diary and in registers. Quite a number of these registers are preserved but only one diary for Valmiera for the year 1675. On the other hand, there are preserved,in the Tidö archives,several summaries and estimates about the usage of statute labour. Statute labour was used for all physical work necessary in the economy of the demesne, namely, preparing the soil for sowing, sowing of grain, carting and spreading manure on the fields, ploughing manure in, clearing meadows and, where suitable, making water-meadows, i.e. putting the meadows for a year under water. There was also work of a very heavy nature such as grubbing trees and burning them to make swidden, but this was sparingly used on the manors. Further work was cutting grass and making hay, reaping and threshing of grain. Produce had to be carted to the city for sale. Building materials had to be prepared, buildings erected and repaired. Cutting of firewood and carting it to the buildings, as well as carting of water, was other work to be performed. Preparation of flax for spinning and weaving of linen were all obligations of the labourers. In other words—rather qualified and unqualified work was their task.

In the Oxenstierna's estates, statute work was applied not only for agricultural pursuits but also to construct the rampart for Valmiera town. The stewards—Behr for the year 1649 and Sprengport together with the secretary Weber for 1653—had prepared specifications of available statute labour and the exploitation of the same. The documents are in the Tidö archives (printed ED 1935, pp. 88–89). In 1653 there was a total of 391 workers with a horse and 199 on foot. Of those, 10 with horses and 50 on foot were employed in constructing the rampart, 24 on foot were occupied in various construction and building works, 10 on foot were clearing meadows, 48 on foot tending manorial animals, 10 were employed as fishers, 28 as servants in the manors, 4 with a horse and 8 on foot in making bricks, one with a horse in carting water, 3 as watchmen. The total of employed in these tasks was 15 with a horse and 181 on foot, which left for agricultural pursuits 376 with a horse and 18 on foot. Spare labour was commuted for 4339 riksdollars.

Count Erik had ordered in his instruction to the steward, that each worker had to sow and work in 6 leaps of rye and 8 to 10 leaps of summer corn. In the year 1653 when the exact data about statute labour in the manors are available this norm was reached. Each worker with a horse worked in on an average 5.7 leaps of rye and 8.9 leaps of summer corn.

The peasants on their farms did not reach this norm, but it must be considered that they did not use their horses exclusively for labour but also for other occasions. As evidenced by numerous folksongs, the horse was the pride of the Latvian peasant and, for instance, played a prominent part if a lad was looking for a bride and on other ceremonial occasions. In 1638 the peasants of the bishopric had a total of 1400 horses and 87 oxen. As recommended in contemporary agricultural literature, a pair of oxen are equivalent to one horse. If the bulls are negelected, we obtain 1443 horse units. For 1638 we have less precise data about the distribution of statute labour as for 1653, but we can estimate that in 1638 377 horse units or 26 % of the total traction power of the peasant farms were engaged in statute labour. Similarly we can estimate that 29.7 % of the total man-power were utilized by the manors.

Like customary dues statute labour also was commuted. On 28 June 1647 the steward David Reimers informed the Chancellor that at the annual wacka-meeting he had suggested to the peasants that leaving the commutation payment for the *otrinieks* as it was at present, the peasants should in addition send the *otrinieks* for six weeks from St. John's to Michaelmas five days a week, like the custom was in all neighbouring noblemen estates. The steward complained that the peasants had rejected his suggestion and therefore he thought it would be advisable to invite some four or five noblemen to come to the bishopric and explain to the peasants that this was the custom of the land (RA, Oxenst. saml.). This letter is important in showing that the manorial management could not increase the statute labour of peasants on its own behalf but needed the consent of the peasants at the annual wacka-meeting. Two years later, in 1649, Count Erik in the instruction to the steward reminded him of this attempt by David Reimers (see page 39), but it seems the attempt to introduce this new custom was abortive.

EVICTION AND DISPLACING OF PEASANTS

At the Tidö archives there are preserved several calculations about the advantage and disadvantage of displacing peasants and using the land of the peasant farms for establishing a demesne. The gain from the demesne to be established was compared with the gain from the revenue from the farms before displacement. Significantly there were no calculations on the line Count Erik was suggesting—to replace statute workers who tended cattle with dairymaids to be remunerated from commuted labour incomes. The management of the estates was so accustomed to statute labour that the possibility did not occur to them of replacing statute labour with paid workers and deriving the necessary funds from commutation.

There were two calculations for the same size of a projected demesne but at different times with different results. The first refers to the 1640's and the second to the year 1670. The first calculation showed that it would not be profitable to displace the peasants for the new demesne, but the second calculation showed the opposite. In the first case the market price for grain was 8 marks a leap, in the second case it was 6 marks. Despite the lower market price, it was more advantageous to displace the peasants because of the improved yield ratio. In the first case the calculated yield ratio was 2.4, but in the second case 4.0. In the first case peasants were willing to commute spare labour, but not so in the second case. We can conclude that the willingness of peasants to commute was dependent on the market price for grain. At a higher price peasants were selling grain on the market and using part of the proceeds to commute statute labour. This shows that market prices of produce were important not only for the management of manors but also for the peasant economy. Regrettably there are no readily available data about the participation of peasants in the market except that there is evidence that peasants sold their own grain at Riga. (Details about the calculations of the manorial government to displace peasants are printed in ED 1935, pp. 91–93.) There is extant a very important document of the year 1665, in which peasants disputed the manorial calculation (see Chapter Eight).

HEREDITARY PEASANTS AND NEW-SETTLERS

In the Introduction it was mentioned that the term *Erbbauer* could be translated in English as 'hereditary peasant'. The instructions of practically all revisions performed by the government demanded making a clear distinction between hereditary peasants and others. In the revision of 1624 (ED 1938, p. 252) the second paragraph of the instruction (dated 16 July 1624) read: 'How long each peasant has lived on his land and which are hereditary peasants or foreign peasants and where to each foreign peasant belongs' (Wie lange Ein jeder Pawr auff seinen Landen gewohnet, unnd welche Erb- oder frömbde Pawren sein und wohin ein jeder frömbder Pawr gehöret). The instruction issued 22 May 1630 by Johan Skytte demands to inquire (*ibid.*, p. 256): 'Is he a hereditary peasant in the estate or where is he from?' (Ob er ein Erb Paur im guethe, oder woher er sey?). The revision's instruction signed by Bengt Oxenstierna on 4 August 1638 combined this question from the previous instructions in the following way (*ibid.*, p. 261): 'Is he an hereditary peasant in the estate or from where he is and how long has he lived on such land' (Ob Er ein Erbpaur im guthe, oder woher er sey, und wie lange Er auf solchen lande gewohnet).

In conformity with the revision of 1638, all peasants there were described whether they were hereditary peasants or not. For instance, at Valmiera Lecis was described as 'Erbpaur' (ARL, p. 501), but Guķis was mentioned as 'ein Churlender' (*ibid.*, p. 502), i.e. from Kurzeme. Ļoļa was described as 'ein Wendischer paur' (*ibid.*, p. 504), i.e. from the Cēsis district. All these farm names were still in existence in modern times, while Jahn Nißke, not any longer in existence, was described as 'ein Reuße' (*ibid.*, p. 507), i.e. a Russian. It is quite clear that a distinction was made in the revision whether a farmer was born in the farm he was holding or not. In the former case he was an *Erbbauer* and had inherited the farm from his father, in the latter case he had settled on the farm from somewhere else.

In the land revision of 1638 in the Cēsis district non-hereditary peasants were 24 % of the total, in Mujāni 21 %, in Burtnieki 19 %, in Valmiera and in Trikāta 15 %. The percentages show the mobility of the peasants and were a result of previous wars and in a way an evidence of the attractiveness of settling in the Oxenstierna estates. Among the non-hereditary peasants the new-settlers were a special group. New-settlers, as previously emphasized, had the benefit of no customary dues and statute labour for three years. In the Tidö archives dated with 1646 there is a list of new-settlers of the Vijciems hundred of Trikāta: 'Voehrzeichniß und Bericht von der Einweisung der gemeßen Lande [. . .]'. The bailiff Nikolai Fabricius together with the wood-ward Johan Maur, the reeve Barovskis and the peasant Jēkabs Līdeks allocated holdings to those who had rendered a safe guarantee (sichere Caution). We are not informed about the nature of the guarantee, but it is interesting that new-settlers needed a guarantee and that the land was allocated to them by a commission of estate officers and with a representative from the peasantry participating.

Another aspect of the life of a new-settler is disclosed by an entry in the cash account of the Oxenstierna estates for 1633 (ED 1935, p. 392). According to judgement of the court, for a peasant who had settled in the Burtnieki district the management had paid 11 riksdollars in settlement of the peasant's debt to the nobleman of the estate the peasant came from. At the first opportunity this amount had to be claimed from the new-settler. Another entry in the cash account for 1641 (*ibid.*, p. 399) stated that for two purchased peasant lads (för twå kiopte Bonde Poyker) 50 riksdollars had been paid. Because of the very short formulation of this entry we are in the dark whether this was in fact a purchase of serfs or whether there was some unspecified transaction behind the entry, for instance, payment of debts. It must be emphasized that this is the only entry of this kind found in the Axel Oxenstierna records. In the eighteenth century purchases of serfs are well documented, but one can have doubts whether the transaction of 1641 really means a purchase of serfs.

Regulations were not always observed. In such cases wronged peasants sought redress and approached in writing the Chancellor or Count Erik. A number of these complaints are extant (RA, TA 269 and 271). Most frequently peasants complained about expropriation of land. In these cases as a rule the peasants stressed that land taken away from them had been in their possession for generations and that they had faithfully paid customary dues and rendered services. There were also complaints about loss of meadows, that a second worker had been demanded, that they had been beaten up after complaining to the bailiff.

In one unique case the peasants complained that when delivering cartage grain in Riga they had been forced to measure it with a heaped leap while at the manor it had been measured with a stroked leap.

Another interesting case is the complaint of the Valmiera freeman, Jēkabs Ūdenskaķis (RA, TA 271: 15 January 1645). He had been sent by the steward Rautenstein to Tallinn to take a bearskin and an elkskin to the tanner. Not knowing the road and the Estonian language and because of want of fodder for the horse, Ūdenskaķis had hired and sent to Tallinn another peasant with his best horse valued at 21 Rd. Later Ūdenskaķis again had to hire another peasant to fetch the tanned hides. As a result, after returning, the horse had perished. When the hides were taken to the Valmiera castle, Rautenstein had them rejected because they were damaged. Then Rautenstein had ordered Ūdenskaķis to be cast in the dark tower where he had to spend three days and nights. After Ūdenskaķis' friends had paid 10 Rd, he had been released and his loss was now over 36 Rd. Later Rautenstein had ordered a soldier to take letters to his brother-in-law in Estonia and again the soldier had taken a horse from Ūdenskaķis, valued at 10 Rd, which again had perished. Thus in short time Ūdenskaķis had lost 46 Rd because of the private affairs of the steward, and he requested the Chancellor to order Rautenstein to repay the amount.

Not all complaints were of an economic nature. Thus a complaint was submitted to Count Erik on 20 May 1647 (*ibid.*) by seven peasants belonging to the Cēsis church. They had been transferred to Mujāni but they had worshiped at the Cēsis church for generations, were christened and married there, paid to the pastor his tithes and to the lord the customary dues. They requested the Count to recind the order and that they not be transferred to Mujāni.

MARKETABLE PRODUCE OF THE PEASANTRY

During the seventeenth century the main oversees export of Riga was flax and hemp. It constituted 59.5 % during the period 1636–1654, 61.0 % during 1655–1699, and 69.0 % during 1700–1718, or 61.5 % from 1636 to 1718 from the total export calculated with Laspeyre's index and 1672 prices (ED Außenhandel 1938). If linseed and hempseed is added the percentage increases to 75.7 % (from 1636 to 1718).

Cultivation of these products demanded special care which was beyond the capacities of the manorial economy and therefore the conclusion is valid that these commodities were mainly produced by the peasantry (Dorošenko, p. 48).

For instance, in 1638 the peasants of the Oxenstierna estates reported that they sowed, on their own fields, 339.6 leaps of linseed, while on the fields of the demesne only 2 leaps of linseed were recorded as sown in 1637 and nil in 1639 (data for 1638 are missing).

Because there cannot be any doubt that the yield of these crops was by far greater on the fields of the peasantry than on the fields of the demesne, the latter shows the minimum of crops harvested by the peasants. The yield of the manors of these technical crops was (in 1637) linseed 9.17 leaps and flax

30 lispounds. Hemp was not cultivated at all on the Oxenstierna demesne and therefore we have no concept about yields. Related to the quantity sown by the peasants, the minimum yield of the peasantry works out at 1557 leaps linseed and 5094 lispounds or 254.7 shippounds flax. To put these figures in a proper context–20,000 shippounds of flax was exported from Riga in 1637. The peasants of the Oxenstierna estates from their produce in 1637 had delivered as customary dues to the manor 3102 lispounds of flax, which means that they had kept some 2000 lispounds which partly was used in the household of the peasants and the surplus carted for sale to Riga. Flax in the household was spun and woven and then tailored into shirts, summerdress and bedding. It is impossible to estimate the amounts used in the household of the peasantry but still it is possible to say that a considerable quantity of flax was sold by them on the market. Assuming that the turnover of flax of the bishopric was representative for total Livonia and judging from the proportion one can say that more than half of the flax exported from Riga had been received by the manors as customary dues of the peasants.

It has to be pointed out that flax, hemp, and seeds exported from Riga came not only from Livonia, but also from Kurzeme, Latgale, and Lithuania. So far there has been no attempt to establish the relative importance of the supply from each of these regions as was made for grain (ED Außenhandel 1938, p. 464), the reliability of which was confirmed by using a different source (Dorošenko, p. 52, note 24). If the relative importance of Livonia or Vidzeme would be known as the region supplying flax for the Riga export, an estimate of the role of the Oxenstierna estates could be attempted. Sources for a calculation of relative importance of regions of the hinterland of Riga trade are the minutes of the commercial court (Wettgericht) of Riga (Dorošenko, p. 48). This means that it could be possible to shed some light on the question of participation of the peasantry in the market.

THE PECULIAR SITUATION OF THE PEASANTRY ON THE OXENSTIERNA'S ESTATES

The situation of the peasantry of the Oxenstierna's estates differed from the position of peasants on the estates of the rest of Livonia. Firstly it was only on the Oxenstierna's estates that Swedish law had been introduced, as detailed in Chapter Six. Secondly the regulations for the management of the Oxenstierna's estates prevented unauthorized exploitation of the peasantry by the personnel of the management. What the attitude of the Chancellor Axel Oxenstierna towards his 'subjects' (a term used by himself) was is disclosed in his testament of 10 February 1650 (AOB, I, 1, p. 659). This certainly is only a

CUSTOMARY DUES, PEASANT DEBTS, AND MANORIAL REVENUE, 1624–1654

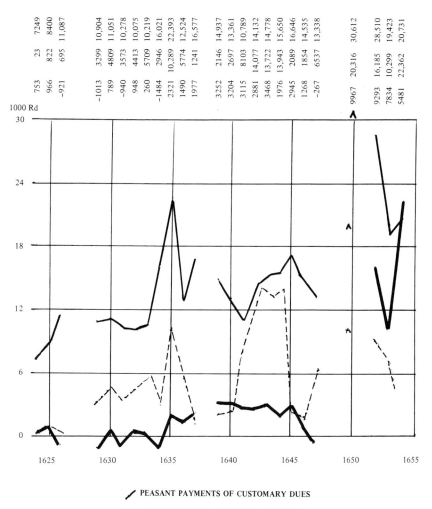

753	23	7249
966	822	8400
-921	695	11,087
-1013	3299	10,904
789	4809	11,051
-940	3573	10,278
948	4413	10,075
260	5709	10,219
-1484	2946	16,021
2321	10,289	22,393
1490	5774	12,524
1977	1241	16,577
3252	2146	14,937
3204	2697	13,361
3115	8103	10,789
2881	14,077	14,132
3468	13,722	14,778
1976	13,943	15,650
2945	2089	16,646
1268	1854	14,535
-267	6537	13,338
9967	20,316	30,612
9293	16,185	28,510
7834	10,299	19,423
5481	22,362	20,731

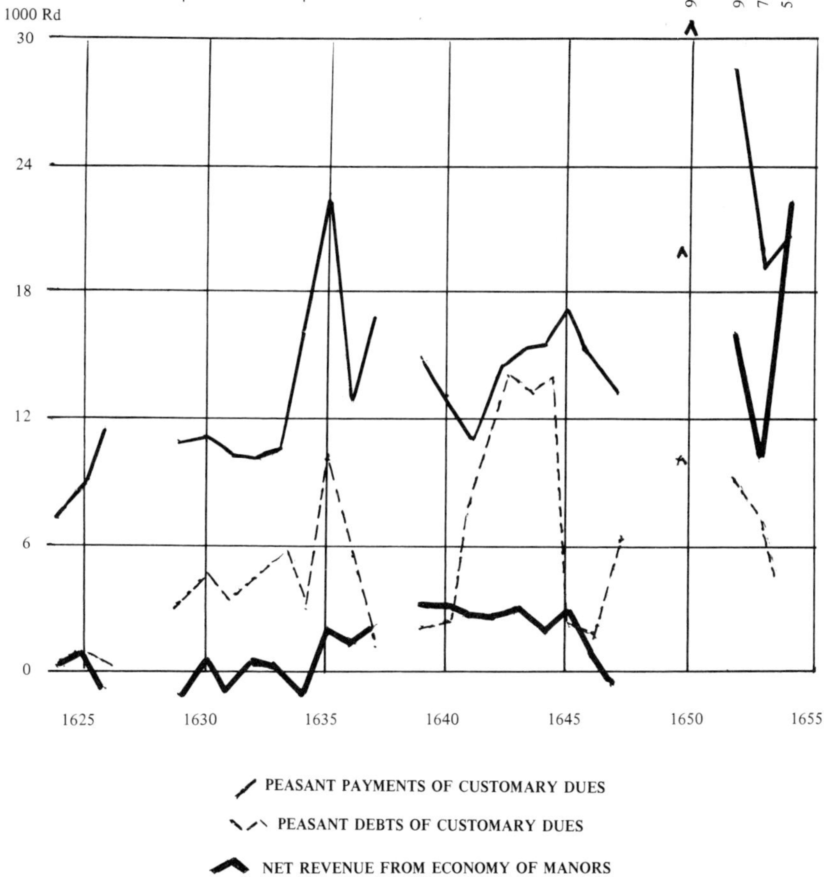

Figures on top of the page are riksdollars and refer to 1) payments in kind and cash of customary dues, 2) debts of peasants for non-paid dues, 3) net income of manors; see pages 58–75.

declaration and reflects in the first place the ideas of Axel Oxenstierna, which on occasions in practice could depart from his pious intentions. Nevertheless, it shows the attitude of the Chancellor towards his peasants not only in Sweden, but also in Finland and in Livonia. The relevant passage is therefore here inserted in translation.

'Wherefore, by manifest holy blessings of Almighty God, our portion has not only been amply sufficient, and has been much increased, but we have also for the most part had good subjects and willing peasants, and seldom had cause to complain about unoccupied homesteads; it has befallen also that we have attained a better outcome than many another, such as have shorn harshly and close to the skin, as well in Livonia as in Sweden and Finland. Therefore I counsel my children and entreat them as a father to follow my example, and that of their dear departed mother and ancestors, and not to be tempted by greed to oppress their subjects excessively and arbitrarily, but to deal with them in a Christian and reasonable manner. Exercise your right to make use of their toil and drudgery so far as you are able with courtesy, compassion, and propriety, not dragging their skin over their ears, but always being mindful that they also are human and like ourselves heirs to eternal life.'

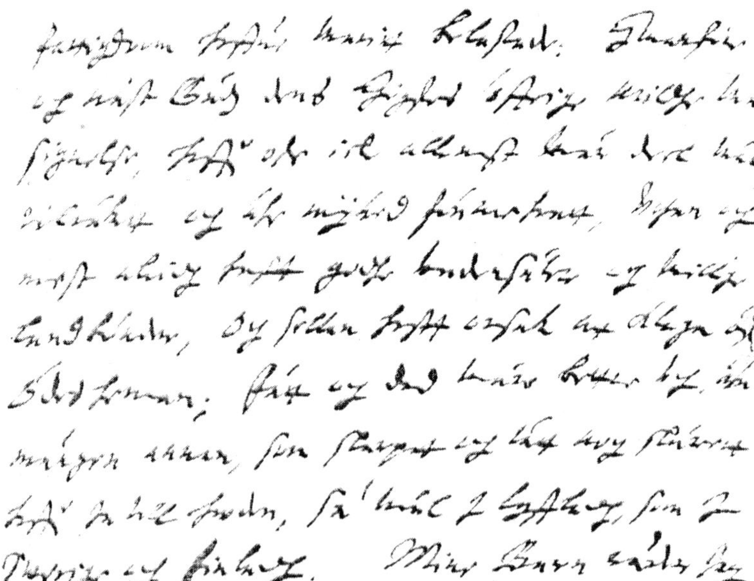

AXEL OXENSTIERNA'S HANDWRITING: FRAGMENT OF HIS WILL

CHAPTER FIVE

RELATIONS WITH THE CROWN

THE KEY OF LIVONIA

The Royal grant of 1622 handed over to Axel Oxenstierna not only a very fertile tract of land in the newly acquired province of Livonia, but also the most important heartland of great strategic significance. The prominence of this region was already recognized by successive masters of the Teutonic Knights Order, who had established their residence at Cēsis from 1297 to 1330, 1429 to 1434, and from 1481 to the end of the domination of the Order in 1561. During the centuries of the Teutonic Knights Order the strongest of its sixty castles was built at Cēsis. King Gustav Adolf also recognized the strategic consequence of this area of Livonia and granted it to his most trusted statesman, the Chancellor. One of the decisive conditions of the fief was that the Chancellor Axel Oxenstierna had, at his own expense, to maintain garrisons in the grant.

With the stipulation that Axel Oxenstierna had to maintain garrisons in the fortresses in order that 'these should not come easily into enemies hands', it was clear that Axel Oxenstierna had to keep these strongholds in good repair and to provide them with the necessary guns and ammunition. The King knew that he could entrust the protection of his most notable military object to his faithful servant, the Chancellor. Maintenance of defence installations certainly diminished the revenue the Chancellor derived from his grant, but he was able to minimize expenses by providing soldiers with land and by utilizing statute labour of peasants in building fortifications.

In the seventeenth century medieval castles certainly had lost their military significance but the location was still important. In the memorial to King Gustav Adolf Axel Oxenstierna wrote (AOB, I, 13: 10 January 1635) that of the Livonian strongholds those along the Daugava and the Gauja rivers should be maintained and improved. As to the latter he wrote: 'Valmiera, Cēsis, and Turaida (Treyden) are significant considering the river Gauja, so is Rauna. The rest [of the strongholds] are of no great importance.' Except the Daugava, the river Gauja was the largest waterway in the Latvian part of Livonia and was used for transport during wartime and by the Oxenstierna estates during the time of peace. Axel Oxenstierna decided to make the centre of the stronghold not Cēsis, but Valmiera some 29 km to the north, situated on the banks of the same river Gauja as Cēsis. Valmiera was the first location which came into the possession of the Chancellor and possibly that influenced his decision. Plans to fortify Valmiera were scrutinized by Axel Oxenstierna personally (see AOB, I, 14, p. 339, no. 459).

THE GARRISONS

On 15 June 1623 King Gustav Adolf permitted 300 Finnish soldiers with their families to settle at Valmiera (RA, RR). These were allocated land in the fields of Valmiera. On 11 January 1625 steward Munck reported to the Chancellor (RA, Oxenst. saml.) that in execution of the Chancellor's orders he had decided not to allow the soldiers to use the land of abandoned farms but to settle them in the town of Valmiera and let them use the land of the castle and the town. On 7 May Munck reported that he had ordered the land measured and that every soldier could sow 2 leaps (one ton) each of rye, barley, and oats, and a quantity of peas, buckwheat, and other crops. The land had been already ploughed and those soldiers who had not their own horse were helped with peasant horses. In 1626, 142 Finnish families arrived. For the year 1626, in the Tidö archives (ED 1935, p. 65), there is a specification about the yield of the soldiers' fields. Lieutenant's Berend Mortenson's field had yielded 355 leaps of rye, 523 and a half leaps of barley, 86 leaps of oats, 26 and a half leaps of peas, and 10 leaps of buckwheat. Of this, 219 leaps of rye and barley and 70 leaps of oats had been reserved for seed; 5 leaps barley and 11 leaps oats had been fed to horses. The rest of the grain had been distributed among the soldiers. Lieutenant's Hans Lydichson's field had yielded 322 leaps rye, 355 5/6 leaps barley, 84 leaps oats, 26 leaps peas. For seed was reserved 203 leaps of rye and barley and 64 leaps of oats. To horses was fed 6 leaps barley and 11 leaps oats. In 1626 the manor lent to the military for seed 292 leaps barley, 63 leaps rye, 58 leaps oats, and 2 leaps peas.

Data are also available for the year 1629. Mortenson's company was harvesting 387 ½ leaps rye, had received from the Valmiera granary 80 ¼ leaps and used for seed 152 leaps. Barley was harvested 346 leaps, received from the granary 215 leaps and reserved for seed 142 leaps. Oats: harvest 146 leaps, from the granary 13 leaps, reserved for seed 60 leaps. Peas: from the granary 14 leaps, all reserved for seed. The rest was issued to 4–5 corporals, 52–62 soldiers and 10–15 boys. Lydichson's company harvested 356 leaps of rye, received from

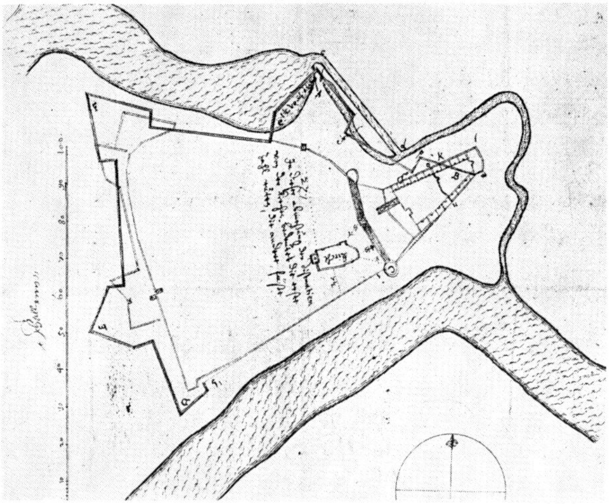

PROJECT OF FORTIFICATION OF VALMIERA (RA, TA 342)

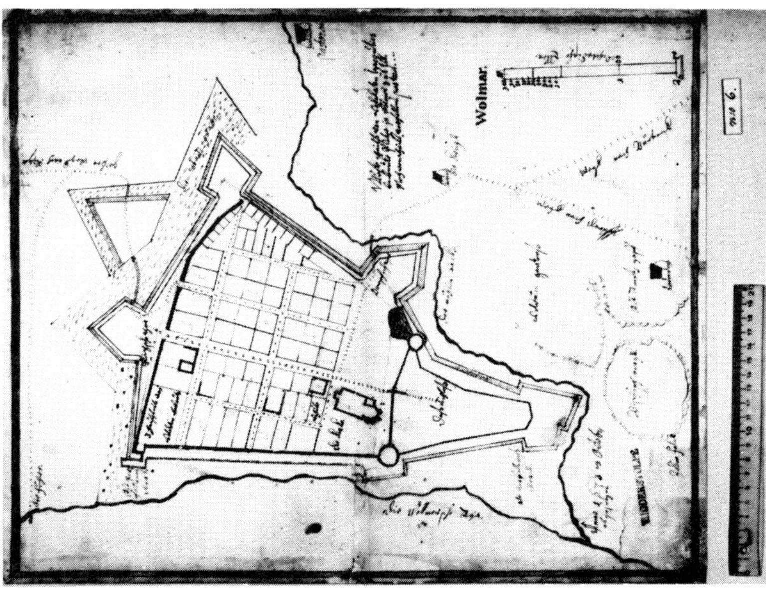

PLAN OF VALMIERA

Kungl. Krigsarkivet, Stockholm

the granary 192 ¼ leaps and used for seed 155 leaps. Barley was harvested 330 ½ leaps, received from the granary 202 ¾ leaps and used for seed 140 leaps. Oats: harvested 149 ½ leaps, received from the granary 34 ¾ leaps, used for seed 72 leaps. The rest was distributed to 4–5 corporals and 25 to 62 soldiers. In the same year (1629) the garrisons at Valmiera, Cēsis, Burtnieki, and Mujāni received from manorial granaries 1565 leaps rye, 1643 leaps barley, 343 leaps oats, 91 ½ leaps peas and 380 ½ lispounds of salt. From the above it becomes evident that in the garrison of the bishopric there were not only soldiers who were settled on land and producing their own food, but also those who were not occupied in agriculture but received sustenance from the manorial granaries.

On 20 September 1637 the steward reported to the Chancellor (RA, Oxenst. saml.) that the fields of the military had been divided into 120 lots of 7–8 tonsteads each (which was the usual land allotment to citizens of a town). On 7 July 1641 (*ibid.*) the steward Ledebohrn reported to the Chancellor that he had entered into an agreement with the soldiers and that they voluntarily (!) had left their land, some 200 tonsteads, for expansion of the fields of the Valmiera manor and had been allocated other land upon which to camp. This document illustrates the precarious economic position of the soldiers *cum* agricultural settlers.

The nominal roll of the soldiers for 1646 (printed ED 1935, pp. 148–154) shows that a reorganization had taken place in the meantime. There was now a distinction in the roll between the soldiers (Soldatesque), the militia (Bürgerschaft) and the 'German' citizens (Teutsche Bürgerschaft). The summary gave for the soldiers two officers, 5 non-commissioned officers, 3 drummers and pipers, and 55 privates, together with the 46 boys, a total of 111 men. In addition the roll listed 10 soldiers in Sweden with the Chancellor. The militia was divided into four squads. The summary mentioned 4 corporals, 2 lance-corporals, 79 privates, 87 boys, 2 widows, and the miller at Mūrmuiža–a total of 175. The names were all Finnish. In the so-called German roll of Valmiera citizens, one was a Scot, two were described as Latvians, the majority of the rest had German names with some Swedish names in between. In 1662, after the First Northern War, there were 66 soldiers at Valmiera (RA, TA 79).

The artillery was a special branch of the defence of the stronghold. When it came to the notice of the Chancellor that the artillery in the bishopric had been neglected, he appointed Antony Hartung as the artillery master (RA, TA 75, pp. 252–255) and issued him with a lengthy instruction on 29 July 1646. Hartung was put in charge of the artillery and the armoury. At the Valmiera castle, rooms had to be set apart for a storage of ammunition and for the cannons, as long as peace prevailed, and a room for the armoury. Hartung was ordered to prepare an inventory of arms and of everything belonging to the arsenal. Damaged cannons had to be repaired, the leather for the cannons, which had disintegrated, was to be replaced. Care had to be taken of the iron cannons sent from Sweden and the necessary shots prepared. Material for these tasks should be supplied by the steward. Artisans of the town should be assigned to work under supervision of the artillery master. If willing lads could be found among the sons of the soldiers, they should be apprenticed in artillery art under the guidance of Hartung. For the armoury 100 pikes from suitable wood should be made. The old muskets should be repaired. In all the business of the artillery master the steward had to help him.

An idea about the armament can be obtained from the inventory prepared on 8 and 9 September 1646 when the steward David Reimers von Rosenfeld assumed his office. There were 21 cannons at Valmiera with 935 shots, 216 muskets (of those 48 issued to soldiers and 79 to the Finnish militia) with 2610 shots. There was a total of 1147 pounds of powder and 40,203 pounds of slow-match. In the town of Cēsis there were 3 cannons. At Valmiera the soldiers had 47 swords and in the armoury there were 219 pikes.

According to the same inventory, the wall of the Valmiera castle was without the cordon and, where a section of the cordon was, it was rotten. The wall of the town was partly in poor repair, the terreplein and observation attachments rotten and partly stolen for fuel. The rampart was in process of construction and in the opinion of the incoming steward it could not be finished until the autumn. Another inventory of 26 August 1651 listed missing balls for which the bailiff of Cēsis would have to pay (RA, TA 342).

In the instructions of Count Erik of 1649 and 1652 what we called here the militia men are called colonists. The instruction of 1649 provided that for the soldiers alongside the Valmiera rampart a barracks had to be constructed according to engineer's Rodenburg's plan. Land was to be allocated to the colonists and they had to pay to the manorial management each tenth shief of grain. They had to live in the 'ryen' (Latvian: rija; this term means the grange adapted for heating and drying of grain and used as dwellings of the poor peasants). In the instruction of 1649 a clear distinction was drawn between the colonists and the soldiers. Count Erik ordered that if some of the colonists enlisted among the soldiers their land was to be kept at the lord's disposal. Both groups had to do military service and Count Erik decreed that they had to drill every forthnight. Both groups were also engaged in guard duties and had to do service in the construction of the rampart.

Count Erik in his privilege granted to the town of Valmiera on 18 May 1652 stated that to provide space for the German citizens all colonists had to be settled on land, except those who were regarded as qualified and had a special permission to live in the town (ED 1935, p. 132).

In appointing Jakob Sprengport as commandant and captain of the garrison on 20 September 1652 Axel Oxenstierna provided him with a twelve paragraph instruction (RA, TA 75, pp. 44–47). He was ordered to go to Valmiera without delay, call together the officers of the garrison and the artillery and show them his commission. He was also ordered to inspect Valmiera and the rampart and organize work on the latter to be continued during autumn to complete the fortification. He should discuss with the bailiffs the material and man-power needed for the construction. The commandant should promote the construction of buildings as ordered by Count Erik and following Count Erik's design. From the very beginning the guard of the fortress should be maintained in the proper order. The keys of the castle and the town of Valmiera were entrusted to the commandant and he should take them into his possession each evening and keep them at a safe place.

The castle of Cēsis should be renovated and Count Erik had already ordered preparation of a design for repairing of it. The commandant should assist in carrying it out subject to further instructions. On the other hand, it had been found that the small fortifications better served the enemy than the defenders and therefore small fortifications should be razed. Consequently the commandant was ordered to demolish the walls and the rampart of Mujāni leaving only the two strong towers. Wrecking should be carried out without great expense. The idea that small strongholds were of little value was expressed already seventeen years earlier by the Chancellor in a memorial to the Queen (AOB, I, 14, p. 55).

The commandant should order the making of an inventory of artillery in the whole bishopric. In all castles he should look after guns and balls which possibly could be found neglected or buried. All found guns and balls should be put in the armoury and repaired if needed. The commandant should rectify all defects regarding the artillery and ammunition but without incurring heavy expenses. It would be necessary to employ the subjects of the Chancellor in cooking saltpetre, making balls and muskets and forging pikes and other arms, but, after considering the opportunities on the spot, the commandant should report, and further instructions would be issued. If the commandant himself cannot solve difficulties experienced with the artillery, he should report to the Chancellor. The soldiers and the colonists should pass review after the arrival of the commandant. The boys of the soldiers and the colonists should be listed and annual accounts kept about increases and departures. The soldiers and the colonists should be properly trained for warfare, they should be alert at guard service and kept in readiness to meet attacks by the enemy. They should be kept in good discipline according to the articles of war. Their salary should be paid properly, but all overbearing and outrage should be suppressed.

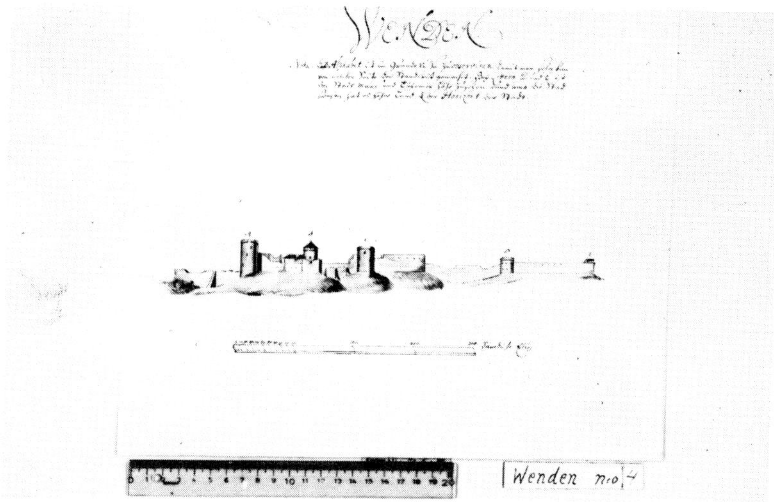

VIEW OF CĒSIS CASTLE

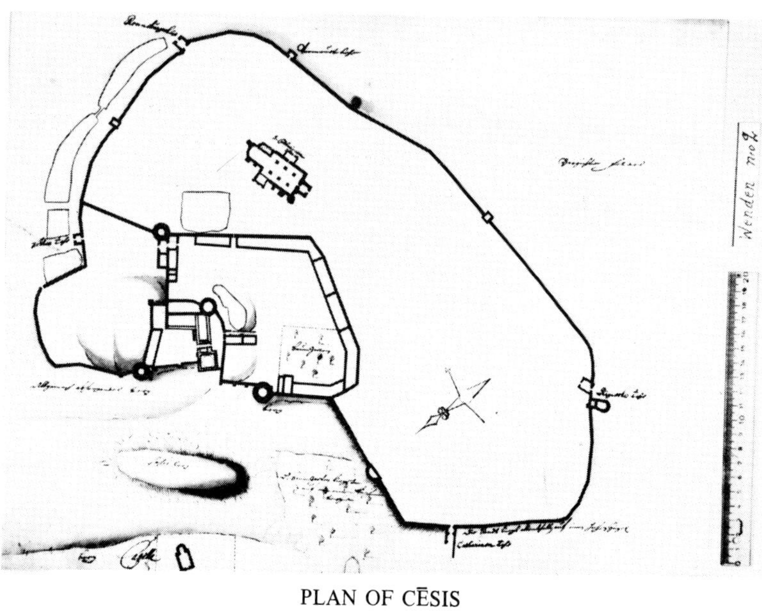

PLAN OF CĒSIS

Kungl. Krigsarkivet, Stockholm

Proper jurisdiction should be kept as previsously ordered and nothing changed until further notice. The commandant had to see that the work of the soldiers should benefit the Chancellor. Free days were granted to them according to previous orders, but the Chancellor would be pleased if the soldiers could be put to work on manufacturing of arms as previously indicated and engaged in building work. The children of the soldiers and of the colonists should be kept within the bishopric and their work organized in such a way that they pay for themselves and the bread they have received would not be spent in vain. Until useful work could be found, to save expenses the commandant should not enlist more soldiers. The officers should not misuse the labour of the privates to their own benefit, and this the commandant should drive home with his own example and proper fines. Every officer could use the services of the marksmen (hunters) from the peasantry which Count Erik had assigned them.

The commandant should see that the officers serve properly and faithfully. Those who were neglecting their service should be suggested for dismissal and more suitable persons enlisted. Count Erik and the Chancellor himself would decide these cases.

The instruction concluded with an exhortation to the commandant to perform his duties as it behoves a soldier and a commandant of a fortress. He had to defend the fortress with his life and serve Her Royal Majesty and the Crown of Sweden in the first place and secondly the Chancellor and his heirs.

THE RETAINERS

Before the Swedish conquest, in Livonia as well as in Sweden, possessors of land were obliged to keep retainers (in Swedish: rusttjänst, in German: Roß-dienst, in Latvian: jātnieku dienests). They were armed horsemen (troopers) and possessors had to maintain them in dependence of the amount of land held, eventually one retainer for every 15 unci of land. While the Chancellor during wartime was freed from the obligation to keep retainers at the bishopric, he had to engage retainers for the noblemen's estates which came into his possession according to the King's grants as *iure caduco*. Thus already in 1625 there was the retainer Wilhelm Möller (in accounts: Wellam Meller) with 3 to 4 horses. He received a salary of 379 to 720 Swedish dollars per annum and was mentioned in the accounts from 1625 to 1633.

To put the retainers' service on a proper footing the Crown carried out the uncus revision of 1630. From 1634 onwards there is evidence that retainers had to be kept for every 15 unci established in the revision of 1630. On 20 July 1635 the steward Ledebohrn wrote to the Governor General that up until that time the bishopric had not provided retainers, but following the order of the

RUINS OF THE CASTLE OF CĒSIS

Drawn by Baron Karl Ungern-Sternberg in 1810

THE RUINS AT PRESENT

(Collection of J.G.Herder-Institute)

THE VAULT OF THE CHAMBER OF THE MASTER

of the Teutonic Order at Cēsis castle

Governor General that nobody would be freed from this obligation, the steward would ask the Chancellor for instructions (EKA, LRKkA, II, 1 a, page 106). The Chancellor then requested the Governor General to free the bishopric from the obligation of keeping retainers (AOB, I, 14, p. 6, no. 297). Nevertheless from 1639 onwards there were, in the rolls of the bishopric, retainers who received land as mentioned in Chapter Two.

On 30 July 1640 the Governor General issued a regulation about the service of retainers (Roßdienstordnung; see Richter, p. 48). The obligation of the landlords was to remunerate the retainers and they were not entitled to dismiss them without consent of the captain of retainers. There were limitations about the period of service during wartime and conditions about service outside Livonia. In general, the retainers were not an efficient military force.

In the Tidö archives from the 1640's there is extant a cost benefit calculation about possible losses in supplying retainers with land as compared with expenses if the horses were to be kept by the Chancellor himself (ED 1935, p. 69).

In the first case the retainers received for each horse 2 unci of land—one settled and the other abandoned. For each settled uncus the retainer had the benefit of two workers who rendered weekly statute work. Those statute workers otherwise would pay commutation of 24 riksdollars. The customary dues of each peasant had the approximate value of 20 riksdollars. The unsettled uncus was used by the retainer as his manor and tilled. Consequently it was worth 60 riksdollars per annum to him. For retainers with 26 horses a total of 52 unci had to be provided, from those 34 ⅔ settled unci, valued at 1223 Rd 84 groschen. This then was the loss to the Chancellor if the retainers were supplied with land from the bishopric.

If the Chancellor would decide to keep his own horses and men, then horses which would pass review cost 60 Rd each, a total for 26 horses of 1560 Rd; 26 men each for salary and food cost 44 Rd 30 gr., total 1152 Rd. To 26 horses each week 1 leap oats had to be fed which totalled, in a year, 450 Rd. For 3 horses one stable attendant was needed, the cost for each 16 Rd, total 144 Rd. The grand total worked out at 3307 Rd 30 gr.

The obvious conclusion, which was not spelled out in the document, was that it was cheaper to grant land to the retainers than to support them on the account of the bishopric. The error in the calculation was that the value of the horses was included in the totals of the second calculation instead of the amortization of the value. But even so, the rest of the expenses exceeds the amount calculated if retainers were remunerated with land and statute labour.

Ruinen des Rodenpoisschen Schloßes. 1791
Rodenpois. Nullum Parochum habet.
6 Augusti visitationem incepimus in Canonicorum Vendensium arce Rodenpois. Ubi cum fundatio pro Parocho a Canonicis fieri debeat, nihil aliud fecimus, (nam et seniores habere non potuimus) quam animas quasdam haeresi infectas cum Deo et Ecclesia conciliavimus, uti uxorem Capitanei, Factorem, et aliquot ex familia arcis.

THE RUINS OF ROPAŽI CASTLE 1791

Drawing and text by Johann Christoph Brotze

The Chancellor managed to economize on the retainers even more. On a question which probably the accountant had asked whether the officers of the garrison could be employed as retainers?—he answered that it did not matter who were the retainers provided only that they had good horses and men who could pass the review (RA, TA 75, pp. 244–245). By employing as retainers officers of the garrison the same persons were engaged in two different capacities and this was certainly a saving for the Chancellor. His suggestion that horses and men should be able to pass the review was a weak point. At the review of May 1639 two retainers with 2 horses were not present and two other retainers, who should have been with two horses each, presented themselves only with one horse.

Under the energetic stewardship of Jakob Sprengport, men able to fight were engaged as retainers but after his time the holdings of retainers were regarded as a sort of a pension to be granted to old bailiffs.

TAXES

A permanent tax levied by the Swedish Crown and paid by the peasants was called statio (Swedish: station, German: Station, Latvian: staciņš). Only the peasants had to pay statio and other taxes, the obligation of the nobility was only to collect them and to deliver them to the Crown. Cartage of taxes levied in kind was done by peasants' statute labour. At the beginning of the seventeenth century, during the Polish and Swedish war, statio was at first a contribution levied on the peasants to prevent burning down of their dwellings (Liljedahl, p. 48). Eventually this became a permanent tax, at first of no fixed size. In 1621 at one estate each peasant household had to pay a loaf of bread, 2 hens, 2 pounds of butter, and a handful of salt. In the first years of Swedish occupation the term statio was applied to all income from the manors managed by the occupying forces. Simultaneously with this income a tax was levied on the peasants. In the ledger of Livonia it was called 'station eller contribution' (EKA, LRKkA). King Gustav Adolf wrote to the Chancellor on 17 October 1622 (AOB, II, 1, p. 203, no. 169) that the peasants had to pay statio for the upkeep of the forces even if it would be hard on them: 'We wish that our forces should be well maintained not taking into consideration the peasants, because we do not know how long we shall be able to keep them [the peasants]'.

The Governor General, De la Gardie, was not happy with the haphazard manner in which the tax was levied. He pointed out to the King that the peasants would run away if handled in this way (Liljedahl, p. 49) and wrote to the Chancellor that grain should be imported from Sweden and Finland because the Latvian and Estonian peasants were not able to pay more (AOB, II, 5, pp.

REVENUE OF THE BISHOPRIC, 1624–1654

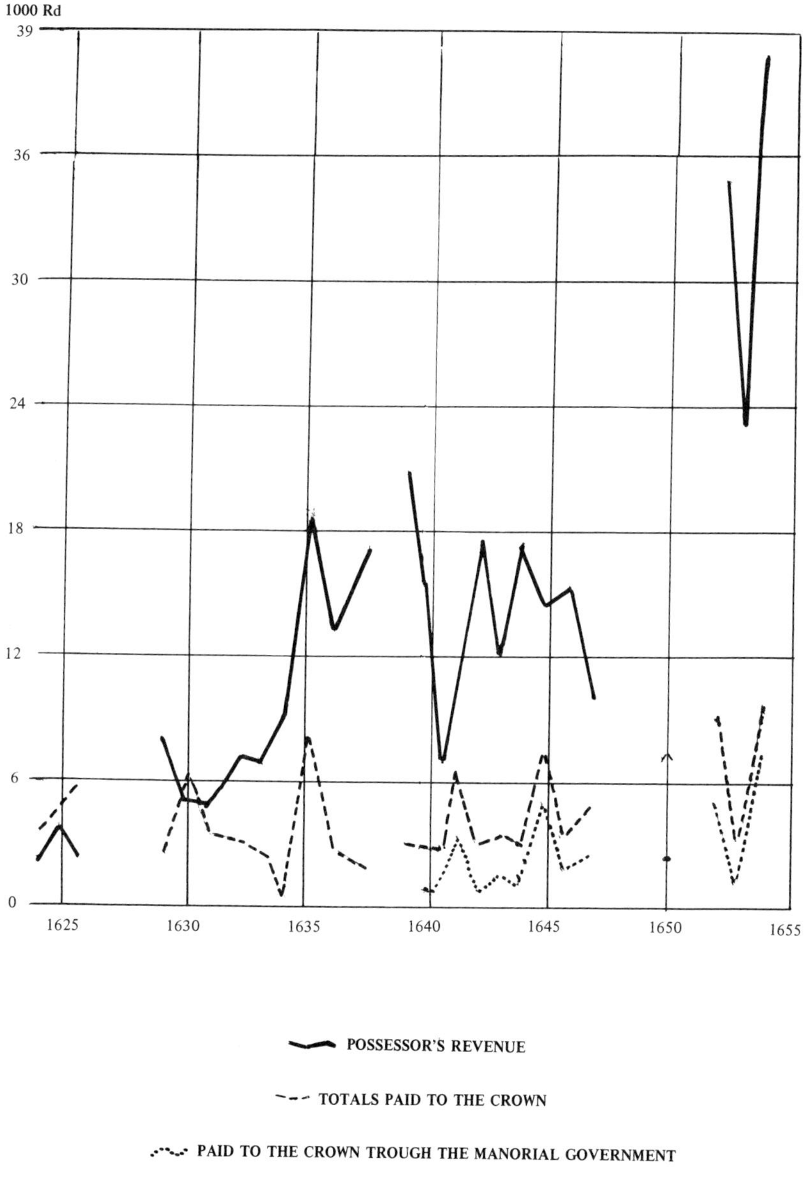

185–186, no. 92). The situation of the peasants was very difficult indeed; what the Swedes did not take, was taken by the Poles (Liljedahl, p. 60). An improvement was only achieved when in 1628 Erik Andersson was appointed to manage economic affairs and when in 1629 Johan Skytte became Governor General of Livonia.

In the bishopric statio was collected from the first year for which accountancy data are available (1624). In 1625 the Crown received the entire income from Trikāta and Cēsis and the Chancellor took for himself only the statio from Otepää and the income from 1 ¾ unci. The situation on the battle-field in Latvia was so difficult that the King asked the Chancellor personally to organize supplies. The Chancellor had to supply the forces not only with bread, but in view of the cold weather the King ordered the acquisition of 200 to 300 fur-coats. The Chancellor was able to collect from the peasants only 100 fur-coats. Nevertheless, it had been observed that the peasants when ordered to provide transport used to dress themselves in up to three coats. It was pointed out that, after they had finished cartage for the forces, these fur-coats could be simply taken away from them (AOB, I, 3, p. 279, no. 142: letter of 23 December 1625).

In the year 1626 the peasants of the bishopric paid (RA, TA) from each uncus: 1 ½ leap rye or 2 Swedish dollars, the same amount of barley, 3 leaps oats or 1 Swedish dollar, half a leap peas or 2 dollars, 2 loads of hay or 1 dollar for each load, 5 peasant pounds of butter or 2 dollars, 1 lispound of pork or 1 dollar, one eighth of an ox or 12 dollars per ox, half a sheep or 1 dollar, half a goose or 16 öre, 10 eggs or 2 öre a piece, 4 hens or 4 öre a piece, straw or 1 öre, the total being 17 Swedish dollars.

The Governor General, Johan Skytte, appointed November 1629, was trying to introduce some order into the chaotic taxation situation. One of the reasons for the Uncus or Land Revision of 1630 was to organize the taxation on a proper basis. Among the questions asked by the commissioners was: How much the peasants had to pay statio in 1628 and 1629? The commissioners had to find out whether the manors had not taken from the peasants more than they had paid to the Crown.

From 1630 the statio was levied from each uncus found in the revision: 3 tons rye, the same amount of barley, 2 tons oats, half a lispound of flax, 2 parmis (each 4 loads) of hay and from each mantal 12 öre cash. From each 15 unci to grind the corn a handmill was required. This was dropped in 1634 and the levy of hay reduced to one parmis to be commuted for one riksdollar. Grain on occasions was shipped by the government to Riga and from there to Holland to utilize favourable prices. The Swedish Crown urgently needed ready money to finance the war in Germany.

For 1630 the fixed amount to be paid was in complete agreement with the amount mentioned in the accounts of the Oxenstierna estates, but in the actual payments were slight variations. The obligation to pay was 1437 leaps (each half a ton) of rye, the same quantity of barley, 958 leaps of oats, 478 parmis of hay, and 136 dollars 16 öre. Rye and barley was delivered in full, oats was delivered 912 leaps, hay 267 ¼ parmis, and cash was paid 421 dollars. In 1633 were put on the accounts as payable 956 leaps each of rye, barley, and oats, 159 lispounds 1 ¼ pounds flax, 509 parmis hay and 17 pairs of millstones. The actual payment was short of 31 leaps oats, 9 lispounds 13 ¾ pounds flax, and 15 pairs of millstones.

The previous paragraph relates to the dealings between the bishopric and the Crown. About payments of the peasants see later.

In 1638, to the cash payment's obligations was added from each uncus half a Swedish dollar for upkeep of mail-coach horses (skiussferds och posthesterness penningar). In its turn, by the revision of 1638 the number of unci of the revision of 1630 for the total of Livonia was increased by nearly 50 % and the definition of uncus was changed in such a way that a peasant holding, which gave the year round weekly statute work to the manor, was regarded as one uncus. The noblemen of Livonia protested against this definition, but they very soon discovered that they could reap an advantage from the increase of settled unci in taking the tax also from the increase, but delivering to the Crown only amounts according to the official number of unci. The next revision happened only in 1688 and during the intervening First Northern War nothing had to be paid, while despite this moratorium some noblemen asked the peasants to pay the taxes in the usual way.

In 1641 the cash payment was further increased by adding a quarter of a riksdollar for timber to be used for fortifications. Peasants could pay this tax in kind supplying the timber, but they preferred to pay in cash because it worked out cheaper this way. In Swedish currency the mail-coach money was 16 öre and the timber money 12 öre from one uncus. In 1647, starting with the financial year on 1 September, timber money was increased to the same amount as mail-coach money–to 16 öre. Until 1672 the statio remained unaltered at 2 tons of rye, the same amount of barley, 1 parmis hay, commuted to one riksdollar, and two thirds of one riksdollar of mail-coach and timber money, which usually was paid with 2 carolines (in 1673/1674 at Riga a riksdollar was valued at 57 silver öre, while a caroline was 51 ⅓ silver öre). In the government's ledger (EKA), beginning with the year 1639, accounts were kept in Swedish silver dollars and one riksdollar was valued at one and a half silver dollars. The official relation which differed from the actual rate of exchange was only changed in the 1680's.

The actual income of the Crown was larger than judging from the received quantities in the accounts of the government's ledger. Firstly, the grain had to be delivered in Swedish tons, but it was issued to the forces in Riga measures. The difference was one sixteenth of a ton on each ton received and this was shown in the gains and losses account of the government's ledger. In 1672 the granaries introduced a new measure resulting in a 9.6 % increase of grain to be delivered. Secondly, from the very beginning peasants had to pay grain with a heaped measure like all deliveries in kind to the manor. From this additional delivery the Crown took one thirty second part of the ton but the rest of the heap was meant for compensation of the grain spoiled by mice in the granary.

The tax, called statio, remained in force during the entire Swedish period and also after the province was conquered by Russia and up to the year 1801. The Russian government also adopted the Swedish approach of conducting land revisions for establishing the number of unci to levy this tax, but, because during the 1680's in connection with the reduction of estates the method of defining the uncus had become very complicated, it was misunderstood, and the so-called Swedish uncus of the Russian period was very different indeed from its original.

EXTRAORDINARY TAXES

The extraordinary taxes were levied by the goverment and by the diet (the Landtag). In the majority of cases these taxes were also paid by the peasants. Extraordinary taxes as a rule were levied for some specific military purpose. The Swedish term for these taxes was *hjälp*, i.e. assistance. In 1629 the peasants of Axel Oxenstierna estates paid 7 Swedish dollars per uncus to finance purchase of artillery guns (artilleri hjälpen). The same tax was levied in 1634. The tax of 1644 to purchase artillery horses (artilleri hästpengar)–2 marks per uncus–was a general tax levied in Livonia and added to the statio. In 1629 the peasants of Livonia had to pay retainers' statio (ryttarnes station) which was also included in the statio tax. In the years 1639 to 1640 the Governor General levied a tax called retainers' contribution (ryttare contribution)–one third of a parmis hay and one third of a ton oats from each uncus. In 1645 a royal retainers' subsidy (subsidi eller rusttjänst contribution) was levied by the Landtag of 400 guilders from each 15 unci. The guilder was valued at a third of a riksdollar. In 1646 this tax was repeated but at the amount of 100 riksdollars from each 15 unci. To establish an additional retainers' company in 1648 the Landtag levied one riksdollar per uncus. In 1653 Sweden introduced an armament tax. In Livonia this levy was 200 dollars from 15 unci to be paid in two years. In 1654 the Landtag levied 30,000 Rd for the upkeep of 2000 soldiers to be sent to Livonia, but the Governor General increased this tax to 9 Rd from each uncus. 1655 the Landtag levied half a riksdollar from each uncus to purchase artillery horses and to pay salaries to officers of retainer companies. To finance expenses of the First Northern War further extraordinary taxes were levied. In the year 1656 this tax was 1.5 tons of rye and the same amount of barley from each uncus. The peasantry of Livonia paid a total of 4955 tons of rye, 1943 tons of barley, and 661 Rd, but the unpaid debt was calculated at 12,036 tons rye, 5181 tons barley and 919 Rd when the war started. (All these taxes and those paid in further years are documented in ED 1936, pp. 97–102.)

TAXES PAID ON BEHALF OF THE BISHOPRIC

In the accounts of Oxenstierna's Livonian estates were included the following extraordinary payments to the government: in the cash account of 1624 was recorded a payment to 'Feldherrn', probably to Gustav Horn–1219 Swedish dollars 29 öre or the equivalent of 1626 Riga dollars 14 groschen. For the purpose of our accounts (see page 58 ff.) this amount has been recalculated to 750 riksdollars and 50 groschen (one riksdollar = 78 groschen). In 1625 to the Riga treasury of the Crown 3000 Swedish dollars were paid, which we recalculated to 1641 Rd 2 ¼ gr. In 1626, 2000 Swedish dollars were paid, which was the equivalent of 948 Rd 13 gr. (the riksdollar was, from this year on, 90 groschen). In 1627, 1000 Swedish dollars were paid, the equivalent of 474 Rd 6 gr. In 1630 the accounts of the Axel Oxenstierna's estates recorded, as expenditure, payments to the Riga merchant Meyer who in 1628 and 1629 had paid to the Crown, for purchase of artillery horses, a total of 1680 Swedish copper dollars. We calculate this to be equivalent to 497 riksdollars 70 groschen.

In 1635 the bishopric paid to the Crown, for war expenses, 5000 Rd. It seems that this was the levy of 1634, which, because of a poor harvest, it was not possible to recoup from the peasants during that year. The royal retainers' subsidy–3733 Rd 30 gr. from 420 unci–was duly paid in 1645. The extraordinary tax of 406 Rd 67 ½ gr. was paid in 1647 and called contribution. The extraordinary tax levied in 1653 was recorded as paid in 1652 from 427 ¾ unci 2851 Rd 30 gr. The 1654 subsidy was paid, inclusive of Ropaži, 2871 riksdollars and 30 groschen.

On page 123 the payment of statio by the bishopric to the Crown has been detailed for the years 1630 and 1633. Quantities received from the peasants were recorded in the ledgers of the bishopric (ED 1935, p. 228 ff.). In 1630, on the debit side 2125 leaps of rye were entered, 93 of which had been received from destitute peasants. In the debit were also recorded debts repaid by peasants, but customary dues and statio had been entered in one sum. On the credit side 606 leaps were recorded as peasant statio debts. Subtracting this from the debit the difference is 1519 leaps, which means that this amount of rye was received as statio payment. Comparing with the credited amount of 1437 leaps paid to the Crown, it works out that 95 % of rye received from the peasants were delivered to the Crown. In 1633, on the debit side 1825 leaps of statio rye were recorded as received from peasants and in the credit 956 leaps as delivered to the Crown. The comparison is obscured by the debts of customary dues recorded together with statio (1038 leaps in the debit and 1133 leaps in the credit).

In 1630 a total of 2126 leaps of statio barley was debited and debts of 953 leaps credited; net–1173 leaps–was received from peasants. On the credit side 1437 leaps were recorded as statio payments on behalf of the bishopric, which means that more was delivered to the Crown than received from the peasants. In 1633 there were 1819 leaps in the debit and 956 leaps in the credit, which shows that only 53 % of the received amount were delivered to the Crown.

For oats in 1630 there were 1354 leaps in the debit and debts of 531 leaps in the credit, which leaves 823 leaps. 912 leaps were delivered to the Crown. In 1633 on the debit side 1806 leaps were entered; delivered were 956 leaps or 53 % of the received amount.

In the cash account of 1630 statio payments of 42 Rd 70 gr. were debited and peasants' debts of 8 Rd 80 gr. credited. In 1633 on the debit side were 76 Rd 60 gr., on the credit side–283 Rd.

One gains the impression that the accountant of the bishopric had difficulties to keep track of the received and delivered statio payments of the peasantry and this may explain the changes in the method of payments, beginning in 1640.

The statio payment was recorded in full on both sides of the ledger as received from the peasants and as issued to the Crown only for the period from 1630 to 1639. Before and after that period only quantities of the differences were entered into the books of the bishopric. From the year 1640 onwards the majority of the peasants of the bishopric delivered the statio directly to the Swedish granary in Riga. The receipts received in Riga were then shown by the peasants to the manorial management and the latter only demanded the unpaid differences (ED 1935, p. 76). The author has estimated the possible direct payments of the peasants to gain an overall picture of actual payments from the bishopric. For this estimate the quantities of 1639 were taken and multiplied by the current market price for rye, barley, and oats. The payments of statio

TAXES PAID BY PEASANTS, 1624–1654

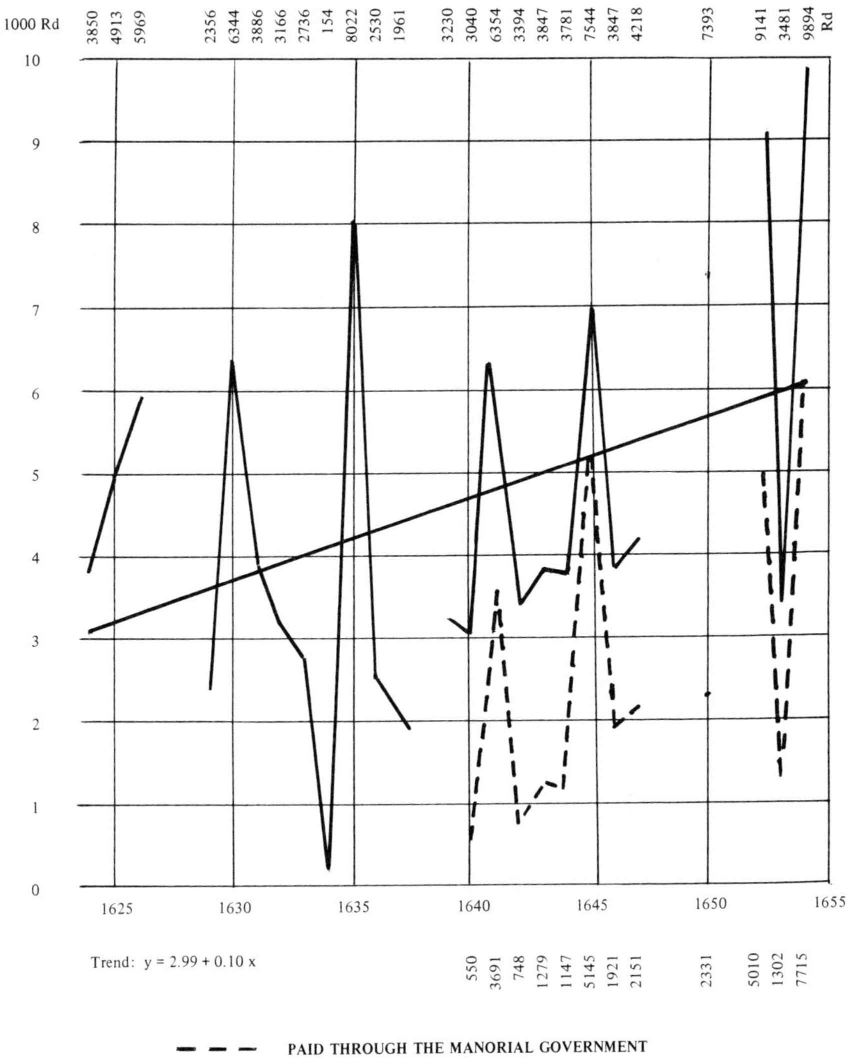

in cash were then added except for the years 1646 and 1647, when these payments were recorded in the estate accounts. The graph shows the results without the addition, as recorded in the accounts, and with addition calculated by the author. It is obvious from the graph that the addition brings the picture of total tax more in line with the general development of the economy of the bishopric. Certainly, the assumption that from 1640 onwards exactly the same amounts were annually paid in subsequent years as in 1639 gives only approximate figures. The peaks in the graph are the results of extraordinary payments. The trend line of the likely taxation payments in thousands of riksdollars is Y = 2.99 + 0.10 X. The value of the trend line for 1624 is 3090 Rd and for 1654 it is 6100 Rd.

That each individual peasant had to deliver statio grain to Riga meant in toto an increase of cartage obligations in comparison with the situation when statio grain was collected by the manorial government and then conveyed by cartage obligations of the peasantry. Unless the peasants cooperated, and there is no evidence to establish this, cartage of small quantities of produce by each peasant meant an increased utilization of horse-power and man-power of the peasants in comparison with the case when full loads were carried. The distance from the farms of the bishopric to Riga was about 90 to 120 km and this was a heavy burden for the peasantry in view of the bad roads.

SHARE OF CROWN FROM THE TOTAL PAYMENTS TO POSSESSOR AND CROWN

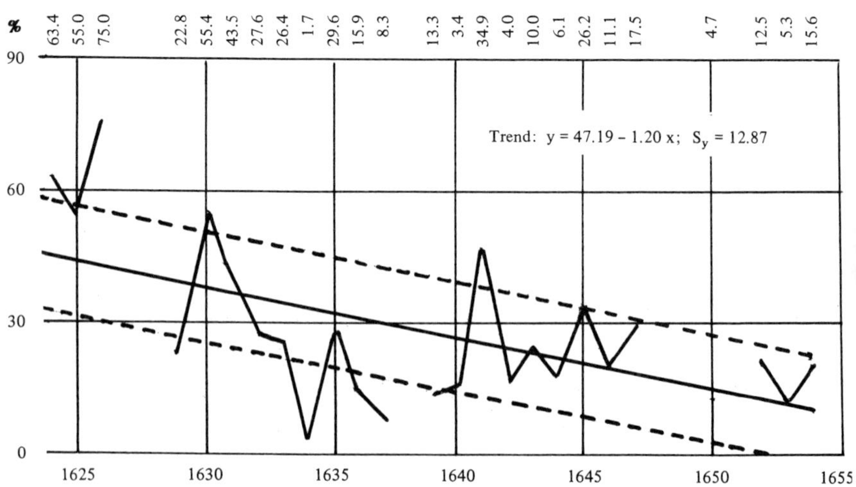

On the other hand, the fact, that all farmers of the bishopric were obliged once a year to go to Riga, had an educational benefit and, if they took with them their own produce for sale, also some economic advantage.

The component of cash payments in percentages of the total from the amended figures also shows a rising trend. The equation is $Y = 14.15 + 1.60\ X$. The value of the payment in cash from the total payment on the trend line for 1624 is 15.8 %, for 1654 it is 63.8 %. The increasing demand of the Crown and the ability of the peasants to pay taxes in cash show that the peasants sold their produce on the market at an increasing rate.

It is interesting to note that, after adding up the possessor's revenue with payments to the Crown, the Crown's share was declining over the years. Expressed in percentages, iterating the trend for the years where data are missing, the trend line is $Y = 47.19 - 1.20\ X$. The trend value for the year 1624 is 46.0 % and for the year 1654 it has declined to 10.0 %. Standard error of estimate $S_y = 12.87$ %.

TAXATION AND PUBLIC FINANCE AFTER THE FIRST NORTHERN WAR

The following summary review is based on entries in the treasury ledgers for Livonia preserved in the Estonian Central Archive (EKA, LRKkA; see ED 1936). Because of the war, only a fraction of the tax, levied on the peasants and called statio, was collected in 1658 and none whatsoever in 1659 and 1660. The King, by a resolution dated 23 November 1660, decreed that all payments not collected were cancelled. Similarly the important revenue in cash derived from customs in Riga (to a lesser extent in Pärnu) had declined during the war from 121,000 Rd in 1656 to 39,000 Rd in 1658 and the same amount in 1659.

With the conclusion of peace in 1660, revenue from these two main sources (statio and customs) grew again and in 1664 the Crown resumed collection of extraordinary taxes, usually by asking the diet of the nobility to levy them.

In 1664, for financing the High Court, one riksdollar from each uncus had to be paid (hovrättspengar). From the total 4265 riksdollars levied in that year only 1802 Rd were received but the outstanding amount was cashed in at subsequent years. The diet of 1665 at Riga levied 2 Rd per uncus for the equipment of two cavalry companies (munterings penningar). From the total of 8496 Rd were received 4215 Rd, the rest was paid in the following years and in 1669 the unpaid amount was only 140 Rd. During the period 1664 to 1666, a tax for building ships for the navy (skepps byggning hjälpen) was levied at the amount of 1.5 tons rye and the same amount of barley from each uncus.

In 1669 from this tax there was still outstanding 242 tons of grain. In 1666 the diet resolved to pay one eighth of a riksdollar per month from each uncus till the conclusion of peace with Russia.

The government had introduced an additional duty. It was disliked by the nobility, because this tax could not be shifted on to the peasantry. The government was prepared to bargain cancellation of the additional duty against a contribution of 6 tons of grain from each uncus, or a total of 12,743.75 tons. From this quantity in 1669 only 6840.25 tons were received as well as 908 Rd, substituting a ton of grain with 4 dollars silver mint. The rest was paid in subsequent years.

In 1674 the diet levied a tax of half a ton grain per uncus for building fortifications. Of this, two thirds were received during the year and the rest in the following year. In 1675 the diet was forced to levy the so-called Livonian contribution of one ton of grain from each uncus. In addition, for the support of the cavalry from each uncus a quarter of a riksdollar or 12 öre was levied and one and a half tons of grain coronation subsidy (krönings hjälpen).

According to the decision of the Swedish riksdag of 1675, a war tax was levied from the so-called donated estates at the amount of half the revenue and from other estates 3 tons of grain per uncus. This met violent opposition from the Livonian nobility when it was attempted to extend this tax to Livonia (Isberg, p. 7 ff.). Nevertheless, the 'half rent' was paid from the estates of the Swedish nobility in Livonia. In the Latvian part of Livonia the bishopric paid for 434.75 unci, Lugaži (Luhde) for 27.75 unci, Cesvaine (Seßwegen) for 55 unci, Vainiži (Wainsel) for 22 unci, Sigulda for 53.75 unci and Rauna (Ronneburg), Smiltene (Smilten), Gaujiena (Adsel), Alūksne (Marienburg) and Gulbene (Gulben) for unspecified unci. In the Estonian part this tax was paid by Tarvastu, Karksi (Karkus), Karitsa (Karritz), Raine, Pärnu, Tekvere, Kirepe, Repina, and some small estates. In 1677 a total of 10,090 riksdollars, 27,768 tons of grain (rye and barley), and 1359 tons of oats was collected. In subsequent years among the estates which paid this tax were recorded: Ērgļi (Erlaa), Limbaži (Lemsal), Ikšķile (Uexküll), Salaspils (Kirchholm), and Nītaure (Nietau), in addition to the previously mentioned estates.

In 1678 a tax for purchasing artillery horses was levied–a quarter of a riksdollar on each uncus. The receipt was 1960 Rd. In the same year Finnish troops were billeted in peasant farms, but those estates, which did not provide this service, had to pay 'militiens förplägning', a total of 3000 Rd. This tax was also demanded in subsequent years.

In 1679 a total of 8482 Albert dollars was levied for the upkeep of the military. Two more taxes were levied during this year: 2 marks, and 3 tons of grain from every uncus. From the 12,724 tons levied, 8900 tons were received and the rest remained in debt. After 1680 the Swedish Crown found a new source of income, which is discussed in Chapter Nine.

All the previously mentioned taxes were paid also by the peasants of the Oxenstierna estates. In addition, a special contribution of them has to be mentioned in this chapter. Being located in the middle of Swedish Livonia the bishopric was on the road from Russia to Western Europe. The Russian ambassadors made their way through the bishopric and travelling in style, with up to three hundred persons in the retinue, were a heavy burden on the peasantry. Thus, for example, in April 1649 the steward Behr reported that the Russian embassy had employed, for cartage, three hundred peasant horses and had six meals in the bishopric (RA, TA 269: 22 April 1649). Again in April 1656 the ambassador with his retinue rested in the bishopric at three peasant farms (*ibid.*, 271: Sprengport to Axel Oxenstierna, 10 and 21 April 1656).

There was more of this kind. Troops were billeted with the peasants if a war was expected. The same happened in the frequent cases of troop movements. This form of tax on the peasantry remained unrecorded and unaccounted for.

Liquidating the debts incurred during the First Northern War, Elisabet and Kristina Oxenstierna on 17 April 1708 stated that during the war in Livonia a peculiar habit had developed. In case there was no way to billet and provide sustenance for troops, they were ordered to go to Valmiera whether they could be accommodated or not (*ibid.*, 72). On one occasion the amount for sustenance of the Grothusen's troops was calculated at 10,092 ½ Rd. As usual, this had to be paid by the peasants.

CHAPTER SIX

SWEDISH LAW IN LIVONIA

APPOINTMENT OF A JUDGE IN THE BISHOPRIC

When the Swedes conquered Livonia they found that jurisdiction there was in a chaotic situation (Axel Oxenstierna wrote: 'alt hafuer varit confus i Livland', AOB, I, 4, no. 254). As early as 1625 the Chancellor introduced Swedish law in his Livonian estates, five years before the Swedish government made an end to the confused situation in the entire province. The Chancellor appointed, in 1625, Jonas Traneus as a judge. In the previous year Traneus had been engaged by him as a secretary of the economy (ED 1935, p. 53). In 1624, the cash account of the bishopric listed penalties received. Because the economic year started with the 1 August, this can be interpreted as the result of activities of the judge appointed in 1625. In 1627 Traneus wrote to the Chancellor that peasants praised God for receiving Swedish law in His Excellency's estates and that other districts and starosties also would like to have Swedish law (Liljedahl, p. 282). It seems this was not only flattery or selfpraise, but a testimony that any law is better than lawlessness. Traneus was eager to put under Swedish law not only the peasants and the town dwellers of the Oxenstierna's estates, but also the nobility living in the precincts of the bishopric. This suggestion was rejected by the authorities and also by the Chancellor (AOB, I, 4, no. 254 and 255). The nobility had its privileges temporary confirmed (on 18 May 1629) subject to later scrutiny by the King, and therefore it was anxious not to lose anything in prematurely accepting Swedish law and jurisdiction. The Oxenstierna court was not the only private court in Livonia. A second private court was established in the county of Pärnu in 1627.

LEGAL REFORMS IN LIVONIA

Legal reforms in Livonia started with organization of county courts (Swedish: landrätter, German: Landgerichte, Latvian: zemestiesas). On 26 November 1629 King Gustav Adolf empovered the Governor General, Johan Skytte, to establish these courts and, in an instruction of 10 December the same year, ordered him to issue appropriate statutes. On 20 May 1630 Skytte issued the first temporary ordinance to establish county courts and later an ordinance regarding castle courts (Swedish: slottsrätter, German: Schloß-gerichte, Latvian: pilstiesas) which were a legacy from the previous regime. The competence of the latter was curtailed and during the period from 1636 to 1639 they were eventually liquidated (Meurling, pp. 72–79).

County courts were established in each of the circuits of Riga, Cēsis, Pärnu, and Tartu. The courts had to sit twice a year–on 1st of May and at Michaelmas (29 September). The judge had four or five assessors from the ranks of noblemen, the stewards, or leaseholders. Noblemen were also subjected to the jurisdiction of the county courts. These courts dealt with cases relating to estates, inheritance, testaments, litigation about property, and also criminal cases, except those where the Crown was involved and criminal cases against noblemen, where the county court had only the function to investigate the cases for transmission to the governor. Fines levied by the court on subjects of noblemen were divided between the court, the plaintiff, and the nobleman.

On the 26 August 1630, the King at his camp at Old Stettin signed a decree establishing a High Court (Swedish: hovrätt, German: Hofgericht, Latvian: hoftiesa) at Tartu. The instructions about the High Court were issued by the Governor General on 27 December 1630. After liquidation of the castle courts the High Court became the court of appeal from the county courts. In criminal cases where the Crown was involved the High Court was the court of first instance and it also decided cases against noblemen, transmitted by the governor.

Appeals from the county courts were permitted only within eight days of sentences passed and if the amount exceeded 50 Swedish dollars. Judgements of county courts referring to life and honour had to be submitted by the governor to the High Court for scrutiny and execution. According to paragraph 25 of the statutes of the High Court, the law to be observed was the local customary law, and the Swedish law was to be used as an auxilliary law. The same was embodied in the revised county court statutes of 1632, in paragraph 29.

The High Court at Tartu was organized according to the Swedish statute of 23 June 1615 (Richter, p. 27, Meurling, p. 46). The court consisted of 14 persons who had legal knowledge. There was a president, a vice-president, six assessors from the nobility and six assessors who were not noblemen. The president was appointed by the king, the rest were self-nominated but had to be confirmed in office by the government. Three councillors were added from the nobility to the body of the court. The jurisdiction of the High Court extended to country and towns of Livonia, Estonia, Ingermanland, and Karelia, except the cities of Riga and Tallinn, which were subject to the High Court in Stockholm. Sessions had to be conducted twice yearly–from

1st March to the end of April and from 1st September to the end of October. The president had to live in Tartu. The fines went half to the Crown and half to members of the court, who divided their share among themselves in equal parts. Supervision of the court was entrusted to the governor general and, differing from the Swedish practice, before each session the court had to submit to the king (if present in the country) or to the governor general a list of persons who were to appear before the court. Sentences of the High Court were not subject to appeal, but only subject to revisions by the king. The fee for submitting the case for revision was 200 dollars. After the First Northern War the High Court was transferred to Riga.

The temporary statute of the county courts of 1630 was in 1632 supplanted by a permanent statute. One more court (at Koknese) was added to the list, but this was united with the Cēsis court in 1638. Each county court needed two assessors and the competence of the court were all civil, criminal, and police matters except which, according to Swedish law, were the competence of the High Court. Litigations before the county courts were only oral. Litigations of peasants against their masters were the competence of the High Court. As in Sweden, only heavy crimes could be punished immediately after the sentence had been pronounced by the governor. All other criminal cases had to be submitted for confirmation to the High Court. To apply torture, permission of the High Court was necessary (Richter, p. 29).

THE CONSISTORIES

In 1633 Governor General Skytte ordered the preparation of statutes of an ecclesiastical court called Overconsistory (Swedish: överkonsistorium, German: Oberkonsistorium, Latvian: virskonsistorija) and in the following year it was promulgated (Richter, p. 36). The Overconsistory consisted of a president, the superintendent, three members of the clergy, and three from the laity. The first two were appointed by the governor general and the other members were selected by him from candidates suggested by the president and the superintendent. The sessions of the Overconsistory had to be held at Tartu annually from 16 June to 18 July. Its competence was to decide matters relating to the church, schools, hospitals, and matrimony. A number of crimes had to be judged, among them the Latvian ancient ceremony of taking a bride by abduction which the German clergy mistook for the real thing.

The Overconsistory delegated to the superintendent the examination and ordination of pastors. The deans had to be encouraged to conduct visitations and call annual synods of pastors of the district. The deliberations of the Overconsistory were secret. Appeals went to the High Court. Revision was possible provided a deposit of 100 Rd was paid. To supplement the activities of the Overconsistory eventually subconsistories (Swedish: underkonsistorier, German: Unterkonsistorien, Latvian: apakškonsistorijas) were established—at first only in Riga and Tartu, but in 1636 in addition at other places. In the same year the Governor General decreed that the subconsistories were to be presided over by the judge of the county court and that they consisted of the dean, one or two members of the clergy, and two assessors of the county court.

LEGALIZATION OF THE COURT OF THE BISHOPRIC

With the organization of the courts in Livonia the need arose to legalize the court of the Oxenstierna estates, which had existed since 1625. The Chancellor petitioned the King to grant him jurisdiction in the first instance, pointing out that the bishopric was one continuous district and could support a court (AOB, I, 6, no. 18). The King granted the request on 8 February 1632 (*ibid.*, II, 1, no. 548).

With the Royal charter of 8 February 1632, the King confirmed to the Chancellor jurisdiction in the first instance at the bishopric of Cēsis and the right to appoint judges (ordentliga domare och häradshöfdinge). The provision was (*ibid.*, II, 1, p. 752, no. 548) that the court did not interfere with jurisdiction of the county courts and the High Court. The King commanded that all persons who live in the fief (lähn) should accept the authority of the judge and obey the Chancellor as their legal lord. The noblemen who lived within the boundaries of the bishopric also now became subject to the jurisdiction of the court.

A misunderstanding very soon developed in the bishopric between the two important officials—the Judge Traneus and the steward Munck. In 1630 the Chancellor commanded Traneus to come to Elbing to answer accusations (*ibid.*, II, 3, pp. 201–202, no. 141). It seems that the latter was able to vindicate himself because in 1631 the Chancellor requested the Governor General to appoint Traneus as an assessor with the High Court and this was done (*ibid.*, II, 10, p. 309: Skytte to Axel Oxenstierna 7 March 1631). Nevertheless, it seems that friction continued between Traneus and the steward who succeeded Munck. In 1633, Jonas Traneus was dismissed and replaced in his post by David Hintelman (ED 1935, pp. 221, 392). The cash account of 1636 shows that in addition to Judge Hintelman two assessors received remuneration (*ibid.*, p. 394), and in 1637 their names are mentioned: Johann von Wahlen and Heinrich Pfeil (*ibid.*, p. 395). Johann von Wahlen resigned in 1643 (*ibid.*, p. 402) and the next year was replaced by Stefan Derenthal (*ibid.*, p. 404), who was still in office in 1652 (*ibid.*, p. 413).

The next judge of the bishopric in 1642 was Franciscus Reiniken. He was appointed by the Governor General on 24 May 1642 and after his appointment went to Stockholm to receive instructions from the Chancellor (RA, TA 75, pp. 27–31). During his absence, his brother-in-law Joachim Kippe was acting judge of Cēsis (Seuberlich, p. 1). On 4 August 1642 the Chancellor replied to sixteen queries made by Reiniken after his return to Cēsis. The town council had claimed its ancient privilege of having the right to judge criminal cases itself. On this claim the Chancellor resolved that King Gustav Adolf had granted him the bishopric and also the town of Cēsis. With a special charter, jurisdiction had been granted to him not only over the county but also over the town, and all cases were under his jurisdiction.

Axel Oxenstierna also then decided on the constitution of the Cēsis court. It was to be directed by a president and the president should be Reiniken. There were to be two assessors. Execution of verdicts was in the competence of the steward. Appeals should go to the High Court at Tartu. Further queries by Reiniken and replies by the Chancellor referred to details of jurisdiction. The main litigations were about landholding. The land of abandoned houses had been illegally drawn under the settled houses. Reiniken asked whether the previous council should not hand over to the present council the landrolls, minutes, privileges, and documents, or clear themselves with an oath that they did not have any. The Chancellor's resolution, as expected, was in the affirmative. The next query was whether the previous burgomaster Bernhard Hirsch should not render full accounts of incomes and expenditures of the town.–It is difficult to see why in such obvious matters the judge needed the authority of the Chancellor and could not instigate action himself.

The next question is of greater interest and might partly explain the need for the previous questions. Reiniken complained of the rebellious behaviour of the town council and that the town's people did not recognize the authority of His Excellency (the Chancellor). He saw the reason in the fact that only during steward Munck's time had an oath of allegiance been administered. He inquired whether the council and the town's people should not be asked to repeat their oath of allegiance to the Royal Majesty and the Excellency in order that they should recognize His Excellency as their lord (RA, TA 75, p. 232). Axel Oxenstierna replied (*ibid.*, p. 236) that to Her Royal Majesty and the Swedish Crown the principal respect had to be paid. Nevertheless, the town in question, the bishopric, and the starosty Cēsis, including jurisdiction, had been given by his Royal Majesty as a gift (sic) to the Excellency according to detailed documents. Consequently the said town should accept His Excellency as their master. Therefore the council and the citizens of the town had in fairness, in addition to the Royal Majesty, to give an oath of allegiance to His Excellency as their direct lord.

Reiniken's further questions were whether, after the oath, the Chancellor, as a sign of special benevolence, would not be willing to donate to the town the newly constructed corn-mill and the public-house outside the town's gate. The lengthy reply was in the affirmative. On the other hand, the question of whether the houses held, before the conquest, by the Catholic clergy should be managed by the town or the castle was resolved in favour of the castle, which means that Oxenstierna kept these houses and the attached land to himself.

The following questions related to the numbers of persons in the town court. The Chancellor resolved (*ibid.*, p. 237) that the court should be constituted of four persons–the president who should be the present and the future judge of the bishopric, two assessors (one from the town's council, the other from the citizens) and the fourth a *Notario Judicy*. On the query about the sources of salaries to be paid to the court the Chancellor resolved that the president would be paid from the revenue of the Chancellor, but the rest were to be paid from revenues of the town, except that the revenue from the town estate Jurğumuiža (St. Jürgen) should be used for upkeep of churches, schools, and hospitals.

In the next query Reiniken again referred to disobedience and asked whether it would not be advisable to station in the town of Cēsis some soldiers from Valmiera (*ibid.*, p. 233). In his reply (*ibid.*, p. 237) the Chancellor wrote that he would order a detachment of soldiers to be stationed in the town (see also RA, TA 342).

THE SUBCONSISTORY AT CĒSIS

In the following question Reiniken asked whether a subconsistory should not be established at Cēsis as in other places (*ibid.*, p. 233). The reply was (*ibid.*, p. 237) that the subconsistory should be established *ad eundem modum ex formam* like the other subconsistories. It should consist of the following. Firstly the director should be the present (Reiniken) and future judge. The dean should be magister Zacharius Holde, the two assessors–those of the county court. Members of the clergy should be the pastor of Cēsis, Bartolomeus Meyer, and the pastor of Valmiera, Joachim Cascheinius.

The question of the subconsistory was dealt with also in the memorial Count Erik issued to the management of the bishopric on 8 February 1653 (ED 1935, pp. 193–195). He stated that there was yet no certainty about the consistories and therefore the composition of the subconsistory had to be postponed until more information would be available. Obviously the reorganization decreeded by the government of the *collegium ecclesiasticum mixtum* to a *collegium purum* (see page 7) had created in practice some difficulties, hence the hesitation of Count Erik to introduce the reforms.

Nevertheless, Count Erik admonished the dean and the pastors to show zeal in preaching and teaching and advised them to be an example to the people. They should reproach from the pulpit and in conversation and punish all vices common in these places as arrogance, haughtiness, luxuriance, wastefulness, insincerity, falsehood, gossiping, and similar wickedness. One could have some doubts whether these human failings were typical of Livonia.

Especial attention should be devoted to education of children. The servants as well as the peasants should be admonished to live a pious life and this should be achieved through visitations. If the clergy found annoying behaviour which cannot be remedied by warning or punishment, they should approach the secular arm. This would not only save their souls, but would also find appreciation from the lords.

If contrary to expectation some of the clergy behaved in an unbecoming fashion as well in conversation as in example and if they voiced opposition to the commands of the lords or made common cause against the lords with the servants, those members of the clergy would suffer not only revenge from God, but they can also expect ingratitude from their superiors and the lords and would receive such a remuneration as they deserve.

The stewards should assist the clergy in their task. With the assistance of the bailiffs the peasantry should be led to a God-fearing life and they should be encouraged to attend divine service and visitations. On behalf of the lords, the steward should have a watchful eye on the churches, to ascertain how the clergy together with the churchward [from the peasantry] collected the tithe, and see that it was properly spent.

About the schools at Cēsis and Valmiera Count Erik promised to issue an instruction. He ordered the steward, the dean, the assessors, the director of the subconsistory, the burgomasters, and the councils of the towns to supervise the schools until the lords would declare themselves on this matter. The aim of the schools was that at least the youth should learn to read in their native language, to write, and to calculate. Each quarter of the year the above mentioned or at least the majority of them should examine the youth. All errors should then be rectified and schools brought to perfection.

The lengthy instruction by Count Erik shows that by 1653 the consistorial reforms of 1648 in the bishopric had not yet been introduced–he still writes about the lay director of the subconsistory. Obviously the need to issue this instruction was prompted by some disarray created by the reforms.

FRICTIONS BETWEEN THE JUDGE AND THE STEWARD

The above discussed letter of 1642 of Judge Reiniken concluded with a complaint against the steward. Obviously the problems Judge Traneus experienced were not only a personal matter but somehow inbuilt into the system. The Chancellor replied in a conciliatory way. He promised to command the steward to show just respect for the court and assist the judge in matters of execution. If the steward would not change his attitude, the judge was asked to report to the Chancellor.

The correspondence further promised to provide better premises for the court at Valmiera and there was a notice that, responding to the request of the judge, he would be sent a model of a seal to be used by the court.

With the subject of the friction between the judge and the steward started the memorial issued by Axel Oxenstierna to the Judge Franciscus Reiniken on 24 August 1643 (RA, TA 75, pp. 27–31), this time written in Swedish, while the previous resolutions were written in German. It appears that Reiniken had been in Sweden and the memorial was handed there to him. His disagreements with the steward, the Chancellor described as insignificant. Each had his own field of responsibility and the Chancellor went on to define these fields.

The judge had to know that the steward was representing His Excellency the Chancellor and that the steward was in charge of His Excellency's people and servants, the bailiffs, the military, and His Excellency's other subjects and officers of high and low rank. The steward was in charge of incomes of the bishopric and had to act according to his instructions. On behalf of His Excellency the steward had to collect fines. He was empovered to defend the rights of His Excellency, the fief, and the garrison. Without the stewards order or knowledge nobody could be apprehended except in *flagranti crimine.* In cases of small disagreements between the servants and the subjects of His Excellency, which were not brought before the court, the steward had to mediate or to punish the wrong doer.

On the other hand, jurisdiction had to be entrusted to the judge and his assessors. Everything which according to a regular lawsuit was submitted to the court, be it a criminal or a civil case, emerging from a contract or from other occasions between His Excellency's subjects and servants or others, ecclesiastics or laity, should be investigated. The judge then had to pronounce judgment which he would and could answer before God, His Excellency, and the High Court.

The steward should not interfere in matters of the judge, demur or intervene in a lawsuit, but keep his office as described previously. If the judge sentenced to prison or to a fine a subject of His Excellency, the judge had to inform the steward who would then take note and execute the sentence. Finally, the Chancellor increased the remuneration of the judge, provided him with a living quarters at the castle of Cēsis, and assigned to him a fisher and a hunter.

With an order, dated 10 November 1647 (RA, TA 75, p. 144), the Chancellor stipulated that the judge had to notify the steward about the location and date of the next sittings of the court. The steward in his turn would notify the bailiffs. The Chancellor further directed that the court should in future sit only in three places of the bishopric: Cēsis, Valmiera, and Burtnieki. This would enable the steward to be present at the hearings and would avoid expenses and complaints.

ENFORCEMENT OF THE AUTHORITY OF THE SUBCONSISTORY AND APPOINTMENT OF PASTORS

Reiniken had complained that the pastor of Rubene (Pappendorf) did not submit himself to the jurisdiction of His Excellency's subconsistory. The Chancellor resolved (*ibid.*, p. 31) that in such a case the pastor was not entitled to be allocated peasants and not entitled to the benefice he was receiving from the bishopric. By hanging the bread basket higher, the recalcitrant pastors could be brought back under the discipline of the ecclesiastical court.

There were some vacancies to the office of the clergy. Regarding Burtnieki, the Chancellor stated that this church was the most prominent in the bishopric and a qualified pastor had to be found who knew German and Latvian. The superintendent was asked to present one or several candidates for the vacancy to His Excellency's steward. After the candidates would have proved themselves, the steward should report to the Chancellor who would decide on the appointment.

Concerning the pastor of Valmiera the Chancellor resolved that if Magister Cascheinius was performing the same duties as his predecessor, i. e. would be in charge of the German, the Latvian, and the Finnish, congregations, he could keep the peasants assigned to the Valmiera pastorate.

CORPUS JURIS LIVONICI

After the establishment of courts by the Swedish government, the Livonian nobility was not happy about the law to be applied in the courts. The nobility wanted a codified law and one which would confirm their privileges. In response to these wishes, the Chancellor Axel Oxenstierna in 1640 asked a previous commissioner of the Swedish Crown—the councillor of the nobility and county judge, Engelbrecht von Mengden—to prepare a codification of the existing law. After three years, in 1643, a delegation of the nobility submitted for approval to the Swedish State Council Mengden's *Corpus iuris Livonici.*

Mengden's compilation was based on a previous project, compiled by Hilchen in 1599, on privileges of the nobility, prescriptive law, German common law, and to a certain extent on Swedish law. Mengden's codex consisted of five books. The first book in seven chapters dealt with the power of the king, dignitaries of the church, the nobility and its privileges, the towns, the peasants and extradition of the same, the servants of the nobility, and then down the social scale with tramps, paupers, gipsies, etc. The second book dealt with police matters and civil law in thirty chapters. Police matters were concerned with roads, rivers, harbours, wreckage, coins, the liberties of noblemen estates, hunting, bee hives, forestry rights, pastures, and lost and found things. Civil law dealt with parental power, the relations between husband and wife, testaments, legal portions, division of inheritance, disinheritance, guardianship, betrothal and nuptials, gifts, prescriptions, hiring out, purchases, eviction, renting, loans, debtors, surety, pledge, deposits, and other matters.

The third book dealt with the court and conduct of cases in nineteen chapters. The fourth book in 25 chapters dealt with the criminal law and the fifth book in only three chapters–with military organization of the country: the retainer service.

The Swedish government promised to examine the project with a view of bringing it more in line with Swedish law because it was influenced too much by Roman law (Richter, p. 48). The examination of the project was entrusted to Fabian Plater, the president of the Livonian High Court, but eventually the project was not confirmed (Buddenbrock 1821, 183, 3).

In 1648 the Livonian nobility made a new move. One of the codes of the Livonian knights' law (Ritterrecht) had been printed in Riga in 1537 with the title *De gemenen Stichtischen Rechte, ym Sticht van Ryga, geheten dat Ridderrecht.* The codex consisted of 249 paragraphs. Not only its language, as can be seen from the title, but also its content was antiquated. According to the legal historian Arveds Švābe, this code had been compiled by order of Habundi who ruled the Riga see from 1418 to 1424 as Archbishop Johann VI. In the opinion of Švābe, this code was accepted by the diet (Landtag) at Valka on 28 January 1422 (Švābe, p. 259). On 17. August 1648 Queen Kristina confirmed this 226 years old law with the resolution: 'The printed land and knights' law, which has been valid previously in Livonia and has been claimed to be in force also at present, Her Royal Majesty graciously permits to be maintained [. . .] ' (Buddenbrock 1821, 222, 6; the original text has been printed with a standard German translation: *ibid.* 1802, pp. 1–295). The confirmed code was a feudal law and contained material, procedure, civil and criminal norms. In 1858 the jurist and historian Alexander von Richter wrote: 'The land law achieved at least from then [1648] on a definite and legalized though, even then, insufficient foundation' (Richter, p. 45). The Livonian nobility also regarded the confirmed codex only as a temporary expedient and requested the Queen for a confirmation of the *Corpus iuris Livonici*. The Queen used delaying tactics (*ibid.*), and consequently the antiquated *Gemene Stichtische Rechte* remained in force till 1864.

DOMESTIC DISCIPLINE

In May 1649 Erik Oxenstierna issued a temporary explanation subject to his father's confirmation about the competence of the economy officers and the county court (ED 1935, pp. 167–169). Four paragraphs of the explanation dealt with the competence of what he called economy officers–the steward and the bailiffs, and the following five paragraphs with the competence of the judge.

The legal power of the steward was what can be called to enforce domestic discipline. The German term is 'Hauszucht'. The first paragraph of the explanation defined this term. It referred to punishment of lazy work by statute labourers, disobedience, non-payment of customary dues, and what was related to these delicts. If peasants were to be punished in cash or monetary values, the bailiffs had to report to the steward who would confirm execution. The second paragraph of the explanation dealt with quarrels among peasants about their land and meadows. These had to be decided by the bailiffs without taking bribes and everything had to be properly recorded. In cases too difficult to decide or if the bailiff was suspicious about the case, he had to request a resolution from the steward and the latter had to arrive personally at the spot to avert partiality of the bailiff. Paragraph three dealt with scuffles among the peasants. If such occurrencies were of no great avail and not punishable with money fines, the bailiff should mediate. In such cases the bailiff should not exact fine or administer hard corporal punishment. Serious cases should be handed over to the county court.

Cases of pilfering of insignificant quantities belonged to the economy. On a first occasion the fine was a threefold replacement of the pilfered goods. Repetition was to be punished with a fivefold replacement and on a third occasion or if the case was more serious it should go to the county court.

It is interesting to compare these stipulations with Count Erik's instructions for his Estonian estates, dated 4 May 1653 (RA, TA 75, p. 151): 'Justice over my peasants and in my estates should be conducted in such a way that if peasants are found to be dilatory in their statute labour, they should be punished by the bailiff. In doing so he has to observe moderation and should not beat up the people in anger with dangerous sticks and truncheons, possibly thus

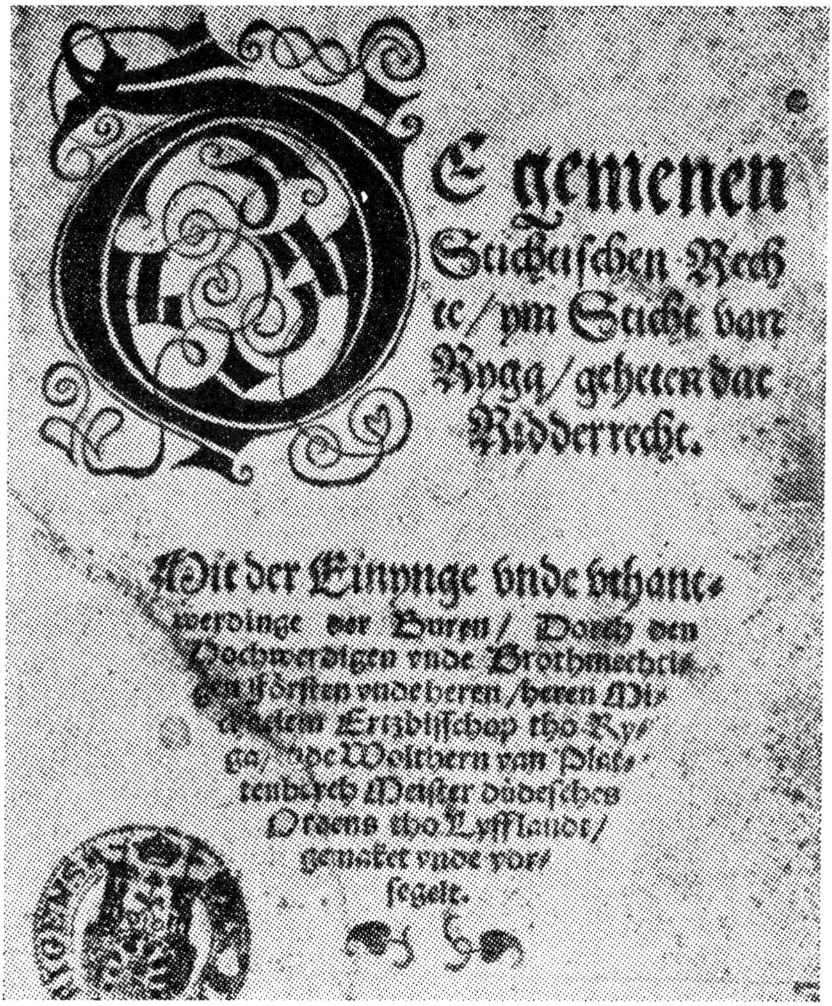
DE gemenen Stichtischen Rechte / ym Sticht van Ryga / geheten dat Ridderrecht.

Mit der Einynge vnde vthhantwerdinge der Buren / Dorch den Hochwerdigen vnde Grothmechtigen Försten vnde Heren / Heren Michaelem Ertzbisschop tho Ryga / vnde Wolthern van Plettenberch Meister dudesches Ordens tho Lyfflandt / gemaket vnde vorsegelt.

TITLE PAGE OF THE LIVONIAN KNIGHTS' LAW (1537)

Municipal Library of Riga

injuring them. Punishment should be done with sense and measure. If a peasant is mischievous he should be punished by birching. If he is a Finn he should be punished by putting in the box (Kasten) and in similar mode. Minor land quarrels among the peasants can be mediated by the bailiff according to custom. Important thefts or serious quarrels with peasants of other lords, which can result in losses to the Count, and criminal cases, the bailiffs should report to the steward and request his decision.'

The question remains open whether Count Erik was treating his Estonian peasants more severely than the Latvian peasants of his father or whether the passing of time was responsible for his far harsher attitude. In the explanation of 1649 he mentions only in passing that hard corporal punishment should be avoided. In the instruction of 1653 corporal punishment seems to be a matter of fact and only injury of people should be avoided. In Livonia during the eighteenth century, after the country was conquered by Russia, inhuman treatment of serfs became commonplace as vividly described by Garlieb Merkel (see his work *Die Letten* vorzüglich in Liefland am Ende des philosophischen Jahrhunderts; published 1796, second revised edition 1800).

THE COUNTY COURT OF THE BISHOPRIC

Count Erik's temporary explanation of May 1649 starting from paragraph five (ED 1935, p. 168 f.) dealt with the county court. Disagreement about pastorate lands, the land of pastorate's peasants, and the land given in fief to noblemen, as well as the land of the towns, was to be arbitrated by the court in cases of dispute. The judge had no power over the bailiffs. If he needed help from the bailiff he should in time notify the steward who would then notify those having to appear before the court. On the other hand, during the court session in urgent cases each bailiff had to assist the judge directly without asking the steward.

If there was no appeal, the judgment of the court should be made known to the steward who should at once execute the sentence but, if the case was urgent, then on the demand of the court the bailiff had to execute. If some outsider sued peasants of the bishopric, then the bailiff should assist the peasants, especially if the interests of the Chancellor were involved. The court had to permit the bailiffs to assist the peasants. The county court had to see that peasants were not in vain delayed by it. This referred to peasants who were not involved in cases and to witnesses as well.

The memorial Erik Oxenstierna issued on 8 February 1653 had also a section on the court (ED 1935, p. 193). The judge and the steward were both reminded to assist each other. If they could not reach mutual agreement, they should approach Adam Hirtenberg (about him see page 34) who either would reconcile them or report to the lord. The latter then would issue an appropriate resolution.

THE COURT AFTER THE FIRST NORTHERN WAR

During the First Northern War the bishopric, being in the war zone, was completely devastated. Axel Oxenstierna and his two sons had died. The minor sons of Count Erik were placed under guardianship (see Chapter Seven), and the guardians from their office in Stockholm directed the business of the bishopric.

The resolution of the guardians of 30 July 1660 instructed the steward to maintain the lay and ecclesiastical jurisdiction in such a way that nothing was lost from the original Royal donation. All previously achieved privileges should be maintained (RA, TA 75, p. 95). The Judge Reiniken should be paid arrears of his salary. His request regarding land and peasants could be satisfied. To show the benevolence of the guardians, the remuneration of Judge Reiniken was increased.

In 1663 the guardians appointed Per Hansson as the new inspector of the bishopric, at the same time appointing the previous inspector, Jakob Reutz, to the office of the judge (*ibid.* 76, fol. 35; 8 July 1663). On 30 June 1665, the guardians reminded both the steward and the judge of the late Chancellor's resolutions of 1643, 1647, and 1652, delineating the different competencies of the steward and the judge.

After the war, the Livonian nobility continued its pre-war campaign in the diet against the private courts of the bishopric and the county of Pärnu. In 1665, the King was induced to issue a decree that these courts should be respected (RA, RR: 8 December 1665; Meurling, pp. 90–91).

On the complaints of Dean Johann Ruhendorf against Judge Jakob Reutz the guardians resolved on 21 July 1666 (RA, TA 75, p. 284). The Dean had complained that Judge Reutz had decided on consistorial matters himself and with assistance of persons not belonging to the subconsistory. The guardians resolved that such decisions were illegal.

In 1668 Jakob Reutz complained in turn to the guardians asking their assistance in a number of cases. The guardians replied with a six paragraph resolution (*ibid.*, pp. 285–288). It was confirmed that for the upkeep of the school in Cēsis the incomes from Jurğumuiža should be used as previously. The Judge had complained that the burgomaster and council of Cēsis had interfered in the jurisdiction of the Judge and the subconsistory. The guardians ordered the steward to achieve cooperation instead of confrontation between the Judge and the town.

The following paragraphs of the resolution dealt with the endeavour of the Judge to receive more remuneration and disclosed that he was in debt to the Oxenstiernas to the amount of 3500 Rd. The guardians suggested that to settle the debt and interest he should alienate to them his estate Lorupe (Chroneborg or Kronenberg). The historian of Livonian estates L.von Stryk was not aware of this phase in the history of Lorupe (Stryk, p. 89) and wrote that the estate was confirmed to Mathias Giging in 1630 (see also ARL, p.255). Actually in 1669 Lorupe, in the Sigulda district, was acquired by the guardians (see page 187). Furthermore, from the private revision conducted in 1672 (RA, TA 371, pp. 224–226) it can be seen that Lorupe was an Oxenstierna estate.

THE ADMINISTRATIVE JUDGES

The final paragraph of the resolution of 1668 in response to Reutz's report (*ibid.* 83, p. 406) dealt with the newly appointed Livonian administrative judges who allegedly were interfering with the jurisdiction of the bishopric court. For the origin of the institution of the administrative judges (Ordnungsrichter) or uncus judges (Hakenrichter) we have to go back in history to the fifteenth and sixteenth centuries. During these centuries, in Livonia special courts were established to deal with recovering of peasant refugees. In the Tartu bishopric administrative judges were appointed as early as 1458. The Riga archibishopric followed in 1498, and in about 1550 the state of the Teutonic Order also appointed administrative judges. With the collapse of the Livonian confederation in 1561, together with other legal institutions the office of the administrative judges came to an end. When in 1648 Queen Kristina confirmed the Knights' Code, to the printed copy was attached the 31 January 1494 ordinance about extradition of fugitive peasants (Švābe, p. 272). The Livonian nobility held the view that together with the code this ordinance was also confirmed by the Queen and consequently in their 1653 diet resolved to renew the office of the administrative judges. It seems that this decision was not implemented because of the war.

After the war peasants more than ever were looking for better masters and, on the other hand, noblemen in their turn were keen to limit freedom of movement of the peasants. One therefore cannot be surprised that some of the administrative judges now appointed were eager to look for fugitive peasants in the bishopric. The resolution of the guardians of the bishopric of 1668 stated in no uncertain terms that the administrative judges were out of bounds in the bishopric and that they were not entitled to interfere in the jurisdiction administered by Jakob Reutz. The guardians informed Reutz that they had written on this matter to the Governor General.

It is not always possible to distinguish whether the fines received by the bishopric were levied by the administration or the court. Cases where executioners were involved: torture, flogging, decapitation, burning at the stake, and hanging, for which executioners were paid, were recorded in the cash accounts. Often it is not possible to decide which sort of punishment was administered by the executioners because of cryptic recording of the payments. In 1637 the executioner was paid, for torture of a girl, 2 Rd 60 gr. The same amount was paid to him for punishment of the same girl and again the same amount for punishment of a peasant from Kurzeme. There is no indication what the punishment was. In addition the executioner received one riksdollar for three meals in the public-house (ED 1935, p. 395). In 1639 an executioner came from Riga, who was paid 11 Rd for punishing (burning at the stake?) a witch. In the same year executioners from Limbaži and Smiltene were invited, who received for their work 5 Rd 6 gr. For capture of a witch, 2 Rd were paid (*ibid.*, p. 396). In June 1640 the executioner from Riga was paid, for burning a witch at the stake and for torturing another witch, a total of 12 and a half riksdollars. In July the same year two sinners were punished and six persons punished at the whipping-post. For this 19 Rd were paid. In November a child murderess was punished and a female sinner thrown into water (the river Gauja?)–paid 17 Rd. The executioner from Limbaži received one riksdollar for undisclosed work. In July 1641 (the same economic year as 1640) one culprit was hanged and one was put on the wheel at a cost of 15 Rd. Some material for torture implements was purchased and an executioner received 3 Rd 30 gr. for undisclosed work (*ibid.*, p. 397).

It seems that from 1641 the bishopric engaged a permanent executioner who was paid 50 Rd per annum and in 1642 received 20 Rd for a suit (*ibid.*, pp. 399, 400). The remuneration of 50 Rd was the same as paid to the assessors of the court. The name of the executioner is only given as Michael. In 1643 the executioner received in addition to his wages travelling expenses of 7 Rd and for sustenance at the Valmiera public-house 1 Rd 54 gr. were paid. A sentinel was paid 4 Rd 60 gr. (*ibid.*, p. 402). The following year the executioner was paid for punishment of six sinners 6 Rd, in addition to his remuneration of 50 Rd, travelling expenses 5 Rd, and for sustenance 4 Rd 63 gr. (*ibid.*, p. 404). In 1645, besides his salary, he was paid for punishment of 6 sinners 6 Rd and travelling expenses 2 Rd (*ibid.*, p. 405). In 1646 the only expenses to the executioner were recorded at 4 and a half Rd, not the salary of 50 Rd (*ibid.*, p. 407), but the following year a total of 129 Rd was recorded as payment (*ibid.*, p. 408). Apparently in 1647 the bishopric terminated the employment of a permanent executioner and in the following years only smaller sums were recorded for occasional work done by invited executioners from other places, as was the practice before 1641. In 1650 three sorcerers (Malifikanten) were punished and a woman was tortured at a cost of 12 Rd 54 gr. (*ibid.*, p. 409). In 1651 no executioner was engaged and the only expenses were for proceedings the bishopric had at the Pärnu county court and the Tartu High Court. In 1652 two persons were punished at the whipping-post at a cost of 5 Rd (*ibid.*, p. 413). In 1653 the executioner had more work which was not specified in the accounts. He was paid 20 and a half Rd (*ibid.*, p. 415). Even more work, unless the charge was increased, had to be performed in 1654 when the executioner received 32 Rd 24 gr. and in addition for the punishment of a female servant 2 Rd 45 gr., and also 3 Rd for undisclosed work (*ibid.*, p. 416; see also ED 1962, p. 389). After the First Northern War a permanent executioner again was employed.

As can be seen from the above review, in the bishopric there were a number of witches and sorcerers punished. Superintendent Samson's six sermons against witchcraft published in 1626 put the need to combat witchcraft before the public, and the first half of the Swedish period in Livonia saw a great number of executions of witches and sorcerers at the stake. In comparison with other Livonian courts, in the bishopric a relatively small number of witches were put to death. In the second half of the seventeenth century the Swedish government intervened and sentences of death were passed on only for accords with the devil and sorcery doing harm. Fortune-telling, witch-healing, and other practices of non-dangerous superstition were punished by birching, caning, or monetary fines. In 1686 the Swedish government prohibited torture and then witchcraft only seldom appeared in the proceedings of the courts. Without torture no confessions of witchcraft could be obtained. In Livonia the last known sentence of burning at the stake occurred in 1692 and the last case of decapitation in 1699.

LIQUIDATION OF THE COURT OF THE BISHOPRIC

In the 1680's the Swedish Crown took over all the important estates in the realm including Livonia. These great revolutionary reforms were called the reduction of estates (see Chapter Nine). With the reduction there was no longer a justification for a separate court of the bishopric and in 1681 it was liquidated.

The Royal decree to liquidate the court was announced to the Livonian diet in August 1681 among propositions signed by Governor General Krister Horn on 12 July 1681 (Schirren, p. 44, § 3). The jurisdiction of the liquidated court was divided among three royal county courts. Under the jurisdiction of the county court of Riga was placed the territory between the rivers Gauja and Salaca. The territory on the other side of the river Salaca was placed under the jurisdiction of the county court of Pärnu and the remaining territory of the former bishopric—under the jurisdiction of the county court of Cēsis.

At the diet the Governor General advised the nobility to deliberate and work out a time-table for sittings of the court—the county courts should sit at different times. He envisaged that because of the reduction there might occur disputes about boundaries between the reduced and other estates and simultaneous sessions of all county courts would delay court proceedings because the commissioner of the Crown (Commissario Fisci) could not take part in the several courts at once.

The reply of the diet to the propositions of the Governor General was in the affirmative (Schirren, p. 48). Reading between the lines one notes a certain satisfaction of the nobility with the liquidation of the court of the bishopric, because the Livonian noblemen had been always opposed to the jurisdiction of this court. They agreed that sessions of the county courts be arranged at different times; the county court judges had already agreed on a time-table.

Thus, after more than fifty years of existence, the separate court of the bishopric was liquidated and its jurisdiction divided among the royal courts.

GENEALOGICAL TREE OF THE OXENSTIERNAS AF SÖDERMÖRE

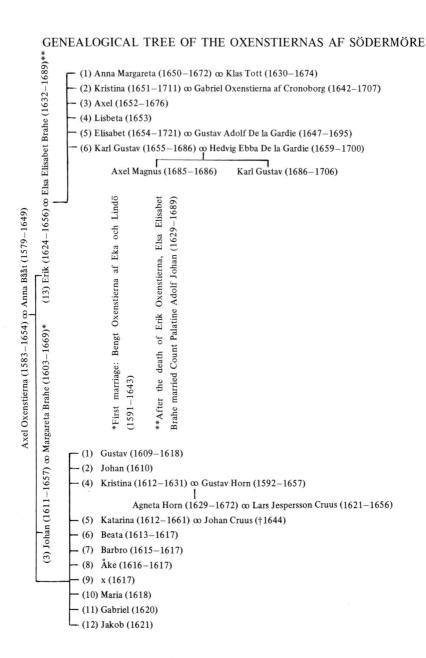

Axel Oxenstierna (1583–1654) ∞ Anna Bååt (1579–1649)

- (13) Erik (1624–1656) ∞ Elsa Elisabet Brahe (1632–1689)**
  - (1) Anna Margareta (1650–1672) ∞ Klas Tott (1630–1674)
  - (2) Kristina (1651–1711) ∞ Gabriel Oxenstierna af Cronoborg (1642–1707)
  - (3) Axel (1652–1676)
  - (4) Lisbeta (1653)
  - (5) Elisabet (1654–1721) ∞ Gustav Adolf De la Gardie (1647–1695)
  - (6) Karl Gustav (1655–1686) ∞ Hedvig Ebba De la Gardie (1659–1700)
    - Axel Magnus (1685–1686)
    - Karl Gustav (1686–1706)
- (3) Johan (1611–1657) ∞ Margareta Brahe (1603–1669)*
- (1) Gustav (1609–1618)
- (2) Johan (1610)
- (4) Kristina (1612–1631) ∞ Gustav Horn (1592–1657)
  - Agneta Horn (1629–1672) ∞ Lars Jespersson Cruus (1621–1656)
- (5) Katarina (1612–1661) ∞ Johan Cruus (†1644)
- (6) Beata (1613–1617)
- (7) Barbro (1615–1617)
- (8) Åke (1616–1617)
- (9) x (1617)
- (10) Maria (1618)
- (11) Gabriel (1620)
- (12) Jakob (1621)

*First marriage: Bengt Oxenstierna af Eka och Lindö (1591–1643)

**After the death of Erik Oxenstierna, Elsa Elisabet Brahe married Count Palatine Adolf Johan (1629–1689)

CHAPTER SEVEN

THE ESTATES AFTER THE DEATH OF AXEL OXENSTIERNA

AXEL OXENSTIERNA'S TESTAMENT

Axel Oxenstierna's first will was written on 21 August 1647. Superseding this he wrote his last will and testament on 10 February 1650, after the death of his wife Anna Åkesdotter Båât (23 June 1649), with a supplement on 31 January 1652 (AOB, I, 1, pp. 638–662).

In his testament the main estates and fiefs according to the law were willed to his sons, but his daughter and granddaughter received from the incomes of the estates a dowry. Two thirds of the inherited estates were willed to the sons and one third to the female offspring and their children. The county of Södermöre and the barony of Kimitho and underlying estates were willed to the eldest son Johan. Axel Oxenstierna then wrote that, because in this way he had bypassed his son Erik, he willed to him all his Estonian estates (*ibid.*, p. 644). The estates were listed in the will. In Virumaa (Wijrland) they were Roela (Rögel), Lähtru (Lechtigal), Püssi (Pyes), Vohnja (Fåvela), Völe (Wolgal), Kavastu (Kapes), Vatku (Wattküll), and in Läänemaa (Wiek): Vöhma (Wemes) in Koluvere (Lode lähn). In the following year (1651) after Axel Oxenstierna had signed his will, he gave all the above mentioned Estonian estates to his son Erik as a gift (RA, TA 63). Thus Count Erik became the legitimate possessor of these estates before the death of his father in 1654.

Count Erik in his instruction to the bailiffs of the Estonian estates, dated 4 May 1653 (*ibid.* 75, pp. 148–160), used repeatedly the expression 'my estates' in sharp contrast to the expression used in the instructions issued about the Latvian estates, where as a rule he referred to his father's estates. There is also a copy of the 'Count Excellency's' list of remuneration of the officers at the Estonian estates (*ibid.*, pp. 36–37). The bailiffs, except those of Lähtru and Vatku, were listed and in addition pastors, sacristans, and pupils, of Kadrina (St. Catharina), Haljala (Halliel), Viru Jaagupi (St. Jacoby), Lüganuse (Luggenhusen), and Kirevere (Kirrefer).

On 1 August 1689 Count Karl Gustav Oxenstierna submitted proofs to the reduction commission on how his grandfather Axel Oxenstierna had acquired some of the Estonian estates (LR, F: 1). Peter Taube had purchased

Püssi in 1621 and on 20 December 1622 Axel Oxenstierna had purchased it from Diedrich Taube's heirs. On 30 August 1623 King Gustav Adolf had donated to the Chancellor 10 unci land and a mill. On 18 March 1635 for 2000 Rd Axel Oxenstierna had purchased Vohnja. This information differs from that published by Paul Johansen.

In a specification of 17 November 1684 (RA, TA 70, fol. 193), the following data about the Estonian estates are extant for the years 1647 to 1672 (total unci corrected):

Estate	Unci of demesne	Total unci
Vohnja	14 ½	103
Kavastu and Völe	35 ¾	86 ½
Roela and Lähtru	8	113 ½
Püssi	13	84
Vöhma	½	28 ½
Vatku	–	10
Kosküla	–	10
Total	71 ¾	435 ½

According to the testament the bishopric was divided by Axel Oxenstierna into two parts. To one part he allocated Valmiera,Trikāta, Mujāni, and Ēvele, to the other part–Cēsis, Burtnieki, and Vecate. Which son gets which part had to be decided by lot. To equalize these parts could be used Ropaži, and also exchange of some small estates could be effected. The expenses of the Valmiera fortification and artillery, and upkeep of the garrison, was a burden to be shared by both sons. Also jurisdiction and the maintenance of the judge was a joint obligation of both.

It is intriguing to discover the method by which Axel Oxenstierna divided the bishopric into two parts. It was not a territorial division because Valmiera with adjoining estates was located between Cēsis and Burtnieki with their adjoining estates (see map page 13). The conjecture of the present author is that Axel Oxenstierna proceeded as follows. In 1650 (see ED 1935, p. 41) Valmiera had 157.5 payment unci and 224.5 mantal. Trikāta had 97.5 unci and 79.5 mantal. Mujāni and Ēvele had 95.25 unci and 130.5 mantal. Thus in the first lot there were together 350.25 unci and 434.5 mantal.

Cēsis had 95.25 unci and 78.5 mantal, Burtnieki–103.75 unci and 282 mantal, and Vecate–113.25 unci and 136 mantal. Thus in the second lot were 312.25 unci and 496.5 mantal. In comparison, in the first lot were 38 unci more, but 62 mantal less. 38 over 62 is 61.29 %. The mantal of each lot multiplied by this percentage results for the first lot in 266.3 mantal, in the second

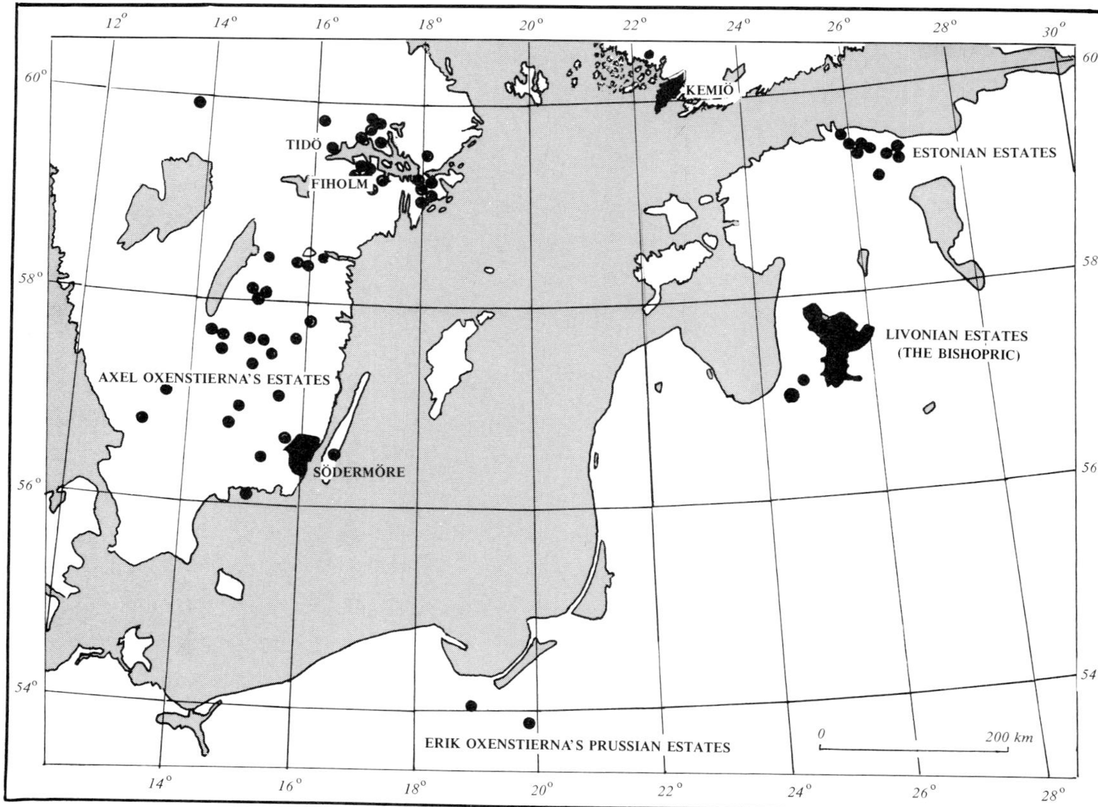

ESTATES OF THE OXENSTIERNAS AF SÖDERMÖRE

lot in 304.3 mantal. Adding the number of unci to these calculated mantal figures we get for each lot exactly the same figure of 616.55. It seems that, in this way manipulating the data about payment and mantal figures for the various estates, the Chancellor had found a formula on how to divide the bishopric into equal parts. Nevertheless, he obviously had some doubts how this artificial division would work out in practice and therefore did not include, in either of the allocations, Ropaži which then could be used for equalizing possible differences. A further escape clause was that the brothers could equalize the lots by exchanging estates at their own decision.

WAR

In the same year (1654) when Axel Oxenstierna died, the neighbouring province of Swedish Livonia, Latgale or, as it was then called, Polish Livonia was invaded by Russia. Vasilij Sheremetiev occupied Ludza (Ludsen) and Rēzekne (Rositten) starosties and part of Daugavpils (Dünaburg) starosty. The Latgalian noblemen requested help from the Swedish Governor General of Livonia, but Sweden was not inclined to be involved in martial conflict with Russia and help was refused. Nevertheless, Livonia was living in the shadow of an expected war, but for a time the worries were relegated to the background because of local calamities. In the bishopric the crop was disappointing. Heavy rain had flooded the fields and damaged the crop. At Trikāta hail had completely destroyed the harvest and the steward Sprengport reported to Erik Oxenstierna that the Trikāta peasants were unable to pay their customary dues (RA, TA 271: 10 July 1654).

In 1655, the First Northern War started and the King of Sweden, Karl X, attacked Poland. Swedish forces occupied Daugavpils. In the early summer of 1656 intelligence reported that a Russian invasion of the Swedish Baltic provinces was to be expected.

On 21 July 1656 the Swedish Commander-in-chief Magnus Gabriel De la Gardie issued a proclamation (*ibid.* 347) that a Russian attack could be expected in Ingermanland and Livonia. He declared that defence was the obligation of all citizens, including the peasantry. He invited the citizens and the peasants in each parish to find a brave man as a captain and with his help to select lieutenants and corporals. In the event of an attack by the enemy, peasants had to hide in the woods and disturb the enemy day and night. They had to fell trees over the roads and keep in touch with neighbouring captains and the commandant of the nearest fortress. For their sustenance they were allowed all grain which the lords of the tracts in enemy hands had not evacuated and also food which could be taken from the enemy. Captains and officers showing valour against the enemy would be remunerated by the King with estates and other benefices for themselves and their children. Peasants who showed bravery and valour, after recommendation by the captain, would be freed from statio tax for six years–for themselves and their children. Nevertheless, they should not refuse due obedience to their lords.

As expected, the Russians invaded Ingermanland and Livonia with a thrust towards Tartu and along the Daugava river towards Riga. Not being able to take Riga after a siege, they retreated marooning and burning the countryside. Even worse was the legacy the Russians left after they had retreated–the plague.

Before the Russian invasion the bishopric was put on a war footing. A colonel of the Royal Swedish army was appointed commander of the Valmiera garrison. Much to chagrin of commandant Sprengport he demanded the keys of the gates of Valmiera, which Sprengport refused (RA, TA 271: Sprengport to Count Erik, 7 April 1656). Sprengport acted feverishly. From Riga he ordered powder, slow-match, balls, and muskets, and recruited men. He wrote to Count Erik: 'I will also further do what is needed because at this time one cannot wait for orders' (*ibid.*, 21 April 1656). On 19 July 1656 Sprengport reported that because of the Russian attack peasants, in general, did no longer obey but 'the subjects of Your Excellency are obedient' (*ibid.*). Several days later he had to change his opinion: 'The peasants are not inclined to obey' (*ibid.*, 24 July).

On 19 October 1656 Lieutenant General Magnus Gabriel De la Gardie ordered the commandant of Valmiera, Sprengport, to provide the fortress of Valmiera with supplies. The Russians advanced as far as Cēsis and pillaged the town. The bailiffs of the district secured an affidavit that there had been nothing left to account for, because everything had been taken by the enemy. It was later said that the Swedish forces had finished off what the Russians had left (RA, TA 347: Elisabet and Kristina Oxenstierna, 30 April 1708).

After the retreat of the Russians a new invasion of Livonia was expected –this time from the south by the Lithuanian and Polish forces. On 13 August 1657 Magnus Gabriel De la Gardie, in view of the fact that Valmiera was infected by the plague and in his opinion could not be defended, ordered the destruction of the fortress and the salvaging of armaments and ammunition. He directed that before this action was taken the advice of Major General Aderkas and of Colonel Toll had to be asked (RA, TA 347). Their opinion was that the Valmiera fortress could be defended and so no evacuation of Valmiera took place. After the Lithuanian and Polish forces had taken Cēsis, its Swedish garrison retreated and came to Valmiera. The commandant Sprengport refused them entry into the town because of alleged shortage of food. They were forced to continue to march to Pärnu without rest. In hot pursuit of the retreating Swedes the Poles laid siege on Valmiera. The 103 or 111 men of the garrison of Valmiera could not defend the perimeter of the stronghold. After five days of siege, commandant Sprengport called together the citizens of Valmiera and the fugitives who had fled from the enemy and suggested they burn down the town, retreat to the castle of Valmiera and defend themselves there. The suggestions were turned down by the citizens and fugitives. As the garrison was not able to defend Valmiera, talks were started with the Poles about conditions of a surrender. On 25 October 1657 Sprengport and the Polish Major General Komorowski signed a capitulation (RA, TA 346). On 27 October the Poles entered Valmiera and the Swedish garrison was permitted to go to Tallinn beating drums, carrying banners, and in full arms with burning slow-matches in hand and bullets in the mouth (§ 3 of the capitulation). Two heavy guns with ten shots were also permitted to take along.

Instead of the agreed road to Tallinn Sprengport marched with his contingent of some hundred Finns and Latvians to Pärnu. The Poles then regarded the agreement as broken. The three officers left by Sprengport with the Poles as hostages were imprisoned and the Poles did not regard the obligations undertaken of not plundering Valmiera and ill-treating the inhabitants and fugitives as binding for themselves (Hornborg, p. 43). Karl Oxenstierna later wrote that in the years 1656 and 1657 the enemy had plundered the whole bishopric and the little which was left was consumed and taken away by the Swedish army and garrison. Not a single creature of the live-stock of the bishopric was left (RA, TA 63).

With the surrender of Valmiera the Latvian part of Livonia (Vidzeme) except Riga was in Polish hands. When King Karl X appointed as Governor General of Livonia Count Robert Douglas, things changed. On 16 July 1658 Douglas arrived in Riga and on 3 August Swedish forces retook the key of Vidzeme–Valmiera. As a consequence the Poles were forced to leave Livonia.

On 7 August 1658 Douglas appointed Sprengport again as commandant of Valmiera in view of his gallant defence work the previous year. In 1659 and 1660 the Swedish general staff was accommodated at Valmiera with Fieldmarshal Robert Douglas, Major Nils Bååt, and secretary Justus Menzenkamp. The commandant was Anders Munck, Junior. There were four companies of cavalry and eight companies of infantry (*ibid.* 72).

The decisive events of the war occurred in Denmark. Late in 1659 the Swedish army in Fünen was forced to surrender to the allied troops of Denmark, Poland, Holland, and Austria (Ogg, p. 450). In January 1660 peace negotiations started. During the negotiations Karl X died (on 13 February 1660) and the Swedish throne was inherited by the minor Karl XI. Peace was concluded and with French help Sweden kept Livonia.

AXEL OXENSTIERNA'S HEIRS

According to the will of Axel Oxenstierna, the bishopric was inherited by Johan and Erik Oxenstierna. It is obvious that because of the war the division of the bishopric as provided in the will could not take place (Meurling, p. 87, based on antiquated literature, thinks that the division happened). Johan Oxenstierna was living in Germany and from 1655 was president of the tribunal in Wismar. Erik Oxenstierna after his father's death succeeded him as the Chancellor of Sweden on 20 October 1654 (Fries, p. 163). He had left his office as Governor of Estonia already in the spring of 1653 and was succeeded there by Heinrich von Turn in 1654. On 2 July 1655, in response to Erik Oxenstierna's request, King Karl X confirmed both Johan and Erik Oxenstierna in the possession of the bishopric (RA, Donationskontoret i Lifland, F: 10, fol. 18). After Prussia was acquired by Sweden, Erik Oxenstierna was appointed by the King as Governor General of Prussia on 10 December 1655 (Fries, p. 234; in the RA, Riksregistratur for December 1655, fol. 2598, the date is not given, but it is mentioned that 'today' Elbing had surrendered, which provides the date of the appointment).

On 24 June 1656, against a payment of 70,000 riksdollars the King granted to Erik Oxenstierna and his male descendents the starosty Christburg (see RA, TA 47, no. 1; Fries, p. 316, writes that Christburg had always been an appurtenance of the governor in Marienburg and consequently was granted him in addition to the salary of 6000 Rd; she does not mention the payment of 70,000 Rd by Count Erik to the King). Further on, on the same date against a payment of 31,000 Rd Erik Oxenstierna was granted Sigismund Güldenstern's estates (RA, *ibid.*) and on 17 September 1656 the estate Schroop. This grant was signed by the King at Frauenburg in Prussia. There on 2 November 1656 Erik Oxenstierna died. He died intestate (RA, TA 63, Gustav Adolf De la Gardie's memorial).

His widow Elsa Elisabet Brahe had two sons: Axel (born 1652) and Karl Gustav (born 1655) and three daughters (Elgenstierna V, p. 608). Before his death Erik Oxenstierna had appointed his brother Johan as guardian of his children.

STEWARD AREND CORNELIUS TURLOW

On 20 April 1657 at Wismar Johan Oxenstierna appointed Arend Cornelius Turlow as chief inspector and steward of all estates left by Erik Oxenstierna in Prussia, Sweden, Livonia, and Estonia. Turlow had been in the service of Erik Oxenstierna as a secretary since 1646, the year Erik Oxenstierna was appointed Governor of Estonia (Fries, p. 322). In his instruction to Turlow

(RA, TA 75, pp. 127–134) Johan Oxenstierna commanded Turlow to go to Prussia and convey his greetings and letters to his sister-in-law. He instructed him to settle the debts of his late brother in Prussia and to engage bailiffs for his brother's Prussian estates. Colonel Reichard held a mortgage over the Prussian starosty Christburg. If Reichard would agree to take an estate instead of the interest on the mortgage this could be granted, but Reichard was not permitted to interfere in the management of the late Erik's Prussian estates. These should be managed by Turlow himself, if necessary, requesting the help of Governor Linde. It is to be noted that the fact that Erik Oxenstierna had estates in Prussia is unknown to historians of Prussia.

Turlow was instructed to ship the corpse of Erik to Sweden and accompany it. He should assist the widow of Erik in every possible way in Stockholm and take the advice of the guardians, Krister Bonde and Israel Lagerfeld; he should help to organize the court of the widow, assist her in the management of her Swedish estates by engaging an accountant, a scribe, and other servants, all according to the wishes of the widow and the guardians–Bonde and Lagerfeld.

After the Swedish affairs were put in order, Turlow should proceed to Estonia. There he should observe the instructions left by Erik, but modify them according to circumstances and what time might demand. Afterwards Turlow should proceed to Livonia. There he should inspect all the estates, but no changes in the disposition should be made. The Livonian estates were jointly possessed by himself (Johan Oxenstierna) and the children of Erik. All suggestions about change, Turlow should report to Johan.

After returning to Prussia the management of the starosty Christburg, the estate Reichandres, and the Güldensterns' inherited manors with the estate Schroop, should be put in order, as well as jurisdiction over the town of Christburg. Turlow had to inspect all the estates in Prussia, Estonia, and Livonia annually or every second year, he had to demand the accounts in time for auditing and preparing a general account (obviously for submission to Count Johan Oxenstierna).

DEATH OF JOHAN OXENSTIERNA

On 5 December 1657 Johan Oxenstierna died. His widow Margareta Brahe (both in their second marriage) had no issue and consequently the only heirs to the bishopric and the other estates became the sons of her brother's daughter Elsa Elisabet Brahe, with the usual obligation to pay a dowry to the sisters of the sons. On 6 October 1658 King Karl X confirmed the Countess Elsa Elisabet Brahe and her male descendents as heirs of the estates including the bishopric and starosty Cēsis (*ibid.*, p. 35). In his letter the King referred to the donations by the late King Gustav Adolf to the Chancellor Axel Oxenstierna and his own previous confirmation of 2 July 1655.

The appointment of Turlow as steward by Johan Oxenstierna remained in force, but he was able to go to Livonia only after hostilities of the war had terminated.

THE STOCKHOLM OFFICE OF GUARDIANSHIP

To handle the affairs of the Oxenstiernas af Södermöre, probably soon after the death of Axel Oxenstierna, an office at Stockholm was established (Oxenstierna stärbhusets kontor). Erik Oxenstierna and his secretary Arend Cornelius Turlow took part in organization of this office. After the death of Erik and Johan Oxenstierna the office became of paramount importance (see Arnold Soom, Introduction to the catalogue of Tidö-arkivet at RA, 1970, p. III). A council of guardians was established. Up to her second marriage to Count Palatine Adolf Johann von Zweibrücken on 12 December 1661, Erik's widow Elsa Elisabet Brahe was very active in directing the management of the estates, but her orders were usually countersigned by one of the guardians. On 1 July 1661 the guardians–Gustav Bonde, Knut Kurck, and Israel Lagerfeld–sent a circular to all stewards that the Countess Elsa Elisabet had invited the three signatories to become guardians. They had accepted this request but with the condition that orders would be issued jointly by all guardians and not by someone individually (Gardberg, p. 30). From 1662 to 1668 documents were signed by Israel Lagerfeld and Knut Kurck. On an extant document of 1671 the signatories are Nikolaus Brahe, Israel Lagerfeld, and Jakob Schnack. This shows that all guardians did not sign documents and that the circular should be interpreted as a hint that Countess Elsa Elisabet had no longer power to sign documents.

The guardians held regular meetings, but drafts of minutes are only extant for 1661 and 1670–1672 (RA, TA 75). For 1660–1669 there is a register of documents (*ibid.* 76–77) and correspondence from the same years (*ibid.* 78–86).

To illustrate the frequency of meetings–beginning with June 1661 meetings were held on 13, 17, 25, and 26 June, 4 August, 2, 9, 17, and 19 September, and 14 November (*ibid.* 75: 'Södermöriske förmyndarförvaltnings protokoll över sammanträden under åren 1661–1670, 1672'). The accounts of the manors were no longer sent to Tidö but instead to the Stockholm office of the guardians, situated in the late Count Erik's house. It was not until relatively late in eighteenth century or at the beginning of the nineteenth century that the archives were transferred from Stockholm to Tidö.

THE GUARDIANS

Gustav Bonde (1620–1667) became chamber councillor (kammarråd) in 1645, governor (landshövding) in 1648, state and chamber councillor (riks- och kammarråd) in 1653, a commissioner in the reduction commission in 1655, chamber president (kammarpresident) in 1660, and minister of finance (riksskattmäster) also in 1660 (Elgenstierna, I). He was not a very active member of the council of guardians because of time needed for his governmental posts.

Knut Kurck (1622–1690) was a member of an ancient family of Swedish noblemen. He had studied in Uppsala and Leiden and had been appointed to several important posts in the Swedish administration. He was also a state councillor. After disagreement developed with King Karl XI, he was relieved of all his posts (Elgenstierna, IV, p. 331). In the council of guardians of the heirs of the Oxenstiernas af Södermöre he was active and showed initiative.

Count Nils Brahe (1633–1699) signed as Nikolaus Brahe. He was the brother of Elsa Elisabet Brahe. He had studied in Uppsala (1647) and had occupied various posts, including that of ambassador to Portugal (1655), Germany (1658), England (1661), and Denmark (1674). He took part as colonel in the expedition to Prussia (1657) and in 1660 was appointed state councillor (until 1682) and admiral of the navy (until 1677). He was reputedly the richest man in Sweden, but lost nearly all his estates during the reduction (Elgenstierna, I, p. 558), including Cesvaine (Seßwegen) in Livonia.

Israel Israelsson Lagerfeld (1610–1684) was ennobled in 1646. He had studied in Uppsala. From 1637 to 1640 he made extensive travels in Europe with his pupil Gabriel Gabrielsson Oxenstierna. At the Brömsebro peace negotiations (1644–1645) he was the Swedish secretary. From 1650 he was vice-president of Abo High Court and from 1653 to 1654 envoy in England and afterwards vice-president of the College of Commerce (kommerskollegium). Before leaving for Prussia, Erik Oxenstierna appointed Lagerfeld as representative in his private affairs (Fries, p. 315). Lagerfeld had some connections with the Baltic by his marriage to Margareta Lennep from Tallinn (Elgenstierna, IV, p. 451).

Jakob Schnack (1625–1697) was the secretary of the office of guardianship. He was ennobled in 1673 and assumed the name of Sneckenberg. He had studied at Åbo, Uppsala, Greifswald, and Rostock, and was a public servant (Elgenstierna, IV, p. 339). Having visited and inspected personally the Baltic estates of the Oxenstiernas in Livonia, Estonia, and Finland, he was regarded as an expert in relevant questions of management. The inspection tour was prompted by complaints about disorders and the decline of income from the estates.

TURLOW'S MANAGEMENT OF THE BISHOPRIC

On 28 February 1659 at Stockholm Elsa Elisabet Brahe, countersigned by the guardian, Israel Lagerfeld, issued a 26 paragraph instruction to steward Arend Cornelius Turlow (RA, TA 75, pp. 107–126). In the preamble of the instruction she wrote that although the chief inspector and steward certainly had full power of authority and instructions to deal with all aspects to benefit the minor children, nevertheless this instruction was issued to confirm the previous authorization and to remind about further mentioned affairs.

In paragraph one of the instruction Turlow was reminded to go to the Estonian and Livonian estates, but in view of the death of Count Johan Oxenstierna all the estates now reverted to her children and therefore he was instructed first to go to Kemiö (Kimitho) in Finland. This was not meant to prejudice Count Johan's widow about what she possibly could be entitled, but nevertheless Turlow should inquire about the administration of Kemiö and make dispositions about what was needed. Turlow should impress on the steward of Kemiö and all other officers of the barony to assist him and in the future to keep in touch with him, for the benefit of the minor heirs.

In this way Elsa Elisabet Brahe settled affairs which otherwise could develop into a family feud. The widow of Johan–Margareta Brahe–was wealthy in her own rights and in fact was claimed to be the wealthiest woman in Sweden. She later remarried and therefore was possessing Kemiö only from 1657 to 1659 (Gardberg, p. 11), when it was ceded to Axel Oxenstierna, Junior, and later possessed by Karl Gustav Oxenstierna until the reduction of estates in 1680.

The next five paragraphs of the 28 February 1659 instruction dealt with the Estonian estates, where Turlow was directed to proceed from Finland. The steward Johan Olofsson Ackerfeld was to be relieved of his post and Johan Georg von Ringenheim appointed instead. The accounts of Ackerfeld should be audited. He had without permission purchased the estates (villages) of Wirrenorm and Kaudenorm and paid too much for them. He had to repay the spent amount including interest and if he wished could keep these estates for himself. Ackerfeld should be directed to come to Sweden to answer charges. In case of disobedience Turlow should request assistance from the government.

At the stronghold of Valmiera and the Cēsis bishopric, which had been retaken from the enemy, Turlow should inspect all castles and estates, and prepare an inventory. At Valmiera he should see that the defences were put in order, but if there still were royal forces in the garrison, he should refrain from action and do as the royal instructions provide. Sprengport should be relieved from his duties and dismissed. After the royal garrison had left Valmiera, Turlow should find out whether the commandant could not be a captain or lieutenant instead of the rank of a major and likewise other officers of a lower rank. This would save in payments, but nevertheless the safety of the stronghold should be considered. If Sprengport would be recalcitrant, Turlow should report to the Countess. All servants provided for in the budget should be paid for their actual performances, but those who had appointed themselves should be dismissed. Those who had not fulfilled their obligations should be sent to Sweden to answer charges. The vacancies for posts of the clergy and judges should be filled with suitable persons. Estates of persons who had sided with the enemy should be taken over. Retainers should be appointed only in such a number as necessary.

Paragraphs 20 to 23 of the instruction dealt with financial matters. The produce of the Estonian and Latvian estates had to be sold as much as possible against ready cash. At Stockholm a debt of 2500 Rd had been taken up. At Riga and Tallinn Turlow should endeavour to collect ducats and specie riksdollars for paying of the debt. Because for debts in Sweden higher interest was to be paid than in Livonia, it was necessary to delay payments of debts there and to send cash to Sweden. Ducats and specie riksdollars should be sent to Tallinn and during the summer transported through the Finnish waters to Sweden.

The final paragraphs of the instruction dealt with Prussian estates. If Turlow was not able to go to Prussia because of warlike activities or other reasons, he should appoint a deputy steward as suggested by himself, namely, Monsignor Lorenz Kempendorf who had been formerly in the services of Johan Oxenstierna. The instruction concluded with an admonishment to act in the interests of the minor heirs and to follow the instructions of the late Johan Oxenstierna of 20 April 1657. At the end of it was mentioned that the instruction had been signed and sealed by Elsa Elisabet Brahe and on her request also by the vice-president of the College of Commerce (kommerskollegium), Israel Lagerfeld.

Turlow was not able to follow the direction to set in order the affairs at Valmiera. He requested Fieldmarshal General Robert Douglas to discharge the enlisted peasants and the Finnish colonists (Erb Bauern und Erb Colonier). The Fieldmarshal refused to discharge them and wrote (RA, TA 75, pp. 250–251: 9 August 1659) that all whom the Lieutenant-Colonel and Commandant Sprengport had enlisted had to remain as soldiers of the Count in the royal service of the Valmiera fortress. What the chief inspector Turlow claimed on behalf of the heirs of the bishopric against Sprengport should be decided by an arbitration commission. On behalf of the heirs of the bishopric two members should be appointed from the county court. From Sprengport's side two officers should be chosen and an impartial secretary selected by both parties. This commission should have only power to investigate the complaints and to report.The next paragraph stated quite tersely that Lieutenant-Colonel Sprengport remained commandant of the fortress and would not be discharged. The letter of Robert Douglas continued that the upkeep of the Valmiera garrison was the obligation of the bishopric, especially because the contribution to the sustenance of the garrison was small and insufficient. The statio of the bishopric had to be paid also in future. Extraordinary taxes remained as before and no changes were permissible. Brewing and bread baking was permitted to officers and privates only for their own consumption. Citizens of the town should be commanded not to overcharge.

About the bishopric a memorial was prepared by Turlow in Riga on 18 September 1659 (RA, TA 75, p. 135). He directed an inventory to be prepared of Valmiera castle listing what was left to the enemy of produce, artillery, ammunition, etc., when Sprengport departed. Valmiera peasants, some 500 strong, should be called to a wacka-meeting at Kauguri or any other convenient place. There the peasants should be examined about the period 1654 to 1658–how much each year each of them had spun flax for the lord and what had not been delivered. How much had been delivered to the Crown, whether excessive payments had not been given to scribes, bailiffs, and others. What cartage had been done, especially for Sprengport to Pärnu, what Sprengport had taken from the peasantry and what had been taken by the scribes and bailiffs; Whether Sprengport had taken anything by force. What live-stock had been taken by the enemy and what the peasants had contributed to the Crown after Valmiera was retaken. Finally, a nominal list had to be prepared of the peasants and their farmhands, who were forcibly enlisted into the military.

The memorial went on that peasants needed not fear Sprengport's revenge because he would not have any power over them. They should be further asked how many horses and live-stock the bailiffs had. An inquiry should be made whether peasants would be willing to pay their debts with live-stock, but at the beginning of the memorial Turlow wrote that the peasants should not be pressed to repay what had not been paid during the war years. An inquiry should be made as to why in last autumn only 732 ⅔ leaps of grain had been sown and not more. A check of Weber's account and Sprengport's land-roll of unci should be made.

Only in 1660 was the management of the bishopric able to cite Sprengport before a court. He was accused and charged on 40 counts, inter alia that he had handed over to the military the storage of the bishopric and carted away provisions. He was further charged of having exploited the peasantry and enlisted peasants into the military forces (RA, TA 346, 347: 1662 and 1663 documents). In 1663 Sprengport was imprisoned at the Valmiera castle. In an instruction to the then inspector (steward) Per Hansson (*ibid.* 75, p. 293) we read that if Sprengport wished at some time to leave the prison, he should behave himself. He had to render satisfaction to the guardians for the great affront committed against the lords of the bishopric and the commissioner (Lagerfeld) who during the winter 1662/1663 was sent to investigate his case.

AFTER THE DEATH OF TURLOW

Chief inspector and steward Turlow died in 1660. In an instruction to the unnamed steward of Valmiera (probably Jakob Reutz), dated 30 July 1660, Elsa Elisabet Brahe and Israel Lagerfeld ordered that the corpse of the chief inspector should be buried in Valmiera with dignity according to his rank on the lords' expenses (*ibid.*, p. 98). In this instruction further the appointment of Nagel as bailiff of an estate near Riga was confirmed. Probably this was Ropaži.

The mentioned instruction was similar to instructions discussed so far. Different from previous instructions were its references to the war. Peace was not regarded as lasting and therefore caution in repairing churches was advised. It had to be investigated who had sworn the oath of allegiance to the Poles. Their estates should be taken over. Instructions regarding fortifications would be issued. On money which Nagel had lent, interest should be paid from the sale of current year's produce. The peasants had been ruined by the war and therefore moderation was advisable, but those, who were able, should pay. The instruction further decided on a number of particular cases.

On 24 November 1660 Elsa Elisabet Brahe had appointed Jakob Reutz as inspector over the Livonian and Estonian estates (*ibid.* 76). His service lasted only 3 years.

THE INSPECTION TOUR OF LAGERFELD

Early in 1663 Lagerfeld was sent by the guardians on an inspection tour of the Oxenstierna af Södermöre estates in Finland, Estonia, and Livonia. A 26 paragraph memorial was issued to him in March 1663 (*ibid.* 80, no. 316; the copy of the instruction is dated March 1664, which is an obvious error). The preamble expressed reliance of the guardians that Lagerfeld would accomplish the task with his usual resourcefulness. The first two paragraphs dealt with Finland, paragraphs 3–10 with Estonia, and, beginning with paragraph 11– with the bishopric. Time permitting Lagerfeld was instructed to inspect all estates or at least the most important. He was empovered to reorganize the personnel of management. He had to enforce execution of the sentence against Lieutenant-Colonel Sprengport. The latter had to pay as much as he could and the rest of his debt should remain in suspense until the heirs came of age, who then would deal with him. In the same way Ringenheim and Olof Nilsson should be dealt with.

The towns of Valmiera and Cēsis had so far not paid anything and they should start to contribute to the lords. If the towns had some complaints, Lagerfeld would see that justice was done and what he could not order he should refer to Stockholm. The town of Cēsis should produce charters about land it was holding and should hand over the illegally possessed land.

Paragraph 15 of the instruction categorically stated that Lagerfeld should bring under jurisdiction of the court and consistory of the bishopric all who live in its precincts. If needed, the assistance of the Governor General should be asked. Paragraph 16 dealt with the Ropaži woods. If the books for 1662 were ready they should with the documents be taken to Sweden (§ 17). If there were noblemen's goods either sold or leased falling under the *iure caduci*, they should be acquired or a court case initiated. If Aßwegen voluntarily handed over Braslava, claims against him would be dropped and he would be granted for life the small estate of Kapūns (§ 18). The debt of Brun Hartman could be liquidated with the widow of Adrian Friberg in Riga (§ 19). Judge Reutz should hand over his charter and pledge for Lorupe against the 2000 Rd which were lent to him, or Lagerfeld should take over Lorupe as provided for in the contract of the lease (§ 20). The contract of the inspector Per Hansson with Johan Nagel and two years free storage lease could be ratified by Lagerfeld (§ 21). An estate could be leased to the inspector (§ 22). Because the instruction of 1663, issued by Jakob Schnack, had not been considered in full by the inspector, Lagerfeld was provided with a copy of the same. Special attention should be paid to questions regarding the court and the consistory, the militia, the towns, the reconstruction of Ropaži, the retainers, the churches at Burtnieki and Ropaži, the saw-mills, and the lime-kilns (§ 23). About the Valmiera stronghold Lagerfeld should approach the Governor General and enquire whether it should not be demolished. In wartime the stronghold did not serve its purpose as shown by experience at the last war when it could be held only for eight days, and it was a burden on the lords (§ 24). The requests of Liphard's widow, as well as Wolmar von Schlippenbach's case and the cases of other private persons, should be resolved by Lagerfeld on the spot or referred to the guardians (§§ 25 and 26).

About the time of Lagerfeld's inspection tour an important change was introduced in the accountancy of the Oxenstierna etates. In addition to the usual accounts of the produce of each estate, called *amts räkningar* (estate accounts), a parallel accounting was introduced by recalculating the produce in monetary terms. These accounts were called *special räkningar* (special accounts). The prices used were not market prices but conventionally established uniform prices for all estates (see RA, TA 309 for the year 1662).

STEWARD PER HANSSON

In 1663 a further important change in the administration of the bishopric was made. For the first time a Swede was appointed steward. Previously, after the Finn Munck, all stewards had been Germans. On 8 July 1663 (*ibid.* 76), with the title of 'Inspector in Charge of the Economy', Per (also Peter) Hansson was appointed and on 11 July a memorial to him was issued. The previous steward, Jakob Reutz, became judge instead of (the blind and old) Franciscus Reiniken who retired. Per Hansson previously had been an inspector of Queen Kristina's estates in Pomerania and, having mastered the German language, had no difficulties in communicating with the bailiffs of the bishopric (*ibid.* 80, 28 August 1663). The memorial issued to him in 1663 was naturally written in Swedish while nearly all the previous instructions were written in German.

The memorial of 11 July 1663 was signed by the guardians Gustav Bonde, Knut Kurck, Israel Lagerfeld, and Jakob Schnack (who signed Schnach), but not by Elsa Elisabet Brahe as previously. The explanation is that she had remarried. On 19 December 1661 she had married Count Palatine Adolph Johann von Zweibrücken.

In the preamble of the memorial the guardians of the Counts af Södermöre stated that they had decided to appoint as inspector of the Cēsis bishopric the commissioner Per Hansson. Their intention had been to issue to him a detailed instruction, but because the documents of the bishopric were left by accountant (kamrerare) Jakob Schnack with the previous inspector Jakob Reutz, the memorial would mention only the discussed items. This preamble was followed by a 17 paragraph memorial and it is difficult to discover what the difference with an instruction would be except in its briefness.

Arriving at Riga, Hansson was ordered to inquire about grain trade. Schnack, during his visit, had entrusted the sale of grain to Johan Nagel, inspector Hans Müller, and the latter's brother-in-law, notary Klas Skütte (see Skütte's letter: *ibid.* 80, no. 85). Together with them Hansson should consider whether it would not be advisable to sell the grain before the new harvest. With the proceeds the loan taken up by Schnack from Nagel, and the interest, could be paid. At Riga Hansson should hand over to Mrs Jäger confirmation of the lease over Jaunburtnieki (Sternhof), which Schnack had contracted. After deducting her claim, she should pay 900 riksdollars to Nagel. At Riga Brun

Hartman should be admonished to pay for the produce he had received in 1659 according to the invoice given to him by Schnack. If he refused to pay, the matter should be dealt with by court. Hansson should also claim a copy of the contract Turlow had drawn up with Hartman about a half uncus at Ropaži and ask the latter to explain how he had paid for the same. While in Riga, Hansson also should ask the bailiff of Ropaži to call and inform him about the conditions of the estate, especially about the lease granted to Zuckerbecker for 60 riksdollars. If Mikel Ridder presented his claim on behalf of his daughter, the widow of Adrian Friberg, Hansson should inform him that as soon as the documents would have been compared with the books the claim would be settled.

Leaving Riga, Hansson should first call at the Ropaži mills–the corn-mill and the saw-mill. From the three saws, two should be taken to the bishopric and installed at Kokmuiža (Kokenhof). He should visit the woods where the artillerists had cut timber for making charcoal and report to the guardians the damage done. During the same trip, he should inspect Nagel's, Zuckerbecker's, and Hartman's rented manors and continue his travel to Ropaži.

From there he should go to Cēsis and see that the fields were tilled, harvested, and other necessary things done. He should do the same in other estates and familiarize himself as much as possible at a first visit. Special attention had to be paid to Kauguri and Renceni, where there were not good bailiffs. These bailiffs nevertheless could remain in office until the guardians decide their fate. The following paragraphs dealt with the former inspector Reutz's appointment as judge and with his salary. A disposition about the salary of scribe Johan Hassel, whom Schnack had appointed instead of Nordenborg, had to be made. Hassel should compile the account of the Livonian and Estonian estates for 1662.

At Kauguri the inspector should look into the opportunity of establishing a new demesne. A quarter of a mile from the present demesne there were two peasants of the bishopric and two priest's peasants. He should negotiate with the priest and offer him as an exchange two good peasants at Valmiera. On the vacated land then even a better demesne could be established than the present one. The inspector should convince the peasants, with kindness, to exchange their farms against others where such could be found, and offer them respite in payment of customary dues and statute labour until they build their new farms.

Regarding the retainers, the late Chancellor's intention was to grant their estates to his old servants who were too old or for other reasons unable to continue service. Nevertheless, in 1658 Lieutenant-Colonel Sprengport had expelled the old retainers from their estates and installed there officers and noblemen who never had served the Count. This, despite the great expenses the Count was suffering in maintaining the garrison. The guardians had resolved to change this and the estate at Valmiera, which Lyttighof possessed for three horses, should be given to Johan Georg von Ringenheim. At Vecate the estate, possessed by Libbert Pfeil for 3 horses, should be given to the old bailiff of Vohnja (Fonal) in Estonia, Andres Holm. Those whom Sprengport had displaced could seek redress from him. Captain of Cavalry Liphard had won his case at the court and the inspector should allocate to him the abandoned farms in the Cēsis district of Sviķis (Swickis), Bucis (Busis), and Zābaks (Sabach). This is an interesting point showing how long it took to get a judgment at the courts. As early as 1638 (ARL, pp. 474–475) Heinrich Lademacher claimed these three farms from the bishopric. The heir of Heinrich Lademacher–his son-in-law Friedrich Liphard who had married Lademacher's daughter Margareta (Stryk, p. 339; he wrote: Magdalena), after twenty five odd years, achieved the addition of the three peasant farms to the estate Dūķeŗi (Duckern). Still the farms were not handed over, there was a further delay when the steward of the Oxenstierna estates started negotiations about exchange of the farms.

The following paragraph of the memorial to Hansson dealt with the arrested Sprengport mentioned above. In the next paragraph was mentioned the arrested accountant Olof Nilsson who should complete the accounts (förplägnings räkningar). All documents and bills, which Schnack had left with Reutz and Hassel, should be sent to Sweden, except the account for 1662. During his travels the inspector should inquire what moneys Reutz and Hassel had taken up, especially after Schnack had left. At Valmiera he had to audit the cash account and make a list of the documents. All litigation documents against Sprengport, Ringenheim, and Nordenborg, should be sent to Sweden–for Sprengport copies, but the others in original. The final paragraph dealt with the claim of Valerius Transe at Ropaži.

How the instruction was carried out can be seen from the report Per Hansson sent to Jakob Schnack in Stokholm on 28 August 1663 (RA, TA 80, no. 23). He had visited all manors and in the first place reported on the conditions of the fields and the prospective harvest. Some of the bailiffs he intended to dismiss, namely, at Ropaži, Kauguri, and Rencēni. He was satisfied with the bailiffs at Cēsis, Kokmuiža, and Trikāta. He intended to live at Burtnieki. Hansson was not happy that a great number of peasants had been leased to other lords and some of the leased ones had been despoiled. As a result of the lease of peasants the acreage of the demesne had declined. At Cēsis only 160 leaps of grain had been sown, at Mujāni–150 leaps, Kokmuiža–160 leaps, Valmiera–80 leaps. Hansson intended to revoke the leases. He ordered that all bailiffs had to report monthly about statute labour. There was a need for good surveyors and land could be found for more than 20 peasants.

Hansson had dismissed Judge Reiniken and appointed Reutz instead. He searched for *caduc* goods and at first intended to take over two one uncus farms used by burgomaster Skult. A nobleman Hirschheyd lived in the town and held Baltāmuiža with 8 peasants and two taverns, which were to be taken over. Another nobleman Aßwegen had a valuable estate [Braslava] which had been donated to the father of Aßwegens wife. He had no male heirs and the estate would fall to the lords of the bishopric. The peasant farms of this estate were intermixed with those of Vecate. The wife of the rentmaster [Jakob Behr] had purchased Munck's estate [Rāmuļi] which had to be purchased from her. Hansson intended to invite all possessors of noblemen's goods situated in the bishopric to come to Riga to show their charters and privileges. He hoped to acquire those estates for which the possessors had no sufficient evidence to prove their possessorship. A doubtful case was the estate of the bailiff of Ropaži.

Some 30 mares and foals had arrived from Kalmar. During the fortnight's travel, six had perished. During the winter the horses were to be accommodated at Burtnieki, Bauņi, and Vecate. There was a need for some 500 to 600 head of live-stock to manure the fields. Horse manure was useful only on alkaline soil. An additional benefit from the live-stock would result from the sale of butter and cheese in the taverns. For 40 Rd, Hansson had taken over old Jörgen Grysenberg's house in the town and had established a new demesne at Kauguri.

Regarding the affairs of Lieutenant-Colonel Sprengport and the accountant Olof Nilsson, the Lieutenant Colonel had replied that he had written to the guardians and expected a reply. The accounts were in a bad shape and to prevent misdeeds Hansson had prohibited all bailiffs from paying out anything without his authorization.

The previous bailiff Oldenburg had some peasants for whom he paid, but he completely ruined them. Hansson requested that such exploitation of peasants be not permitted.

Those who had peasants on lease drove them so hard that the peasants could not till their own land and were pauperized. The result would be seen at the next wacka-meeting. In all eleven estates statute labour was rendered by 270 peasants with, and by 22 without, a horse, but statute labour of 146 peasants with a horse and 84 without was leased. In these figures was not included peasants who served at the granges, worked as servants, tended live-stock, and who were new-settlers. Regarding allocation of fishers and hunters Hansson requested an instruction and complained that the commandant, during his absence in Holland, had his fisher and two hunters assigned to Colonel Arenstorf and thus the lords were deprived of the work of three peasants.

The letter closed with a report about exchange of land with Captain Liphard at the estate Dūķeŗi (Duckern) and again Hansson stressed the need to conserve the land and the peasants. The farm Zābaks had been handed over to Liphard, but Bucis and Sviķis had been retained by the bishopric and exchanged with other land. As compensation for the inferior quality of the allocated land Liphard had received an eighth of an uncus more–all subject to ratification by the lords.

CASH INCOME AND EXPENDITURE, 1661–1670

There is extant a summary of cash income and expenditure of the period 1661 to 1670 (RA, TA 133, no. 30) for all the estates of the Oxenstiernas af Södermöre. Incomes were specified as to the Swedish county (greveskap räntor), Finnish estates (friherrskap räntor), the inheritance estates (arvegods räntor), the fief (länegods räntor), the bishopric (stiftiske räntor), the Estonian estates (estniske räntor), and various incomes (diverse upbörder). Expenditures were specified: for the recipients own behalf, paid debts, paid interest, remunerations to the office, and purchases. (Expenditure figures in the source were added together for 1666–1667 and 1668–1670.)

Incomes and expenditures were divided between Erik Oxenstierna's two sons: Axel and Karl Gustav, and his three daughters: Anna, Kristina, and Elisabet. These accounts were given in Swedish dollars and öre.

Only Axel's account showed a surplus for all years, but Karl Gustav's account only for 1663, 1664, and 1666–1667. The account for the daughters showed a deficit for all years because of the large payments of debts and interest from their share.

The incomes from the Swedish and Finnish estates went undivided to the eldest son Axel. The income from the inheritance goods as well as from the Estonian estates was divided allocating 28.6 % for each of the sons and 14.3 % for each of the daughters. The income of the fief and the bishopric was divided in equal parts between the sons. The various incomes were divided in five equal parts and allocated to each of the heirs.

From the total income the share of the bishopric was: 1661–33.5 %, 1662–4.1 % only, 1663–44.8 %, 1664–34.6 %, 1665–1 % only, 1666–43.1 %, 1667–46.3 %, 1668–43.4 %, 1669–40.4 %, and 1670–35.8 %.

Recalculated from silver mint dollars to riksdollars at the rate of 2 silver dollars per riksdollar, the absolute amounts derived from the bishopric were: 1661–8016 Rd, 1662–1065 Rd, 1663–19,186 Rd, 1664–8456 Rd, 1665–148 Rd, 1666–9395 Rd, and the same amount the following year, 1668–9882 Rd, and the same amount in 1669 and 1670.

FIHOLM

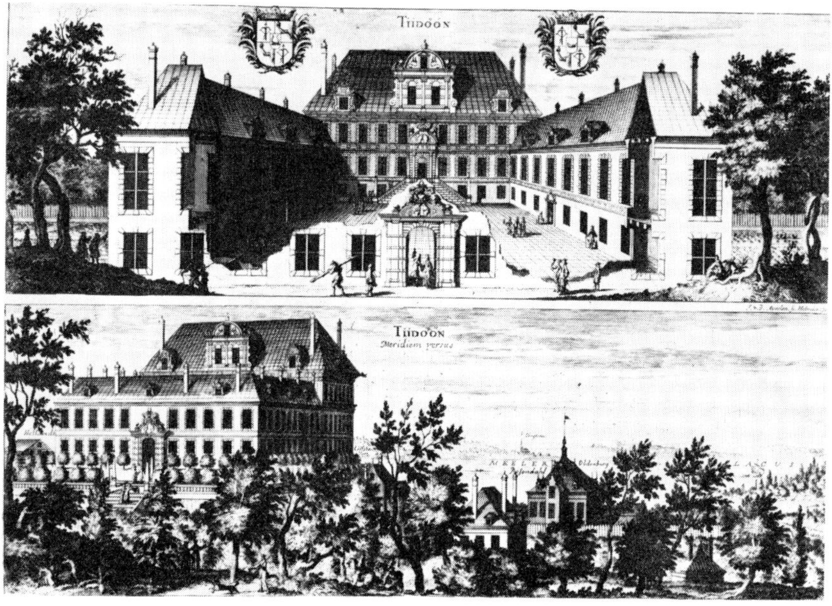

TIDÖ
From Erik Dahlberg's *Suecia antiqva et hodierna*
(Kungl. Biblioteket)

INCOME & EXPENDITURE

	CASH & PRODUCE		*MANORS*	
	Dr	Cr	Dr	Cr
1662				
Balance	6653	8181	–	–
Sales	3990	3442	3442	3990
Customary dues	18,991	3424	–	–
Transfer	2262	33,703	3119	5519
Demesne	20,757	4091	4091	20,757
Remuneration	–	2574	2574	–
Produce refined	5717	2955	2955	5717
Gains & losses	–	–	19,802	–
Totals	58,370	58,370	35,983	35,983

Referring to page 170–the extremely low income for 1662 and 1665 and the repetition of the same figures in two cases for subsequent years does not inspire confidence in the figures.

To check on the figures we rework the data of the capital account of the ledger (RA, TA 335, Huvudbok, fol. 8–20) for 1662 on the same pattern as on page 58 ff. of the present volume. The result for the total bishopric (including Ropaži) is presented in the above table.

The same ledger shows that in 1662 the merchant Johan Nagel had received (from 13 estates of the bishopric) grain to a total of 17,538 Rd. If we add to this the amount of 19,186 Rd appropriated in 1663 to Axel and Karl Oxenstierna, the total is 36,724 Rd which by approximately 3000 Rd exceeds the amount we calculated from the ledger as allocated to the possessor's account. It must be pointed out that the accountants of the Oxenstierna estates entered in the ledger amounts calculated at conventional prices, not market prices, while our calculation on page 58 ff. is in market prices.

From the above consideration it follows that the amounts appropriated to the heirs only incompletely reflected the economic activities of the bishopric. This refers particularly to the low income years.

THE SPRENGPORT CASE

It was mentioned above of the difficulties the previous commandant Jakob Sprengport experienced after the war was over and the fortress of Valmiera was returned by the Swedish Crown to the management of the Oxen-

OF THE BISHOPRIC

PEASANTS		*THE CROWN*		*POSSESSOR*		*BALANCE*	
Dr	Cr	Dr	Cr	Dr	Cr	Dr	Cr
–	–	–	–	–	–	8181	6653
–	–	–	–	–	–	–	–
3424	18,991	–	–	–	–	–	–
–	–	3458	3119	33,703	201	–	–
–	–	–	–	–	–	–	–
–	–	–	–	–	–	–	–
–	–	–	–	–	–	–	–
15,567	–	–	339	–	33,502	–	1528
18,991	18,991	3458	3458	33,703	33,703	8181	8181

stiernas af Södermöre. The latter started litigations against Sprengport in the courts. He was accused (RA, TA 346, 347) of 1) improper management as a steward and illegal handing over of the possessions of the bishopric to the Crown; 2) enlisting the Latvian peasants of the bishopric in the military forces and releasing enlisted peasants from payment of statio tax and of customary dues, to the prejudice of the lords.

The indictments of the first item, as usually in similar litigation cases against manorial officers, were petty and do not deserve detailed discussion. Of a more substantial nature were accusations of the second kind. Paragraph 13 of the indictment bill stated that the defendant had an order from his superiors to recruit a company of cavalry and a squadron on foot, to billet the recruits in the estates of the bishopric, and to require the necessary sustenance from the peasants. In executing this order the defendant had used force and recruited hereditary peasants, the subjects of the bishopric.

To this accusation Sprengport replied that no proof could be advanced that he had recruited a single hereditary peasant. On the contrary, he had prohibited recruiting of these. As emerged later, Sprengport had in mind with this denial that he had not ordered the recruitment of farmers but only enlisting of farmhands.

Further on (§ 15) the defendant was accused of misinterpreting the order that peasants who had shown valour against the enemy had to be rewarded. The order allegedly referred only to the release from paying statio, but the defendant had without a special order from the lords released peasants from statute labour and customary dues. The losses suffered by the lords on this account had to be repaid by the defendant. On this Sprengport replied that he had followed the manifesto of Magnus Gabriel De la Gardie. He suggested that the peasants in question be interrogated and they would be able to prove that they had fought against the enemy and well deserved the liberty granted.

As to the alleged forcible recruitment of the peasants, the management of the bishopric instigated an inquiry and listed all the names of the recruited and the circumstances of the recruitment. Results of the inquiry are extant for Rencēni, Cēsis, Bauņi, Valmiera, Kokmuiža, Mujāni, Ēvele, Jaunburtnieki, Burtnieki, and Vecate. A total of 267 peasants complained and among the complaints recruitment of 81 soldiers was mentioned. From these, 36 were farmhands and 17 foster-sons of the peasants, who also were regarded as farmhands; 12 were sons and 15 relatives of the farmers. Only one was himself a farmer and his wife had complained.

In further investigations (*ibid.* 346: 4 February 1663) the wording of the indictment bill was slightly changed. Regulations provided that retainers could be only Swedes, Germans, or Finns, and not Latvian or Estonian peasants. Contrary to this Sprengport had recruited the subjects of the counts or their farmhands and relatives and even some citizens of Valmiera, their servants and people. By using force even before the door of the church which should have been a safe refuge, he had taken 86 men from the peasantry and their servants and the inquiry had not yet been finished, so there would be even more. Peasants who had been engaged in his party he had relieved from customary dues, statute labour, and statio, and in this way disposed of the lords' income like a lord himself.

Sprengport once more maintained that he had not ordered recruitment by force and that at the time of recruitment nobody had complained. To those peasants who had shown merits before the enemy he had, according to Count Magnus' 1656 decree, promised that they would be free from statio and other obligations. If it was desired not to permit this, nor to follow the decree, nor to distinguish between merits and vice, the lords could demand repayments from their subjects. This argument by the defendant created some difficulty with the accusers. They voiced the opinion that the statio had to be paid to the Crown and consequently there was no loss to the lords if statio was not paid, but the defendant had to deduct the amount of other benefits granted to the recruits from the statio paid to the Crown from the other peasants. Because he had not done this, he was obliged to repay the losses suffered by the lords.

From the instruction to Lagerfeld (see page 165) it emerges that the sentence of the court went against Sprengport. Nevertheless, he was not dismissed from the Swedish army and was later the commandant of Nöteborg in Ingermanland (Elgenstierna, VII, p. 440).

CHAPTER EIGHT

UNDER NEW MANAGEMENT

PROBLEMS TO BE SOLVED

Guardianship of the Oxenstierna estates came to an end on June 1671 when Axel was 19 years and Karl Gustav 16 years of age. The brothers had received university education according to habits of the time befitting members of the high aristocracy and they did not want any longer to be under the tutelage of the guardians. They were declared to be of age (RA, TA 63, Gustav Adolf De la Gardie's memorial). Lagerfeld and Schnack nevertheless continued to assist the counts in the management of the estates.

Before the declaration of age of the heirs, the first task was to carry out a revision of the Livonian and Estonian estates. Such a revision had been planned since 1665 but it now became urgent to prepare data for a division of the estates between the heirs who were to be declared of age. There was also a plan to implement changes in the management of the estates: firstly it was considered to expand the manorial economy and secondly instead of managing the estates by bailiffs and a steward the heirs wanted to lease them. For these plans too, an inventory of the estates–the revision–was necessary.

Both these ideas–to expand the manorial economy and to lease the estates–did not augur well for the peasantry. Added to this there was at the same time a movement to tighten the screw of serfdom and to limit the personal liberty of the peasants.

In the background loomed another problem for the management of the Oxenstierna af Södermöre estates. With the coming of age of the heirs, claims for settlement of the not yet fully paid dowries to the female members of the Oxenstierna clan were advanced by their husbands. It appeared too, that debts of the Chancellor Axel Oxenstierna had not yet been paid in full.

A PLAN FOR REVISION OF THE OXENSTIERNA ESTATES

On 30 June 1665 the guardians of the Oxenstierna estates answered several questions of the inspector. Regarding his question about surveying of the unci and establishing proper boundaries between peasant farms they suggested the continuation of the procedure of the old Chancellor (Axel Oxenstierna; his son Erik is referred to as the young Chancellor). The guardians explained that the aim of ordering peasant affairs was that peasants should have no more land than that for which they paid and rendered service according to their uncus (RA, TA 75, p. 295). As to the land of the citizens of Valmiera town, the guardians decided that in case 576 leapsteads were not sufficient, some land of the militia men (coloniae länderne) or some waste land from the Kokmuiža or Valmiera estates could be added. The guardians demanded that the terriers (wackeböker) should contain the obligation of each uncus, the income of the lords and the Crown, disregarding whether the peasant farm was occupied or waste, or granted as a fief in subinfeudation. For the latter, each bailiff had to keep a special register which should include the retainers' farms, abandoned farms, farms of free peasants, etc. These registers should be inspected at the wacka-meetings, signed, and put into the accounts. For the debts of peasants a special roll had to be prepared. It was decreed that the debts of the war years of 1659 and 1660, when the peasantry experienced great difficulties, were to be cancelled and no bailiff should demand them unless the peasant voluntarily wanted to pay.

Besides decisions in particular cases, a question of general interest was dealt with in paragraph 20. The inspector had to pass review of the officers and soldiers of the Valmiera garrison and find out what service every man had rendered to the lords. He should investigate the reason why such a great number had deserted.

Of great importance is the resolution of the guardians Knut Kurck, Israel Lagerfeld, and Jakob Schnack, dated at Stockholm on 6 August 1668 (*ibid.*, pp. 265–279). The inspector and the accountant had reported that there were great discrepancies between the data in the terrier (wacka-books) and the unci actually held by the peasants. A number of peasants had more land than their uncus provided for. These peasants had appropriated their neighbours' land which had became waste during the war or because of pestilence. There were even more peasants who had less land than shown by the uncus register and some of the land was infertile—water-logged and sandy. The result had been that the peasants who had received in the measurement inferior land had become paupers and therefore every year their obligations had to be reduced. The entire situation was confusing and had created errors in the terriers and in the calculations of the income.

To remedy this deficiency the guardians had decided that surveyors, after being put on oath, should conduct a new land revision and survey the land in the whole bishopric Cēsis and in all estates there without any exception, disregarding whether they were under management of the lordship, retainers'

AXEL ERIKSSON OXENSTIERNA AF SÖDERMÖRE
(at an age of six years)

Painting by Werner Rothfinck 1658
Photo Svenska Porträttarkivet, Stockholm

manors, granted *ex gratia*, leased, or given as a fief. The two surveyors of the bishopric should start this work at once. They should allocate to each peasant farm either one, a half, or a quarter of an uncus in proportion to good arables, meadows, and woodland, so that each peasant could fulfil his obligations. To those who had useless sandy or water-logged arables, meadows, or wood-land, more land in quantity should be given to correspond to good land. The survey should establish definite boundaries between every village and farm. If convenient and if there were sufficient peasants, in preference to a whole uncus to every peasant half an uncus should be allocated. After a village had been surveyed and the boundaries marked, the bailiff, the surveyor, and the peasants of the village should ride along the boundaries to ascertain that justice had been done to the lords and to the peasants and to show where the boundaries were. If the inspector and his deputy Liphard could take part in this, it would be better and safer.

For a correct referrence later, after each village had been surveyed, the surveyors should draw a map showing the situation of each land, a description of its quality and quantity in leapsteads, and the boundaries and their marks around each village. After each estate and its demesne had been surveyed, the surveyors should draw a general map including the nobility estates lying within the precincts and also the free estates of the nobility. The surveyors had to inquire how many unci the nobility estates had.

For this work the surveyors should receive for each uncus they survey and place on the map two riksdollars from the lords and two riksdollars from the peasants. If it was found that the surveyors could not finish the work within two years, the inspector was empowered to engage one or two more surveyors with the same remuneration and conditions. In this way the total work should be finished within two years. After the survey was finished, all maps should be copied and for each estate the bailiff, and for each farm the peasants, should receive a copy. In addition a general map of the total bishopric should be drawn. For this work the surveyors should be specially paid. The inspector should drive ahead this work. Other business permitting, he himself or his assistant should take a keen interest in it.

DISCUSSIONS ABOUT CHANGED PRINCIPLES OF MANAGEMENT

The second paragraph of the instruction is also of importance. It shows a changed approach to the principles of management of the economy. It voices the opinion that demesne established at a convenient place and provided with necessary workers was more profitable than land utilized by peasants. Therefore the inspector was instructed to find convenient locations as to arables and meadows, where in the neighbourhood there were sufficient workers, not needed by other estates, and where there was sufficient live-stock to manure the fields. At those places new demesne should be established. This should be effected, but without harming established demesne.

By 1670 the idea that demesne husbandry was more profitable to the management than receiving customary dues from peasants was hardened by a calculation referred to in Chapter Four. The calculation (ED 1935, p. 92) reviewed the situtation in the bishopric as to totals of grain sown, the need of horse-power, and the numbers of peasants put on cash payments. The conclusion was that there was in the bishopric a surplus of 116 and a half peasant farms which neither performed statute labour nor had it commuted to cash payments. To establish a six unci demesne six one uncus peasants had to be displaced and settled on half an uncus each. The loss in customary dues in kind and in cash and statio from the six whole uncus peasants would be 121 Rd 65 gr. On the other hand, income from the six half uncus peasants would be 75 Rd 78 gr. The new demesne would have 720 leapsteads of land less 120 leapsteads unsuitable land, or a total of 600 leapsteads remaining for tillage. When divided into three lots and one lot left in fallow, 400 leaps of grain could be sown. At a yield of the fourth corn above the seed this would give 1600 leaps of rye and barley and at a price of 6 marks per leap the revenue would be 640 Rd. Adding to this the income from the six half uncus peasants and subtracting the loss from the six whole uncus farms, the net profit would be 594 Rd 13 gr.

The profitability of eviction of the peasants and establishing a new demesne was calculated not only by the manorial management but also by peasants. There is extant a very interesting document of this kind, dated 1 November 1668 and received at Stockholm on 5 February 1669, i. e. exactly when the manorial administration thought it profitable to displace peasants (RA, TA 84). Two peasants–Jānis Ošenieks and Toms Spruks (Spruck)–submitted their considerations with the request to pass those on to the authorities in Sweden. The peasants thought that in far away Sweden the local conditions in Vidzeme were not properly understood.

The peasants pointed out that, in the bishopric, displacement of good peasants was going on and that there were plans to evict even more of them. The management had gained an income from the peasants as safe as from deposited cash. If war broke out, as frequently was the case in Livonia, the peasantry was an unexhaustable treasure. Peasants paid annually 30 5/9 leaps of grain. Calculated at ¼ Rd the sum was 7 Rd 57 ½ gr. The amount paid in lieu of hops was 1 Rd 22 ½ gr., for flax and hemp 2 Rd, for various produce 4 Rd 66 gr. The peasants with a horse paid for commuted statue labour 14 Rd, and work of an *otrinieks* for 6 weeks was commuted to 2 Rd. Cartage was worth 4 Rd. In addition the upkeep of the military was to be considered.

If one uncus peasant was displaced, at least three statute labourers with a horse would be needed to till the land. The labour was worth 51 Rd. For seed 60 leaps of corn were needed, which was equivalent to 15 Rd. The yield could not be estimated more than a third grain which would give 180 leaps or in money terms 45 Rd. Not calculating the labour of the *otrinieki* who had to harvest and the workers at the grange, cattle tenders, guards of the manor and the fields, the expenses of the unnecessary buildings and the remuneration of the bailiff, the loss to the lords from each uncus was 56 Rd 56 gr. From these facts the lords could see how large had been the loss from the 12 peasants who during these years had been evicted to establish a new demesne.

The peasants continued that they thought the people in command were so keen to establish new demesne because they wanted to court favour with the lords. In the opinion of the peasants, the expansion of the officialdom of the bishopric was a dead loss and the wealthy peasants would be prepared to commute statute labour. Those who could not pay cash could till the fields of the existing demesne. The peasants considered that in this way the lords would gain three times more than by evicting peasants. Because of want of live-stock, the demesne yielded less than the farms managed by peasants. Further, in case of an enemy attack the demesne would be destroyed and no gain would be forthcoming, while the peasants fulfilled their duty permanently.

Ošenieks and Spruks concluded their petition writing that they did not intend to teach the lords proper husbandry but that they prostrated themselves before the lords in their misery. The evicted peasants were chased away like wild animals because they were not given other land in the bishopric. They prayed that they should not be displaced until the heirs of the bishopric came of age, who then would be able to decide their case. In the meantime the peasants begged the guardians to consult some impartial Livonian husbandman who was familiar with local conditions, and they hoped the guardians then would reinstate the evicted peasants on their farms.

One of the differences between the cost benefit calculations of the manorial management and that of the peasants was that the former calculated the yield at the fourth grain, while the peasants calculated the third grain. Further, the manorial government planned to settle the displaced peasants each on half an uncus of land (conveniently neglecting the custom that new-settlers were granted three free years), while the peasants stated that they were chased away. A further difference, and a fundamental at that, resulted from the fact that the manorial government did not include in the calculation the cost of statute labour, i. e. the loss from foregone commutation. They did not also include the remuneration for the bailiff and other manorial officers, which the peasants mentioned though not expressing this in monetary terms.

Obviously as a reply to this calculation of the peasants the manorial government submitted a calculation about the profitability of two recently established demesnes–Jaunā muiža (Axelshof) and Kārļa muiža (Karlshof). The reader will notice that these two estates were named in honour of the two heirs of the bishopric; the first name being unpronounceable for the Latvian tongue, the estate in Latvian was named The New Estate. These names show the subtlety of the peasants' remark that manors were established to court favour with the lords.

The expenditure and revenue were calculated by the management for the years 1668 to 1670, and it seems that the calculation was submitted in the year 1671 because it was stated for Jaunā muiža that the 1670 yield could not be included in the calculation as threshing had not been finished (RA, TA 317).

From the calculation can be seen that in the foundation of Jaunā muiža six peasants with 4 ¾ unci had been evicted and for the foundation of Kārļa muiža also six peasants with 3 unci. These were the 12 peasants referred to by Ošenieks and Spruks. The calculated loss by the management included customary dues, commutation of labour, cartage, and expenditure on sown grain, and for Jaunā muiža also hops. The yield in 1668 for Jaunā muiža (yield divided by sown grain) was: rye 2.99, barley 3.97, oats 2.30, or on the average 2.47. For Kārļa muiža in 1668 rye yielded 6.81, barley 5.19, or on the average 5.88. For 1670 rye yielded 6.72, barley 2.62, oats 3.32, or on the average 4.17. During the year 1669 there was a failure of crops and therefore no results for that year were recorded. Conventional prices used by the peasants were different from those used by the manors, except for commutation of labour which for both sides were identical: 14 Rd for a worker with a horse. Commutation of the work of the second labourer and of cartage was calculated by the manorial management at a lower price than calculated by the peasants. The net result of the calculation by the manorial government gave a profit for 1668 at Jaunā muiža of 38 Rd 27 gr. and at Kārļa muiža for two years (1668 and 1670) 468 Rd 44 ⅜ gr. or 234 Rd 22 gr. per annum.

The major difference with the calculation of the peasants was that the manor did not include the costs of tilling the land of the demesne. This was an obvious error because the physical use of statute labour meant loss of income from commutation of labour. As stated by the peasants, for tilling one uncus three workers were needed. The fields of both manors had 7 ¾ unci. Calculating 14 Rd for each of the tillers and ignoring the *otrinieki*, we have to add to the expenditure 325.5 Rd and the loss from both manors then works out at 53.2 Rd per annum. The conclusion is that the peasants in their submission were more up to date with the facts than the anonymous author of the project and the accountants of the two manors, who opposed the calculation of the peasants. The failure of crops also had to be considered. On the manorial fields the failure in 1669 was total. On the other hand, in bad years peasants certainly remained in debt with their customary dues but even in the worst of the years they paid something to the manor.

THE REVISION OF 1671/1672

The revision, ordered for 1665, did not take place. In a memorial dated 13 June 1668 (RA, TA 83, nos. 339–343) the inspector Per Hansson wrote that the revision he had suggested three years ago could not be performed, but he repeated again previously advanced reasons why a revision had become imperative: 1) The surveyors had allocated to peasants unsuitable land, therefore the latter had been pauperized. 2) During the times of the plague peasants had appropriated land of their dead neighbours. Therefore a general survey of land was necessary to allocate to each peasant appropriate proportions of good and bad land. Only then would each of them be able to pay his customary dues. Because a royal revision could be expected, it was important to prevent the consideration of poor quality land.

The revision in the Oxenstierna estates eventually was conducted in the years 1671 and 1672, though not in the form as planned by the guardians and the inspector. The reasons for the project were not only those mentioned previously: to record the correct uncus corresponding to each peasants holding and to find out the possibilities of establishing new demesnes. There was another urgent reason prompted by the coming of age of the heirs of the bishopric. The bishopric had to be divided and this became the overriding cause of the revision.

Because Erik Oxenstierna had died intestate, it was decided that the estates were to be divided between his two sons Axel and Karl Gustav as established by the precedent of the testament of the Chancellor Axel Oxenstierna, which provided that the bishopric should be divided between his two sons: Johan and Erik. In the text of the revision (*ibid.* 32) it was alluded to twice that the aim of the revision was to prepare material for the division of the bishopric.

The revision started at Cēsis on 13 November 1671 and continued during December at Kauguri, Mūrmuiža, Mujāni, Trikāta, Kokmuiža, and Valmiera. On 17 January 1672 Burtnieki was investigated and in February the revision took place at Ropaži, finishing on 12 February at Lorupe. The minutes of the revision are preserved in the Tidö archives (*ibid.* 321). The volume is bound in parchment with an inscription on the spine: Ny Formerade Wacken Böcker

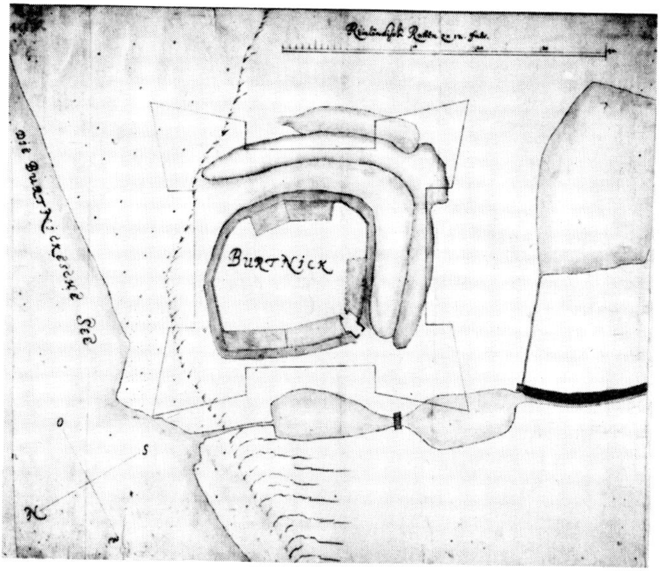

PLAN OF BURTNIEKI CASTLE

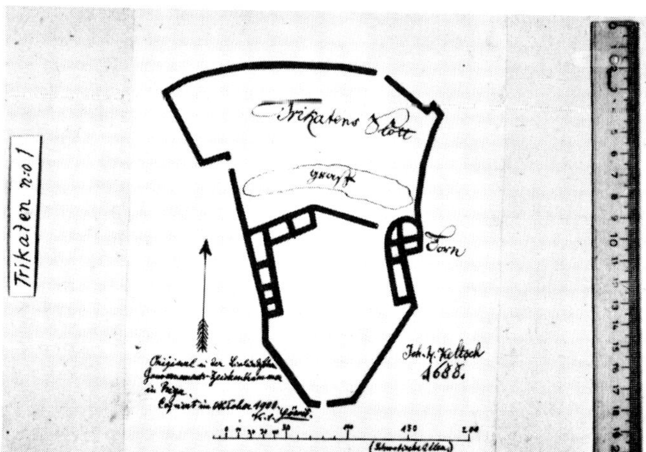

PLAN OF TRIKĀTA CASTLE
Kungl. Krigsarkivet, Stockholm

sampt hålldne Protocoller Wyd Lifländske Revisionen A 1672, fol. 82, no.8. Pages are numbered from 1 to 221 and a second series from 40 to 257.

About the peasants the following data were recorded: name, the uncus of 1651 or 1652, and the uncus set at the revision; if and when land had been measured–in such a case the results of the measurement in tonsteads and the quality of land were mentioned. An enumeration of man-power was given and the relation of people living on the farm to the farmer was registered. Finally it was stated whether the farm had obligation to perform statute work and, in such a case, whether on foot or with a horse and how many days per week, or whether statute labour had been commuted. For some farmers it was mentioned that they had a hop-garden. There were no data about peasants' livestock and sown area with grain.

The fields of the demesne were also described as to their quantity and quality and the names of the fields were given. Meadows were also mentioned. In some cases the names of displaced peasants were recorded where the fields of the demesne had been established.

The measurements of land were recorded as performed in 1653 and 1654 in Cēsis and, after the interruption caused by the war, continued up to 1669. There were measurements also for Kauguri. It seems that the command by the guardians of the 6 August 1668 about surveys and mapping of the estates was not executed.

The following is a summary of data comparing 1652 with 1671/1672, calculated by the author. Fractions are calculated to two-figure decimals.

LANDS OF THE BISHOPRIC IN 1652 AND 1671/1672

Estates	1652			1671/1672		
	Demesne unci	Payment unci	Mantal	Demesne unci	Payment unci	Peasant farms (number)
Bauņi	4.00	48.75	65.0	7.00	54.50	79
Burtnieki	6.00	53.50	74.5	5.00	50.25	84
Braslava	–	–	–	2.66	3.75	11
Cēsis	8.00	96.00	137.0	5.83	95.13	167
Ēvele	6.00	45.25	60.5	6.00	42.62	72
Jaunā muiža	7.00	22.75	27.5	2.00	21.25	29
Kauguri & Mūrmuiža	5.00	42.75	52.5	4.00	42.38	59
Kokmuiža	4.00	43.00	178.5	2.50	34.50	49
Valmiera	3.50	78.00		4.25	77.25	128

Mujāni	4.00	54.75	82.0	2.33	46.87	73
Rencēni	7.75	49.25	70.5	8.00	49.13	79
Trikāta	11.00	107.00	139.5	12.00	136.50	189
Vecate	5.00	47.25	69,0	4.00	57.12	113
Subtotal	71.25	688.25	956.5	65.57	711.25	1132
		Unci			Unci	
Leases and fiefs		–			23.88	
Unsettled and not paying dues		177.25			34.25*	
Reeves and freemen		23.75			7.25*	
New-settlers		34.00			–	
New estates		–		12.62	7.87	
Bānūži: settled land		4.75			4.25	
unsettled land		1.00			0.75	
Brenguļi		32.50			**	
Veļķi		9.00			9.00	
Rentmeistera muiža (including demesne)		8.50			8.00	
Retainers' peasants		39.50			42.00	
demesne & unsettled		30.25			17.00*	
Peasants of the clergy		22.13			21.75	
unsettled land		1.00			4.13	
Total		1071.88			891.38	
Added demesne from subtotal		71.25			65.57	
Added new estates		–			12.62	
Grand total		1143.13			969.57	

* Not strictly comparable with data for 1652 because of different classification.

** Included in Trikāta in 1671/1672.

To make the payment unci more comparable between the years 1652 and 1671/1672, we add Brenguļi to the total of 1652. The payment unci for 1652 then are 720.75. In 1662, just after the war, payment unci had declined to 647.5 which is 89.8 % of unci for the year 1652. By 1671/1672, payment unci had increased from the low of 1662 to 711.25 which is 98.7 % of the figure for 1652. If the grand totals for the years 1652 and 1671/1672 are compared, the decline is from 100 to 85. The greatest loss was of unsettled land which was overgrown during the war with trees and bushes and was not any longer regarded as potential arables.

Ropaži has been excluded from the above comparison because of missing data for the year 1652. At the revision of 1672, Ropaži had 79 peasant farms with 32.5 unci of land. In the demesne there were 230 leapsteads of land divided in three fields, but because of want of manure only 102 leaps of rye and 60 leaps of barley had been sown. In addition, there were 80 leapsteads of exhausted land and 40 leapsteads of swidden. Meadows there were for 150 cart-loads hay. Not included in these figures was an estate with the name Naglumuiža (Sissigall) belonging to Ropaži and leased to the Riga merchant Nagel's widow, consisting of 10 peasant farms, in total of 2.5 unci. The chief inspector Turlow had leased 3 peasant farms to the Riga citizens–Johann Zuckerbecker and Mrs Derenthal. The demesne of Naglumuiža had been established on peasants' land and contained 80 leapsteads or 1.5 unci.

SURVEYS OF LAND

As mentioned before, land was not measured in 1671/1672. Instead, in the minutes of the revision, measurements for some estates of previous years were given with the annotation that they had been revised in 1672. It appears therefore that the recorded adjustments reducing the quantity according to quality were performed in 1672.

At Cēsis out of 167 peasant farms only 84 or 50 % had data about land measurement. The 84 surveyed farms had a total of 6832.5 tonsteads land, but to account for the quality this was reduced to 4263.5 tonsteads. The total number of unci of these 84 farms was 59.25 which equals to an average of 115.32 tonsteads of real acreage, or 71.96 tonsteads of adjusted acreage, per uncus. The principle of adjustment becomes clear if we look at the quality of land. Good arables and good swidden were valued at 100 %. Good arables and heathland swidden in combination were valued at 77 % and so were medium quality arables. Average quality swidden was estimated 67.5 %. Average quality arables and heathland swidden were estimated 66 %. Sandy arables were estimated 65 %. Sandy fields and heathland fields were estimated 50 %. Waterlogged fields were estimated 50 to 64 %, but heathland and poor quality fields were estimated 25 %. In some cases there was acreage added to compensate for defects. For instance, the peasant Bērziņš received 29 % of acreage on top of his land to compensate him for want of meadows.

A difference is discernible in the adjustments as to the various number of unci. The land of one peasant who had 1.75 unci was adjusted to 94.8 %. One peasant who had 1.5 unci land had the benefit to be adjusted to 75 %. Five peasants who had 1.25 unci each had their land reduced to 70.2 %, 19 peasants with one uncus–to 68.8 %, 23 peasants with 0.75 uncus–to 61.8 %, 21 peasants with 0.5 uncus–to 58.5 %, and 12 peasants with 0.25 uncus–to 36 %. This shows that the smaller the uncus number of a farm, the larger the benefit from adjustment. On the other hand, the adjusted areas were not proportional to the uncus number. For instance, adjusted area of land on the average in one uncus farms was 65.4 tonsteads, while in 0.75 uncus farms it was 48.8 tonsteads (if proportional the figure for the latter would work out at 49.1 tonsteads). In farms with half an uncus it was 34.9 tonsteads (and not 32.7 as one expects with proportional figures), and farms with a quarter uncus had 20.4 tonsteads adjusted land (while the proportional figure would work out at 16.4 tonsteads). This shows that the fractions of unci were not proportional to the acreage–smaller unci had relatively more land than larger unci.

Of the estate Kauguri all peasant farms had been surveyed in the years 1665 and 1666, i.e. before the resolution of 6 August 1668 to survey all estates. The revision of the measurements was undertaken in 1671. The total acreage of the 38 farms was 3017.5 tonsteads which was reduced to account for the quality to 1793.8 tonsteads, i.e. to 59.4 % corresponding to 27 and one eighth unci. There were 14 one uncus farms with total acreage of 1376.5 tonsteads, which was reduced to 899.7 tonsteads or to 65.4 %. Three quarter uncus farms were 9 with 724 tonsteads reduced to 425 or to 58.7 %. Eleven half uncus farms had 739 tonsteads reduced to 405.5 tonsteads or to 54.9 %. Three a quarter uncus farms had 163 tonsteads reduced to 56.2 tonsteads or to 34.5 %. One farm of an eighth of an uncus with 15 tonsteads was reduced to 7.5 tonsteads or to 50 %. The average size of the one uncus farms before adjustment for quality was 98.3 tonsteads with a standard deviation of 8.1 tonsteads. For the three quarter of an uncus farms the corresponding figures were 80.4 ± 16.3, but for the half unci farms 67.2 ± 11.1.

After the war an estate in the Sigulda district was added to the bishopric. It was the earlier mentioned Lorupe (Kronenberg). In a resolution dated 7 June 1663 the Governor General prohibited any infringement by neighbours into the boundaries of this estate (RA, TA 75, p. 106) and in 1669 it was acquired by the Oxenstierna heirs (*ibid.* 134). The estate was revised by Niclas Nordenborg on 12 February 1672 (*ibid.* 321). There were 7 peasant farms estimated at 2 unci and two unsettled farms with five eighths of an uncus. The land had been measured and the seven peasants had a total of 131.25 tonsteads good land and 50.58 tonsteads of inferior land. The latter was proportioned at 43 to 68 %

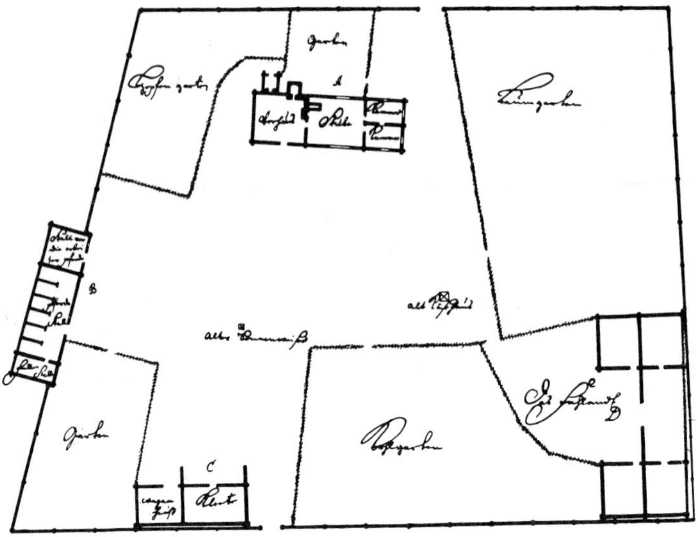

LORUPE

Surveyed by J.H.Keltsch 1692 (EKA)

of good land and three peasants were reduced in their uncus number because of want of meadows. The demesne had in the first field 34 leapsteads of winter crop and 40 leapsteads of summer crop, in the second field correspondingly 28 and 33 leapsteads, and in the third field–12 and 16 leapsteads. In addition there was old swidden of about 50 leapsteads. Some seven to eight years ago the yield had been the seventh grain, but during the time of the revision only the third grain (it is not clear whether this was meant to be above the seed or not). Nevertheless, hope was expressed that in five and a half years previous fertility could be regained. There were three meadows yielding 16 cart-loads hay.

The minutes of the revision of the bishopric of 1671 and 1672 were signed at Valmiera on 7 May 1672 by the inspector Per Hansson, his assistant Friedrich Liphard, and the scribes Johan Hassel and Anders Brunman. They stated that the estimates of the unci had been done with utmost care after their own knowledge and the testimony of the reeves and old peasants. The necessary ocular inspection could not be done because of winter time and the urgency of the inquiry in connection with the forthcoming division of the estates. The results were sent to their lordships for confirmation (p. 257 of the minutes).

THE PEASANTS IN 1671/1672

Of considerable interest is the demographic situation that can be gleaned from the revision. The average number of inhabitants per farm was in Bauņi 9.31, Braslava 8.82, Vecate 8.81, Rencēni 8.51, Jaunburtnieki 7.44, Burtnieki 7.29, Mujāni 6.16, Valmiera 6.08, Trikāta 5.69, Cēsis 5.49, Lorupe 5.57, and Ropaži 5.08. The large difference between Bauņi and Ropaži can be explained by the fact that in the estates at the top of the list females are included, while with descending figures females are less and less enumerated. For instance, if in Trikāta the obviously omitted females are added, the average is 7.81 instead of 5.69 and Trikāta advances from the ninth to fifth position in the above series of estates (*ceteris paribus*).

Because Bauņi had the highest number of inhabitants in the peasant farms, it is only worth while to present a frequency distribution of the inhabitants of this estate.

FREQUENCY DISTRIBUTION OF INHABITANTS IN PEASANT FARMS AT BAUŅI (1672)

Number of persons per farm	Frequency	Number of inhabitants	Per cent of total inhabitants
3	1	3	0.4
4	–	–	–
5	4	20	2.8
6	5	30	4.1
7	10	70	9.6
8	9	72	9.9
9	18	162	22.3
10	10	100	13.8
11	3	33	4.6
12	8	96	13.2
13	4	52	7.2
14	4	56	7.7
15	–	–	–
16	2	32	4.4
Total	78	726	100.0

To illustrate the situation on the peasant farms, let us take the two farms at Bauņi with the largest number of inhabitants: Mūsiņš and Pavārs, both with 16 inhabitants. Both farms were still in existence in the year 1688 (see ED

1974, map p. 127 and list of farm names p. 116). Some time before 1736 on the large fields of these two (Mūsiņš and Pavārs) and on the land of some five or six peasants in their neighbourhood the estate Pučurga was established named, in German, Galenhof after one of the peasant farms Gallan shown on the above mentioned map. The name of Pavārs disappeared, but Mūsiņš was transferred some five kilometres to the northwest and the farm name was preserved until the recent collectivization of Latvia by the communist regime.

Mūsiņš had on his farm (of three quarters of an uncus) his wife, one son and six small children (sex in the record not specified), two farmhands and one maidservant. One of the farmhands was married and with his wife had three small children. So on the farm there were two nuclear families and two single persons. As a rule, farmhands were not related to the farmer and in the rare cases where this was so, it was specially noted in the record.

Pavārs held a farm of one uncus. He had with his wife one married son and one married daughter. The latter had five small children. The farmer's sister's four small children were living on the farm, but there was no information where his sister lived and whether she was still alive. Then there was one maidservant. This was a consanguineous family except for the maidservant.

To sum up the total recorded population of Bauņi in the year 1672, the structure appears as follows:

STRUCTURE OF FARM POPULATION AT BAUŅI ESTATE IN 1672

Males		Females		Sex not known	
Farmers	78	Their wives	77		
Sons	159	Daughters	111	Their children	81
Sons-in-law	3	Daughters-in-law	16		
Brothers	23	Their wives	9	Their children	16
Sisters' husbands	5	Sisters	2	Their children	1
				Foster-children	6
Farmhands	51	Their wives	8	Their children	11
Non-related inhabitants	8	Their wives	6	Their children	11
		Maidservants	44		
Total	327		273		126

It seems from the above that even at Bauņi, where females were most completely recorded in comparison with other estates, there too the records were incomplete. Under the assumption that there was a balance of sexes, 16.5 % of females were not recorded among the grown up population, which would add 54 to the grand total. There is a probability that girls also were missed out among the children whose sex was not mentioned in the source.

MEDIATE SUBDITI

The legal position of the Latvian peasants and the actual position with legal implications of the Finnish colonists at Valmiera considerably worsened after the First Northern War. The secretary of the corps of Livonian nobility, Kaspar von Ceumern, had prepared a draft of a new statute, which was submitted for approval to the Governor General Klas Tott. Tott sent the draft written in German to Sweden on 25 January 1668 (RA, Livonica, II, 83) and signed another copy himself on 28 January ordering it to be discussed at the next diet (Landtag). The draft was discussed at consecutive diets in October 1668, October 1669, and July 1670. In July 1671 Klas Tott went to Sweden and obtained Royal assent on 22 September (RA, RR, 22 September 1671, § 9) with the title 'Land Ordnung'. There was no Swedish translation of the German draft and Royal assent was obtained probably on the recommendation of the Governor General,without reading the text. The draft is extant in Riksarkivet and the Latvian State Archive, and has been printed by G.J.von Buddenbrock.

From our point of view the important chapter is in Part Six with the title 'Von Ausantwortung der Bauern' (On the extradition of peasants). By this law the Latvian hereditary peasant became an inherited peasant. There was no definition of the term *Erbbauer* in the law, but the following points apply. Inherited peasants were: 1) those who were born from inherited peasants, 2) children of foreign peasants who lighted a fire in a hearth on the land of a nobleman, 3) everybody who arrived and settled on the land of a nobleman and lighted there a fire, 4) every peasant who had lived on the land of a nobleman for ten years and whose previous master was aware of this, 5) every fugitive about whom the nobleman had informed the previous master and who was not claimed within three months, 6) children of peasants who had married into the land of a nobleman, 7) foster-children, the issue of farmhands; foster-children of farmers could be claimed after their marriage together with their children, 8) children who were born at one place and afterwards had moved to another place remained inherited peasants attached to their birthplace, 9) children and parents of foreign [Russian, Lithuanian, Courish, etc.] farmhands if born in Livonia; 10) children born out of wedlock became inherited peasants of the nobleman on whose land they were born.

By this legal act a new principle was formulated and peasants whose status before this act could be regarded as semifree (hereditary peasants and new-settlers) now became unfree (inherited peasants). In other words, they became serfs, i. e. peasants legally attached to the soil. In order to establish whether he was a serf (if born on a nobleman's land) or free (if born somewhere else, for instance, in a city) it was important for the peasant to establish where he was born. The rule certainly did not apply to noblemen themselves who were born on noblemens' land, and not to other people who were not peasants.

In actual fact it took a considerable time until the new legal concept was implemented. Even after promulgation of the new law, peasants left the land where they had settled, became fugitives and looked for better opportunities. As late as 1697, Governor General Erik Dahlberg issued a proclamation against fugitives. The law of 1668–1671, for the first time in Livonian history, also attempted to attach the previously free farmhands to the soil, but this also was not implemented. The court of the Oxenstierna estates at Cēsis in 1671 found that farmhands were 'uncertain' and female farmhands by no means were bonded (Buddenbrock 1821, p. 1475). Nevertheless, the road towards serfdom had started and it culminated during the eighteenth century when Russia became overlord of Livonia with its outspoken sympathy for the nobility, which was not the case with Sweden.

The general revision of the Oxenstierna estates previously discussed in this chapter shows that the same terminology was applied as was used by commissioners in the first half of the century. For instance, at Ropaži there a distinction had been made between 'Rodenpoyscher Erbpaur' and 'Churländer', while according to the new law the peasants from Kurzeme also were 'Erbbauern' in the sense of the new terminology. Tradition was stronger than forms invented by lawyers and accepted by politicians.

Ropaži was the only estate where in this particular revision details about where each farmer had come from and how long he had lived on the land if he was not born at Ropaži were recorded. Out of 80 farmers for whom data are available 24 were hereditary peasants, born at Ropaži (30.0 %), 20 (25.0 %) came from Kurzeme (the Duchy of Courland), 28 (35.0 %) from other estates of Vidzeme (Livonia), and 3 (3.8 %) from Estonia. One came from Lithuania (1.2 %). One (1.2 %) was born at Ropaži, but he was not a hereditary peasant. For 3 (3.8 %) data are missing.

For 18 peasants or 22.5 % the year was recorded when they settled at Ropaži: three in 1642, one at each of the years 1657, 1658, 1663, and 1667. In the year 1669 settled five, 1670–three, 1671–two, and 1672–one.

There is no other information of this kind available for other estates. Regrettably we cannot be certain that the figures for Ropaži can be generalized. Ropaži was nearer to foreign countries (Kurzeme and Lithuania) than the rest of the bishopric and the major part of Livonia.

The economic situation of the Finnish colonists of Valmiera was more precarious than that of their Latvian neighbours. Since 1644 they had to pay a tenth part of the yield of harvest of their fields, while the Latvian peasants paid a fixed quantity and the 'tenth part' (which actually was a quarter of the harvest) only from abandoned land which they illegally tilled. The payment of the tenth part from the harvest was regarded as a more stringent demand.

In 1641 the Finnish colonists were resettled and had to leave tilled land of 200 tonsteads. Resettlement of Latvian peasants to acquire land for the foundation of a new demesne was proceeding only after negotiations and with the consent of the peasant concerned, which admittedly could be forced upon him. The Finnish colonists as a paramilitary force had simply to obey orders. Similarly, by order, the Finns had to leave the town of Valmiera and resettle on land as ordered by Count Erik in 1646. The statute work demanded from the Finns was lighter than demanded from the Latvian peasants: only four days a week as compared with five days a week from the latter. The Finns very likely were not required to send a second and a third worker as the Latvian farmers had (which usually was commuted), at least nothing on this account is mentioned in the sources. We can therefore conclude, that the economic obligations of the Finns were more precarious as far as customary dues were concerned but advantageous in relation to statute work. On the other hand, the Finns were engaged in military training, guard duties, and fortification work, on top of their statute work, which to a certain extent cancelled this advantage.

Their legal position from the point of view of tenure was worse than that of the Latvian peasants. Nevertheless, their legal position as to personal freedom was beyond any doubt at first (ED 1962, pp. 59–81). On 1 May 1629 King Gustav Adolf explained to the Livonian nobility that Finnish and Swedish peasants in Livonia could be occupied only with remuneration and that they could not be forced into serfdom (RA, LTR 1629). Queen Kristina repeated this and on 20 August 1634 decreed (VA, Ea IV, B 35) that Finns who settled in Livonia did not lose their freedom and did not become servile slaves (leibeigene Schlawen). The usage of this terminology was a bad foreboding for the Latvian and Estonian peasants in Livonia, especially when on 27 April 1682 King Karl XI in anger and exaggeration described the legal situation of the Latvian, Estonian, and Pomeranian peasants as slavery (Swedish text: VA, Vba; German translation: Schirren, p. 19).

A sympton that the Finns in Livonia were on the road to bondage can be discovered as early as 18 October 1636 when the steward Ledebohrn reported (RA, Oxenst. saml.) that he could not pass review of the children of Finnish soldiers because nearly all of them were working as farmhands on the farms of peasants. Farmhands certainly were not bondmen, but assimilation into the Latvian population with its inferior legal status did not augur favourably for the future. In 1637 the steward again asked the Chancellor whether the soldiers of Valmiera were permitted to give their children to whom they wished (att Wollmarske Solldater gifwa deras barn åth dem som dhe willia) or whether they had to receive sustenance until they came of age (RA, TA 75, p. 248). The Chancellor's reply was that it was permissible to hire out children until they came of age, but then they must be required back. Only if sustenance could be cheaply arranged could they be kept on the expenses of the bishopric. To require back the hired out children would presuppose the keeping of a register, but there is no evidence that such a register was kept. It then seems that children after coming of age did not return and therefore on 10 August 1642 the Chancellor ordered the issue of sustenance to the children, but the parents had to guarantee that after certain years the children would enter the Chancellor's service in the garrison or as artisans (*ibid.*, p. 270).

This condition reminds one of bondage. Nevertheless, a list of 1646 shows that several Finnish children were farmhands with Latvian peasants, certainly not detailing at which farm. The problem of the Finnish children was mentioned in the Chancellor's instruction for the steward Sprengport on 20 September 1652. On the 8 February 1652 Erik Oxenstierna ordered (RA, Oxenst. saml., Ser. D II, 1 and RA, TA 75, p. 90, also ED 1935, p. 192) that for a better education some of the Finnish children should be billeted at the Valmiera castle and should be taught to spin, weave, read, and be instructed in piety. The spinners and weavers in the estates then could be used for other work. The rest of the children who received monthly stipends should be taught prayers and then assigned to artisans to learn a craft. Notwithstanding these instructions, it seems that a number of Finnish children remained with the Latvian peasants and eventually became Latvian peasants themselves. The account of the estates also mentions cancelled debts of Finnish soldiers who had fled. These too probably were absorbed into the Latvian peasantry.

It seems that the Chancellor was worried only about the Finnish boys—the prospective soldiers—not the girls. An interesting case about a Finnish girl is documented in 1645 (RA, TA 342). The Latvian peasant Pēteris Baile at the Valmiera town court had sued Peter Pounenen who had hired out his daughter to him for a year, but she had left her service prematurely. The court ordered the girl to return and serve the full agreed time.

Count Erik, in the instruction issued for the Oxenstierna's Estonian estates (*ibid.* 75, pp. 152–153) on 4 May 1653, ordered that bailiffs would have to pay for losses if and when, because of inappropriate handling of a peasant, he became a fugitive. If a peasant escaped for other reasons, he had to be followed and captured. If a Swede or a Finn escaped one could not demand that he should be returned, but nevertheless it had to be found out to where he had fled. His debts had to be recovered either voluntarily or enforced according to Swedish law. The law was to be enforced if he had not served his full time or had not given notice in time that he would leave. The distinction made between an Estonian peasant and a Swedish or Finnish peasant, as this ordinance shows, was wearing thin. Probably the development in the legal position of the Swedish peasants in Sweden itself was influencing the attitude of the lords in the Swedish overseas provinces.

The First Northern War undoubtedly worsened the legal position of the Finns at Valmiera. After the recapture of Valmiera Governor General Robert Douglas on 15 August 1659 decreed that the 'Erb Bauren und Erb Colonier', whom the commandant Sprengport had enlisted in the military forces, should remain in royal service (RA, TA 75, p. 250). This is the first time the author has found the expression 'inherited colonists' in describing the Finns. It is possible that the Governor General as a newcomer to his office was not aware of the legal connotation of this term and used it only as a figure of speech. On the other hand, there can be no doubt about the resolution of the guardians Knut Kurck, Israel Lagerfeld, and Jakob Schnack, given on 6 August 1668 in reply to a query of the steward Per Hansson (*ibid.*, p. 270). Referring to the late Chancellor's order of 1642 they resolved that children of Finnish soldiers at Valmiera had to be maintained with annual sustenance if parents guaranteed (giöra honom den försäkring) that they would remain in the Count's service at the garrison. This was nothing new, it was only a repetition of decrees before the war in the same matter. What was new, was paragraph 35 in the same document (*ibid.*, p. 278). This paragraph stated that the inherited soldier (Arv-soldat) Simon Kobias had requested to be allowed to become a citizen of Valmiera. He was given permission provided he could supply, instead of himself, another soldier as good as he was. Nevertheless, he had to remain for lifetime an inherited Finn (grevl. husets Arvfinne). By 1671 this term was well established: Paul Kokain and Matz Hervon complained about the commandant of Valmiera, Edmund van der Brug, and signed: 'Eder Hoghgrefl. Nåder arme och arfegne Soldater' (*ibid.* 270).

We have no longer a possible case of misused terminology or a misunderstanding. Within a generation the free Finns, whose freedom was safeguarded by Gustav Adolf and Kristina, had become serfs. This is confirmed by the opinion volunteered by Jakob Fleming at the Chamber College on 16 July 1680 (KA, at present RA, Kammarkollegii arkiv, Protokoll). On the suggestion that the Finns from Livonia be resettled back to Finland he replied: 'Livonia like Finland is a Royal province. The Finns populate the country. It depends on the will of His Royal Majesty to repatriate the old Finns. About the young [Finns] who are born on the estates the nobility claims a right and the resettlement cannot be as easily executed.'

The case of the Finns in Livonia in general and in the bishopric in particular is an interesting example about the origin of serfdom. These Finns within living memory had become serfs. The development foreseen in another context by Per Brahe in 1650 had been fulfilled: 'We all are *subditi regni*, the peasants are *mediate subditi* but we are *immediate*' (quoted by Heckscher II, p. 333).

DIVISION OF THE BISHOPRIC

On 7 March 1672 on the insistence of Count Karl Gustav (Eriksson) Oxenstierna a ballot about the division of the bishopric took part. The preceeding discussion and the outcome of the ballot are recorded in the minutes of the guardians office (RA, TA 75: Södermöriska förmynder-förvaltning protokoll). Counts Karl Gustav Oxenstierna, Nils Brahe, Knut Kurck and Jakob Schnack, and also Israel Lagerfeld, were present. Count Karl Gustav insisted that the division should take place at once so that the advantage of the season could be utilized and the estates could be leased. The guardians were reluctant to conduct the ballot because Count Axel Oxenstierna was not present. But Karl Gustav declared that if his brother would not accept the outcome of the ballot he would agree that a new ballot be arranged and that the present ballot should be regarded to be only provisional. It was agreed that the division should in principle follow the plan set down in the will of the grandfather of the heirs, Axel Oxenstierna (see Chapter Seven), but Knut Kurck pointed out that the land of Mujāni was intermingled with the land under Cēsis. Schnack's opinion was that at least the Mode hundred (wacka) of Mujāni should be added to the Cēsis lot. After discussion it was agreed that the Mode hundred should temporarily be added to the Cēsis lot and that to equalize the lots Ropaži and Lorupe could be used, as was provided about Ropaži in Axel Oxenstierna's will.

In the ballot Count Axel was represented by Count Nils Brahe. Count Karl Gustav took the first draw and received the Valmiera lot, but in Count Nils Brahe's hat remained the Cēsis lot. The schedule of how to divide the bishopric is extant (*ibid.* 124) and printed here in facsimile. As can be seen, the schedule was based on the 1652 terrier and not on the 1671/1672 revision which was finished on 12 February, but the results of which had obviously not yet arrived in Stockholm. Calculating on the 1652 payment unci Axel Oxenstierna had received 10 unci more than Karl Gustav Oxenstierna, but on the

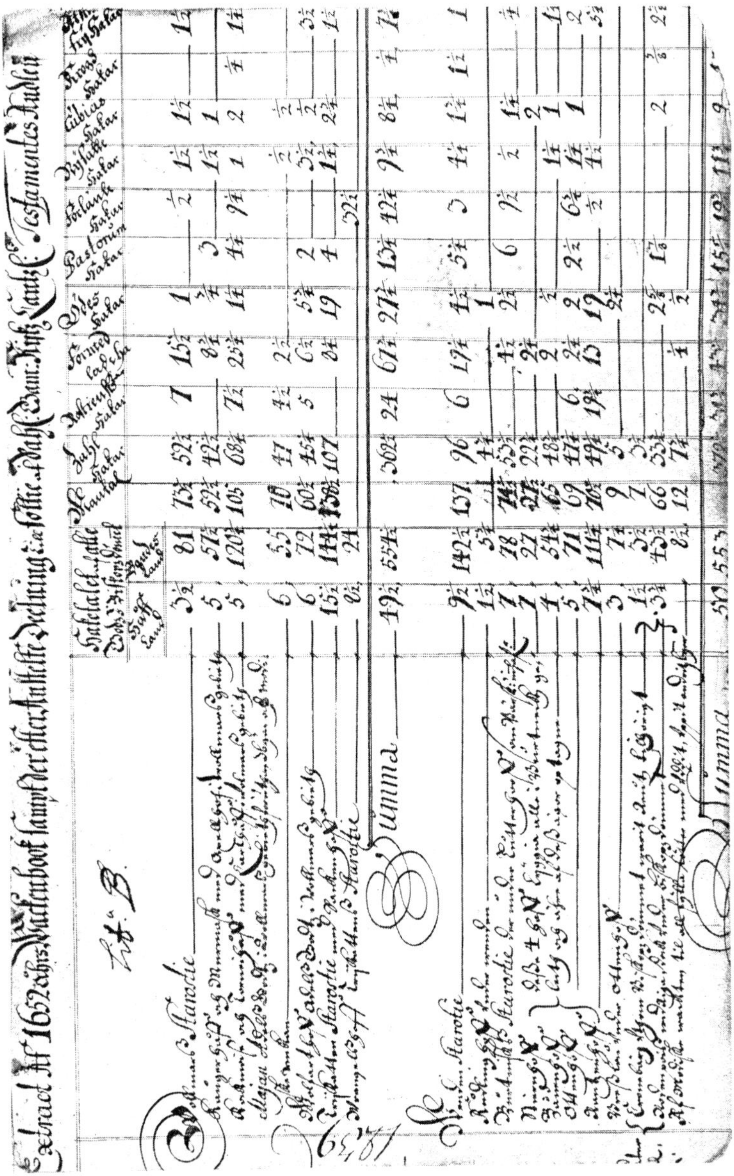

DIVISION OF THE BISHOPRIC BETWEEN THE SONS OF ERIK OXENSTIERNA

(RA, TA 124)

base of 1671/1672 unci Axel fared worse in the ballot. Karl Gustav had received 43 and seven eighths payment unci more than his brother.

After the ballot of the Livonian estates a ballot of the Estonian estates was also performed. Count Axel received the Roela (Rögel) lot, but Count Karl Gustav the Vohnja (Fonal) lot. In Axel's lot were included Roela and Lähtru with 105 ½ unci, Püssi with 84 unci, a half of Vöhma with 13 ¾ unci and Kosküla with 10 unci or a total of 213 ¼ unci according to the 1647 wacka-book. In Karl's lot was included Vohnja (without Vatku) with 103 unci, Kavastu and Völe with 86 ¼ unci, half of Vöhma with 14 unci, and Vatku with 10 unci. The total was also 213 ¼ unci (RA, TA 70, fol. 19).

FINANCIAL RESULTS AFTER THE DIVISION

For the part of Karl Gustav Oxenstierna ledgers are available written in riksdollars (RA, TA 336–338), but at conventional prices, not market prices. The accounts are for the Valmiera starosty and they include: Valmiera, Kauguri, Mūrmuiža, Jaunburtnieki, Kokmuiža, Tarnisa, Mujāni (except the Mode hundred), Ēvele, Trikāta, Vāle, and Brenguļi. The accounts have been reworked by the author from the capital accounts of the ledgers into the same schedule as on page 58 ff.

INCOME & EXPENDITURE OF THE LOT

	CASH & PRODUCE		MANORS	
1672	Dr	Cr	Dr	Cr
Balance	3679	17,788	–	–
Customary dues	29,481	2691	1757	12,886
Transfer	–	8649	–	–
Demesne	438	6346	855	695
Remuneration	2024	230	230	4487
Produce refined	125	43	43	125
Gains & losses	–	–	15,308	–
Totals	35,747	35,747	18,193	18,193

The item Sales is included in the items debited to the Possessor's account.

It is noticeable that for the two years 1672 and 1673 the previously observed tendency–that revenue from the manorial economy exceeded the revenue from the customary dues of the peasants–continued. We further notice that the payments to the Crown were relatively small during the presented three years. In the years 1672 and 1674 Karl Gustav Oxenstierna was personally present at the starosty, as can be seen from the expenses: in 1672 he was greeted on arrival by an orchestra hired in Riga and in 1674 his consumption of produce was recorded.

Axel Eriksson Oxenstierna's income from the Cēsis lot (Cēsis, Liepmuiža, Burtnieki, Jaunā muiža, Bauņi, Vecate, Renceni, Vilzēni, Priekuļi, Ropaži, and the Mode hundred of Mujāni) was recorded in a lump sum among his incomes from the Swedish and Finnish estates (*ibid.* 96–102). The accounts were written in Swedish silver dollars. Assuming that 2 Swedish dollars equal one riksdollar, the income as recorded from the Cēsis lot was: 1672–4496 Rd (or 17 % from the total income including the Estonian estates, the fief, Finnish estates, and Swedish inherited estates), 1673–3573 Rd (15 %), 1674–13,300 Rd (47 %), 1675–5533 Rd (28 %), 1676–10,684 Rd (44 %). The results of the Cēsis and the Valmiera lots are obviously only comparable for the year 1674. For the previous years the accountancy technique for the Cēsis lot precludes comparison with the results for the Valmiera lot.

OF KARL GUSTAV OXENSTIERNA

PEASANTS		*THE CROWN*		*POSSESSOR*		*BALANCE*	
Dr	Cr	Dr	Cr	Dr	Cr	Dr	Cr
–	–	–	–	–	–	17,788	3679
1586	18,005	1388	–	–	–	–	–
–	–	–	–	8649	–	–	–
–	–	–	–	5748	–	–	–
2463	–	–	–	–	–	–	–
–	–	–	–	–	–	–	–
13,956	–	–	1388	–	14,397	–	14,109
18,005	18,005	1388	1388	14,397	14,397	17,788	17,788

Source: RA, TA 336–338.

1673	CASH & PRODUCE Dr	Cr	MANORS Dr	Cr
Balance	17,798	13,938	–	–
Customary dues	21,671	5931	–	7410
Transfer	–	16,132	–	–
Demesne	60	1013	–	7187
Remuneration	–	2515	2515	–
Produce refined	–	–	–	–
Gains & losses	–	–	12,082	–
Totals	39,529	39,529	14,597	14,597

1674	CASH & PRODUCE Dr	Cr	MANORS Dr	Cr
Balance	13,938	16,289	–	–
Customary dues	25,139	2162	227	8099
Transfer	–	9483	–	–
Demesne	–	9730	–	–
Remuneration	46	1721	1721	272
Produce refined	262	–	–	262
Gains & losses	–	–	6685	–
Totals	39,385	39,385	8633	8633

LEASE OF THE BISHOPRIC

In the ballot of the lots between the heirs of the bishopric, Count Karl Gustav mentioned the idea of leasing the estates. To establish the rent, the following scheme was worked out. Statute labour was calculated to be worth with a horse 16 Rd, on foot 11 Rd, the *otrinieks* 2 ½ Rd. Commutation money was added to the total and also the value of customary dues calculated according to standardized conventional prices. The calculations were performed on the basis of the terrier (wacka-book) for 1671.

The total for all eleven estates was calculated at 28,773 Rd. To this amount were added the savings made from not having to pay bailiffs (1503 Rd), savings on the differences of measures on sold grain (1184 Rd), and savings on

PEASANTS		*THE CROWN*		*POSSESSOR*		*BALANCE*	
Dr	Cr	Dr	Cr	Dr	Cr	Dr	Cr
–	–	–	–	–	–	13,938	17,798
2393	14,261	132	–	3406	–	–	–
–	–	873	–	15,259	–	–	–
–	–	–	–	8140	–	–	–
–	–	–	–	–	–	–	–
–	–	–	–	–	–	–	–
11,868	–	–	1005	–	26,805	3860	–
14,261	14,261	1005	1005	26,805	26,805	17,798	17,798

PEASANTS		*THE CROWN*		*POSSESSOR*		*BALANCE*	
Dr	Cr	Dr	Cr	Dr	Cr	Dr	Cr
–	–	–	–	–	–	16,289	13,938
1315	15,202	847	–	–	2065	–	–
–	–	–	–	9483	–	–	–
–	–	1205	–	8525	–	–	–
–	–	–	–	226	–	–	–
–	–	–	–	–	–	–	–
13,887	–	–	2052	–	16,169	–	2351
15,202	15,202	2052	2052	18,234	18,234	16,289	16,289

expenses to the clergy, the court, the salaries to military and to officers of the economy (1968 Rd). The grand total rental in this way was calculated at 33,427 Rd 76 ½ gr. Because from 1666 to 1669 the bishopric had yielded on the average only 19,501 Rd 21 ¼ gr. per annum, the additional profit in leasing the estates was calculated at 13,926 Rd 55 ¼ gr. (RA, TA 134, Lit. A).

Another calculation showed that, after leasing, the burden imposed on the peasantry would be substantially increased. It provided that the peasants who held one uncus and those with ¾ uncus should be placed respectively on half and ¼ uncus and on the saved land new settlements established. Because the half uncus peasants rendered the same amount of statute labour as one uncus and ¾ uncus peasants, new-settlers would give an additional income from statute labour and from customary dues, estimated at 8857 Rd (*ibid.*, Lit. C).

Notwithstanding the argument of Count Karl Gustav Oxenstierna during the meeting with the guardians on 7 March 1672 that the division of the estates was urgently needed so that the estates could be leased during spring, it seems that the estates were not leased for several years. Axel Eriksson Oxenstierna drew income of varying amounts from his lot until his death in 1676. Similarly also Karl Gustav received a varying income from his lot. The variations of the income show that the estates were not leased. If they had been leased the amount received would have been the same for a stretch of years.

Only from 1678 do we have indications about leasing of estates of the previous bishopric. After the death of Axel Eriksson Oxenstierna the divided bishopric had been united again into the possession of Karl Gustav Oxenstierna. He travelled to Livonia and on 20 September 1678 leased the bulk of the bishopric to the Riga merchant Johan von Reutern (RA, TA 68). On 10 October 1678 he leased Ropaži to the same merchant. Before the lease Reutern had advanced to Karl Gustav Oxenstierna more than 20,000 Rd at 10 % (later reduced to 8 %) interest. Reutern also advanced, for the estates, statio to the Crown, provided clothing to the Valmiera garrison, leased storage space for the grain of the estates, which he took on consignment, supplied the Count's court, paid freight on commodities which the Count shipped to Sweden, and paid remuneration to the officers of the estates including the judge and assessors. Against these advances Reutern received grain on consignment and other produce from the estates and, after the contract of lease was signed, accounted for the rent of the estates.

The rent for Burtnieki, Bauņi, Braslava, Vilzēni, Jaunā muiža, Mujāni, Lenči, Kokmuiža, Kārļa muiža, Tarnisa, Ēvele, and Rencēni, in 1678 was 7030 Rd 45 gr. In 1679 the rent for Trikāta, Cēsis, and Priekuļi was 3000 Rd, but because of failure of crops in 1679 Reutern was credited with 1200 Rd (*ibid.*). The rent for Ropaži contracted 10 October 1678 for ten years was 5000 Albert Rd per annum (*ibid.*).

CLAIMS BY THE HEIRS

The will of Axel Oxenstierna (AOB, I, p. 644) provided a dowry to his daughter Katarina (in the will: Karin) and his granddaughter Agneta Horn, or their children. Johan Oxenstierna according to the will on inheritance of the Södermöre county had to pay to Agneta Horn 3000 Rd, on inheritance of the barony Kemiö and Nynäs 1000 Rd, and to Karin 2000 Rd from the county and 1000 Rd from the barony. Erik Oxenstierna from the Estonian estates had to pay to Agneta Horn 5000 Rd and to Karin also 5000 Rd. From the Cēsis bishopric and underlying starosties, fiefs, and estates, 8000 Rd had to be paid to both ladies without delay, before division of the bishopric between Johan and Erik Oxenstierna. The total dowry stipulated in the will was 16,000 Rd (sic) to each of the ladies, either in specie or its value, from the fiefs in Sweden, Finland, Estonia, and Livonia. As soon as the brothers took possession of the estates they were to pay interest on the dowry at five per cent unless the fief and the estates were devastated by the enemy. If this should occur, payment of interest should stop but the capital should not be curtailed. Apparently war was permanently on the mind of the Chancellor.

In his will Axel Oxenstierna provided also about settlement of his debts. These debts he had contracted mainly in the service of the Crown abroad (AOB, I, 1, p. 640). He wrote that he would endeavour to repay the debts during his lifetime in order not to aggravate his heirs, but if he was not successful, he commanded that the debts should be paid from the Cēsis bishopric and all underlying and added estates. The revenue from these possessions were not to be used by the heirs until the debts were paid, except expenses for upkeeping the economy, payment to the staff, and expenses of the garrison. After curtailing these expenditures the rest of the revenue should be used in settlement of the debts.

During his last years Axel Oxenstierna was borrowing money from his daughter and granddaughter probably to repay his other debts contracted during his diplomatic service abroad, which he mentioned in his will. On 21 January 1650 he borrowed from his daughter Katarina 4000 Rd at 10 % (RA, Oxenstierna af Södermöre, E. 1070) and on 1 January 1653 further 16,000 dollars copper mint at 10 %.

After the death of Axel Oxenstierna, negotiations began about payment of the dowry and repayment of the loans to Katarina and Agneta. Johan Oxenstierna was prepared to pay 3000 Rd, but Erik paid 13,000 Rd. On 1 May 1655 Erik borrowed 2000 Rd at 10 % from a Katarina's servant to pay the dowry and took up a further 926 Rd on 1 August 1655. He obliged himself to pay 8000 Rd at 5 % interest and a further 5000 Rd.

After the death of Erik and Johan Oxenstierna, the undertaken obligation to pay the debts fell on the heirs of Erik Oxenstierna and the heiress of Johan —his widow Margareta Brahe. According to Johan Oxenstierna's will, she inherited the Oxenstierna estates in Finland. In an accord of 28 August 1661 she agreed to pass on her inherited counties and baronies to the eldest of Erik's sons, but half of the Norrköping rules estates which Count Johan had inherited should go to both sons and the rest of the estates to all other heirs.

Among the heirs was also Count Erik's widow. After she remarried in 1661 she too reached an accord with the guardians of her and Erik's minor children. The accord was challenged by her husband, Count Palatine Adolf Johan, but was confirmed by the court (RA, TA 63).

After these accords the obligation to pay the dowry and the debts rested with the guardians of Count Erik's children, but the legal situation was complicated and led to disputes. The guardians argued that the recipients of the allodial estates also had to participate in the payment. They further argued that because of the Russian invasion in Livonia Count Erik's heirs did not take possession of the Livonian estates before 1660 and that only a third of the debt could be claimed from them. These arguments were rejected by the claimants.

Countess Katarina died in 1661. In 1678 when a case came before the courts the unpaid dowry was calculated at 11,000 Rd and the interest for 23 years at 12,650 Rd, so the total sum was 23,650 Rd. Compound interest even with a relatively low interest rate was a scourge upon every debtor.

The question of payment from the revenue of the estates entered a new phase with the marriage of Count Erik's daughters. Anna Margareta 1665 married Klas Tott, Kristina married Gabriel Oxenstierna of Cronoborg 1673, and the same year Elisabet married Gustav Adolf De la Gardie. On behalf of their wives the husbands advanced claims for incompletely paid sisters' lots. Despite settlements by the widows of Johan and Erik, claims were also advanced by the husbands in their second marriage: the husband of Elsa Elisabet Brahe, Count Palatine Adolf Johan, and the husband of Margareta Brahe, Landgrave Friedrich von Hessen-Homburg. The first was especially active. He challenged the declaration of the coming of age of Axel and Karl Gustav Oxenstierna, as well as the division between them of the estates and advanced several claims (see RA, TA 63).

It was a sorry sight, all the members of the high Swedish aristocracy jockeying for a share of the revenue from the landed estates.

On 3 June 1682 the High Court of Sweden adjudicated that the various claims should be put before a liquidation commission. The minutes of this commission of 7 June 1687 (*ibid.* 71) recorded decisions on claims of the heirs of Erik and Johan Oxenstierna and of the heirs of Axel Oxenstierna and his brother Karl Gustav. The liquidation commission calculated how much should be paid to Elisabet and her husband Gustav Adolf De la Gardie and how much to Kristina and her husband Gabriel Oxenstierna from the inheritance left by Karl Gustav. By June 1690, to the unpaid claims interest was added—it was a fortune exceeding available assets.

CHAPTER NINE

THE END

LIVONIAN PUBLIC FINANCE SINCE 1680

The year 1680 was a watershed in the agrarian and fiscal history of Sweden and of Livonia. The Swedish parliament had decided that the government should take over all manors which earlier sometimes had been public estates. The decision was applied not only to Sweden proper but also to its overseas possessions. In Livonia it met a violent opposition from the local nobility. Nevertheless, King Karl XI decided to go ahead with the expropriation of former public estates. These reforms were called reduction of estates (for a modern concise discussion of the reduction see Ågren). To prepare the reduction in Livonia, on 20 April 1680 Karl XI ordered the organization of a new uncus revision in order to replace the official number of unci in force since the revision of 1638. The method of the uncus revision was discussed by the Swedish Chamber College (Kammarkollegium). It was decided at first to survey all lands in Livonia and this was started in May 1681. After efforts lasting five years it was decided to revert to more primitive methods as used in 1638. On 7 February 1687 the King appointed the Livonian commission entrusted with the Livonian uncus revision. Disagreements in the Chamber College about the principles of the revision delayed its implementation but finally in 1688 it was carried out (for details see ED 1950, pp. 28–36).

Simultaneously with the beginning of the surveys in 1681, the Crown started reduction of estates taking over those which previously at some time had been public possession. Oxenstierna's estates in Livonia were among the first to be reduced. The estates taken over were leased to interested persons. Despite the great increase in revenue from the lease of the estates and the increased uncus number after 1688, the Crown continued to levy extraordinary taxes. Before the reduction, the main cash income of the Crown came from collection of duties in general and from the duty called licent in particular. In Livonia, the Swedes started to collect licent in 1629 at Riga and Pärnu. In addition to the licent other duties were collected. The first duty collected in Riga was called portory. It was introduced in 1581 by the Polish Crown and was shared between the city of Riga and the Crown. After the Swedish conquest of Riga, the Swedish Crown took half of this duty leaving the other half to the city. Other customs collected by the Swedish Crown were: payment for the upkeep of beacons, convoy money, load money, customs collectors' money, extraordinary customs, payment to benefit paupers, and others.

With the conquest of Lithuania and Poland by the Swedes in 1655 and 1656, a Lithuanian duty was introduced. After the loss of Lithuania and Poland this duty was collected in Riga; it was extended to all merchandise arriving in Riga by the Daugava waterway. In 1668 the Lithuanian duty was replaced by a customs called the royal addition, or simply: supplementary customs. After the reduction, the main cash income was from rent of the leased estates, although because of increase of exports and imports the revenue from duty also increased.

A summary of revenue and expenditure of the Crown in Livonia, prepared on the basis of the treasury accountancy data (ED 1936, pp. 64–65; source in EKA) shows the difference before the reforms of Karl XI and after. The selected year 1680 was yielding revenue above the average and the year 1694 was also a favourable one. Cash in hand and grain in storage at the beginning and the end of the year has not been included in the tables because of the difficulties of obtaining reliable figures from the records.

REVENUE AND EXPENDITURE OF LIVONIA IN 1680 AND 1694

REVENUE	1680		1694	
	GRAIN (TONS)	RD	GRAIN (TONS)	RD
Duty:				
Licent	–	86,092	–	162,956
Portory, excise, and others	–	41,916	–	40,107
Supplementary customs at Riga	–	–	–	72,571
Taxes for the army:	–	–	–	21,800
Deductions from salaries:				
1 % from public servants	–	–	–	1862
5 % from members of the reduction commission	–	–	–	1275
Statio:				
Rye	10,278	–	14,971	–
Barley	10,280	–	15,175	–
Oats	5678	–	7558	–
Cash	–	8912	–	10,287
Contributions:				
Rye	4010	–	–	–

	1680		1694	
	GRAIN (TONS)	RD	GRAIN (TONS)	RD
Barley	340	–	–	–
Cash	–	843	–	–
Revenue from the reduction:				
Rye	–	–	4862	–
Barley	–	–	338	–
Cash	–	–	–	188,997
Profit on exchange	–	1854	–	–
Profit of the Riga manufactory	–	–	–	122
Total: Rye	14,288	–	19,833	–
Barley	10,620	–	15,513	–
Oats	5678	–	7558	–
Cash	–	139,617	–	499,977

EXPENDITURE

Salaries of public servants	–	21,764	–	18,007
Pensions	–	2754	–	3677
Clergy	–	2827	–	1732
Schools	–	2008	–	5441
Courts	–	5173	–	10,822
Repayments of debts	–	1775	–	26,748
Repaid rent to reduced estates	–	–	–	1761
Various	–	5920	–	2180
Transferred to Sweden	–	–	–	140,504
Expenses for shipment of grain	–	–	–	579
To the garrison:				
Cash	–	99,221	–	284,800
Rye	24,968	–	37,801	–
Barley	8594	–		
Oats	7408	–	10,148	–
Total		141,442		496,251

From the various attempts by historians to get a comprehensive picture of the incomes of the Swedish Crown we can quote the calculation by G.E.Axelson (Axelson, p. 112 f.). The estimates are not very reliable because incomes in kind have been calculated at conventional prices and not at market prices and to these estimates as well can be applied the caution expressed about the method as to how such exact historical statistics were compiled by nineteenth century scholars (Ågren, pp. 245 ff.; compare also ED 1950, p. 104– about data by W.E.Svedelius).

Nevertheless, the estimates give a rough relative picture about the significance of Livonia and other provinces of the Swedish realm before sunset. From the total revenue in the year 1699, amounting to 6,576,724 dollars silver mint, Sweden proper yielded 54.7 %, Livonia 14.1 %, Bremen and Verden 8.8 %, Finland 8.7 %, Pomerania 6.5 %, Estonia 4.0 %, Ingermanland 2.9 %, and Wismar 0.3 %.

With the loss of the foreign provinces Sweden, from being a world power, became an insignificant country on the fringe of Europe. When Karl XII, on 11 November 1714, arrived from Turkey in Stralsund, he had established an endurance record by his ride on horseback through Europe, but from Swedish overseas possessions only Stralsund and Wismar remained in his hands (Ogg, p. 470). Financially the result of this political catastrophe was that the deficits of the Crown were twice the amount of gross receipts.

REDUCTION OF THE BISHOPRIC

The decision of the Swedish parliament to reduce estates was in Livonia, in the first place, applied to those granted after the conquest to the Swedish magnates. Already in 1681 the total bishopric of Valmiera and Cēsis was taken over by the Crown and leased to the same Riga merchant Johan von Reutern who since 1678 had rented a part of it from Karl Gustav Oxenstierna. The rent to be paid to the Crown was 19,000 Rd (RA, Livländska Donationskontoret, D VI b: 4, fol. 2).

Reduction was applied to and in the rent were included all estates of the bishopric–not only those which King Gustav Adolf had granted as fiefs to the Chancellor Axel Oxenstierna, but also those purchased and established by the Chancellor himself. About the estates which could be regarded as private and therefore according to law not subject to reduction, Karl Gustav Oxenstierna approached the reduction commission (RA, Reduktionskommissionen i Livland, F: 10, fol. 911–921, received 13 February 1682). He requested firstly compensation for the seed sown on the fields of the bishopric, according to the parliamentary decision that compensation for seed on reduced demesne should be paid to previous possessors. Secondly he requested exemption from the reduction of estates purchased, exchanged, or otherwise acquired at his grandfather's time and later, listing: 1) Braslava (acquired in 1668 from Aßwegen by a court ruling), 2) Ēvele, 3) Mujāni, 4) Lenči, 5) Vāle, 6) Bānūži,

KARL GUSTAV OXENSTIERNA

Photo Svenska Porträttarkivet, Stockholm

7) Lorupe, 8) Skaņkalne, 9) Buxhövdenhof (Offerlachs), 10) Kunğēns (Doctormoise) and Vilkamuiža, 11) Rūte and Baloži, 12) Ķoņi, 13) Rentmeistera muiža, 14) Brenguļi, 15) Mūrmuiža and Kokmuiža, 16) Veismaņi and Liepmuiža, 17) Ropaži, 18) the estates of the towns Valmiera and Cēsis

CONCESSIONS TO COUNT KARL GUSTAV OXENSTIERNA

On 31 July and 5 August 1682 in response to Karl Gustav's request the reduction commission at Stockholm resolved to exempt from the reduction some private estates of the Oxenstiernas af Södermöre in the bishopric. The commission listed: Ēvele, Skaņkalne, Mujāni, Völkersams Hoflage, Strīķi, Tarnisa, Kauguri, Rūte and Baloži, Blanka, Lenči (in the extant copy of the letter Lenzenhof was misspelt: Räntrenhof), Stiene, Negurska, Rentmeistera muiža, Vilkamuiža, Kunğēns, Brenguļi, and Braslava (RA, Oxenstierna af Södermöre, E 1069). Following this decision the rental to be paid for the bishopric by Johan Reutern for 1682 was curtailed to 13,000 Rd (RA, Livländska Donationskontoret, D VI b: 4, Räkenskaper över reducerade gods, Livland 1681–1690, fol. 46). Nevertheless, it seems that the estates were not immediately handed over to Count Karl Gustav; in 1683 the rent to be paid by Johan Reutern was 19,600 Rd and the same amount was fixed for 1684 (*ibid.*, fol. 62).

A comparison with the petition of Count Karl Gustav shows that from the requested 22 estates he was granted 10 and in addition 8 estates which were not mentioned in the petition extant. Obviously he had submitted more than only one petition. On 30 October 1682 he once more requested the exemption of Ropaži from reduction (RA, Reduktionskommissionen i Livland, F 1: 10 D, fol. 936), pointing out that his grandfather had paid a hypothecary debt on that estate.

In 1683 the Swedish parliament resolved to leave the complicated question of exemption from reduction to the King's disposition. Referring to this resolution on 30 January 1684 the King considered the petition of Count Karl Gustav. The Count and his wife were granted for life half of the noblemen's estates listed in the resolution of the reduction commission of 1682 (RA, Oxenstierna af Södermöre, E 1069). This concession was granted in view of the great merits of the ancestors of Count Karl Gustav and of his own bravery and integrity.

Executing this decision, on 15 February 1684, the reduction commission wrote to the Governor General Krister Horn that half of the specified estates should be vested for life to the Count and his wife and the other half to the Crown. The Governor General was requested to inform the commission which estates had been vested to the Count and which to the Crown (*ibid.*).

On 6 September 1684 the reduction commission wrote to Jakob Sneckensköld who was in charge of the reduction in Livonia that the Governor General had requested details of how to implement the division of the granted estates between the Count and the Crown. The commission entrusted the task to divide the estates to Sneckensköld and indicated that consolidation of estates by exchange with neighbouring Crown land in the division would be desirable. In such a case the unci of the exchanged land should be equal, including the demesne. The Count could be permitted to make a choice provided the interests of the Crown were safeguarded. A formal exchange project should be drafted and sent for confirmation to the reduction commission.

The outcome of the exchange and transfer of possessions becomes evident from the contract of 16 February 1685 between the Count Karl Gustav and Johan Reutern who rented the estates left to Karl Gustav. Copies of Karl Gustav's calculations about the prospective rent are extant as well as lease contracts in original and copies, signed 1685 (RA, TA 134). On 13 February 1685 a contract was signed with Johan von Reutern leasing to him Ēvele and Ķeiži, Mujāni, Lenči, and an estate named Schiltkornshof (Latvian name: Šilkoris), Buxhövdenhof, Kauguri, Skaņkalne, and Braslava, for nine years from Easter 1685 to Easter 1694. The total amount of the contract was 5275 Rd minus discount 105 Rd, i.e. net 5170 Rd per annum. Half was to be paid at Easter and half at Michaelmas. In addition Reutern had to provide two retainers. Reutern pledged himself not to increase the customary dues and statute work of the peasants. Fugitive peasants had to be recovered or restituted, except if the reason for abandoning land had been a failure of crops or other unavoidable reason. Otherwise failure of crops was at the risk of the leaseholder but could be deducted from the rent at a maximum of 400 Rd per annum.

Taxes and billeting of military forces were to be paid and provided for by the peasants. Upkeep of the clergy, the court, and occasional commissions, was to be paid for by the leaseholder. He was not entitled to deduct from the rent debts of peasants. He had to conserve the peasantry and the equipment and should be careful with swidden and clearings not to curtail the value of the estates. In case of an enemy invasion or the plague the leaseholder could subtract the loss from the rent of the last year of the contract. Live-stock taken over with the lease was to be delivered at the end of the lease in the same quantity and quality, except if a general epidemic of live-stock in the country had happened, but this had to be notified and proved to the representative of the lord in the same year when it occurred.

Braslava was subleased to the assessor of the Overconsistory, Jakob Hempel. The rent was 800 Albert Rd per annum. The conditions were similar as in the contract with Reutern. Exceptions were, that for failure of crops a quarter of the contracted lease could be subtracted. The Count was obligated to keep a retainer, but the leaseholder had to conduct court cases in the county and the supreme courts and if need be pay the expenses. Peasants were prohibited from taking anything to the city for sale unless they had paid their customary dues, and they had to offer commodities to be sold first to the leaseholder at a price they could fetch at the city.

On 16 February 1685 Mujāni and Lenči were subleased to county judge Captain Fabian von Tiesenhausen within the framework of the general contract concluded with Johan von Reutern. The rent was 1330 Rd plus the upkeep of a retainer.

A copy is extant from Count Karl Gustav's calculation about details of the leased estates to Johan Reutern (RA, TA 134). Braslava together with Kunğēns was leased for 800 Rd, Ēvele with Ķeiži and Jērcēni–1567 Rd, Kauguri and Jaunā muiža–1400 Rd, Mujāni and Lenči–1331 Rd, Skaņkalne and Buxhövdenhof–177 Rd. This gives the gross amount of 5275 Rd of the contract with Johan von Reutern.

It appears that, from the grant of the reduction commission, Karl Gustav had received Braslava, Ēvele, Kunğēns, Lenči, Mujāni, and Skaņkalne. From his original request he received Buxhövdenhof and in addition three estates which probably were granted in exchange as suggested by the reduction commission on 6 September 1684. These three estates were Kauguri, Jērcēni, and Jaunā muiža.

On 23 January 1686 the reduction commission resolved to grant to Count Karl Gustav Oxenstierna possession of Lorupe, which was acquired by the guardians of the Oxenstiernas af Södermöre in 1669, and Vāle which was confirmed to Axel Oxenstierna by King Gustav Adolf in 1630 (*ibid.*, fol. 11–12). According to the calculations made by the Count (*ibid.* 134), the rent from Lorupe was estimated by him at 80 Rd and from Vāle at 428 Rd. With these two additional grants the Count had received 13 estates from 51 estates of the Oxenstiernas af Södermöre.

CALCULATION OF THE RENTAL

The principle of how the rental of the leased estates was calculated can be seen from copies of personal notes of Count Karl Gustav (*ibid.*), which probably refer to 1685. For each estate he took into account two variables: 1) the availability of statute labour, 2) the amount of customary dues.

Statute labour was estimated in horse-units by converting services rendered on foot into horse-units and adding this to the number of workers with a horse. It was then estimated that with each horse-unit 14 leaps of grain could be sown. The estimated total amount sown was divided in three equal parts for rye, barley, and oats. The yield was calculated at the third grain for rye and barley and at the second grain for oats. Multiplying this by conventional prices, the total estimated sum for the harvest of the estate was obtained.

Customary dues were also calculated at conventional prices and added to the sum obtained for the harvest. After rounding off the total, the result was the rental to be received from the leaseholder.

As an example let us take the calculated rental for Mujāni. This estate had 20 peasants rendering statute labour with a horse and 10 ½ peasants serving on foot (the fraction was derived from summing up part-time workers). The work of the latter was regarded to be equal to 6 horse-units, thus the total of horse-units was 26. Multiplying by 14 it was calculated that 364 leaps of grain could be sown–121 ⅓ leaps each of rye, barley, and oats. At a yield of three the sown quantities of rye and barley resulted in an estimated harvest of 364 leaps of rye and the same quantity of barley, and at a yield of two in 242 ⅔ leaps oats. Multiplying this by conventional prices the received amount was 424 Rd. We can only guess what the conventional prices were as used by the Count. If we take for a leap of rye 45 groschen, for barley 40 ½ groschen, and for oats 29 groschen, we obtain approx. this total (the Rd equalled 90 groschen). The total of customary dues for Mujāni was estimated by Karl Gustav at 396 Rd. The total rental thus worked out at 424 + 396 = 820 Rd. There was obviously some deduction from the rental calculated and Mujāni was leased for 800 Rd.

In exactly the same way, the Count calculated the rental of his other estates. The profit of the leasee was, firstly, the excess of the yield over the third and second grain and, secondly, a potential profit if the market price exceeded the conventional price at which the produce of the demesne and the customary dues were calculated.

It seems that the described method of calculating the rental was not invented by the Count but was the common approach used in Livonia by other landlords. It is of interest to compare this method with that used by the government to calculate the rental in leasing of reduced estates. For estates which were leased before the reduction the government at first charged exactly the same rental that had been paid by the previous leaseholders. Then over a period of seven years, from 1681 to 1688, a peculiar method was developed. It is possible to follow the development of ideas step by step (ED 1950, pp. 87–105) from the minutes of the Chamber College (RA, Kammarkollegii Protokoll), the ensuing correspondence, regrettably scattered over four archives (RA, VA, EKA, and fragments of correspondence at the library of the University of Uppsala), and, last but not least, from the letters of the King (RA, RR) who took a great interest in this matter.

A major step in the development was when the Chamber College succeeded in freeing itself from two medieval concepts: 1) that land could be measured only in terms of area; 2) that the quality of land must be adjusted by allocating a larger area to compensate for poorer quality of land (as, for instance, was done in the revision of 1671/1672; see page 186). The modern solution to both problems was to calculate land in monetary terms. During the debates, the Chamber College also succeeded in rejecting sectional interests of those who wanted for Livonia a larger tonstead than was in use in Sweden, Finland, Ingermanland, and Estonia–it was suggested to take 18,000 square ells for a tonstead instead of 14,000. New principles for the taxation unit, the uncus, were also established. An achievement was that against the violent opposition of the Livonian nobility the demesnes were included in fiscal calculations, at least for reduced estates.

As an example to show how these new ideas were implemented we can take the same estate which was used to illustrate the calculation of the rental by Count Karl Gustav Oxenstierna, namely, Mujāni. For our example we select the year 1700, long after the death of the Count and when Mujāni was no longer possessed by his heirs and the new method of calculating the rental was well established.

The document is the 'Special calculation on the Crown's estate Mujāni of the Riga circuit and Valmiera parish [note the new secular territorial division in parishes instead of the previous castle districts] showing how much it can yield for 1700 according to the survey and description by the surveyors and the grades of fertility set by the Royal Commission and the evaluation of each grade as fixed by the King' (RA, Livländska Donationskontoret, D VI b: 5).

The 'special calculation' consisted of three parts–two parts in the debit and the third in the credit. The first part was somewhat misleading entitled 'Demesne revenue' (Hovs revenüer) and actually was a schedule of the area of the three types of land and its fertility grade expressed in money terms. The second part was entitled 'Customary dues of peasants from the unci' (Bonde hakarnas ränta) and was an enumeration of the produce to be paid, expressed in physical terms and calculated at conventional prices. To this the income from the tavern, the mill, and that from the reeves was added. The third part (in the credit) was entitled 'Deductions' (Avkortningen) and was specified–statio, militia, retainers, the pastor, and the bailiff. After deduction of the credit from the debit the balance (Saldo) was obtained.

At some time before 1700 Dūķeŗi as a cattle farm had been added to Mujāni and was included in the calculation. Fortunately Dūķeŗi was partly recorded under a special heading thus partly permitting a direct comparison between Mujāni in 1685 and 1700. Regrettably the customary dues of the peasants in 1700 have not been recorded separately for Mujāni and Dūķeŗi, which prevents a complete comparison.

The quoted document in a slightly recast form (simple fractions converted into three-figure decimal fractions; explanatory reiterative text shortened) is presented in the following. It must be added that the riksdollar was equal to 90 groschen.

SPECIAL CALCULATION: MUJĀNI FOR 1700

DEBIT

Demesne revenue; 14,000 Swedish square ells per tonstead

GRADE OF FERTILITY		RD: GR. (a tonstead)	RD: GR.	SPECIE RD: GR.
	Arables			
2	98.375 tonsteads	1: 85	191: 25.125	
3	65.125 "	1: 50	101: 62.500	292: 87.625
	Fallow			
3	22.5 tonsteads	: 70	17: 45.000	
4	3 "	: 52.5	1: 67.500	19: 22.500
	Woodland			
2	16.125 tonsteads to be divided into 20 yearly lots for swidden, 0.806 tonsteads to be sown [with grain] for three consecutive years = 2.419 tonsteads	2: 45	6: 4.219	
3	170.125 tonsteads to be divided into 22 yearly lots for swidden, 7.733 tonsteads to be sown [with grain] for two consecutive years = 15.466 tonsteads	2: –	30: 23.864	
4	182.25 tonsteads to be divided into 24 yearly lots for swidden, 7.594 tonsteads to be sown [with grain] for two consecutive years = 15.188 tonsteads	1: 45	22: 70.313	59: 68.395

Dūķeŗi, the new cattle farm of Mujāni

Arables

3	53.5 tonsteads	1: 50	83: 20.000	
4	3.75 „	1: 50	4: 33.750	87: 53.750

Woodland

4	75.5 tonsteads divided into 24 yearly lots for swidden, 3.146 tonsteads to be sown [with grain] for two consecutive years = 6.292 tonsteads	1: 45		9: 39.375
				97: 3.125

DEBIT: INCOME

Income of the demesne according to the previous calculations

The old demesne of Mujāni	312: 20.125	
Woodland of the same	59: 68.375	371: 88.500
The new cattle farm	87: 53.750	
Its woodland	9: 39.375	97: 3.125
Subtotal		469: 1.625

Customary dues of peasants according to the new wacka-book for 1700, including statio and tax to keep militia

333.5 leaps rye at : 45 each	166: 67.500	
396 leaps barley at : 45 each	198: –	
373.5 leaps oats at : 22.5 each	93: 33.750	
98.5 lispounds flax at : 30 each	32: 75.000	
13 lispounds 6 pounds hops at : 45 a lispound	6: 58.500	
45.5 sheep at : 45 each	22: 67.500	
89.5 cartloads hay at : 22.5 each	22: 33.750	
125.75 Albert Rd converted to specie Rd	120: 45.938	663: 21.938

Tavern

There is a tavern without land and of little significance.

Mill

There is a mill which is only used during the autumn and spring by the demesne and there is no income.

Reeves

The reeve of Mujāni paid annually 12.5 pounds of wax which equals 0.625 lispounds at a price of 3: 30		2: 7.500
The same was paid by the reeve of Dūķeŗi		2: 7.500
	Total	1136: 38.563

CREDIT

Deductions

Statio for 20.25 revision unci at 7: 2.25 each	142: 23.063	
Tax for the upkeep of the militia for 20.25 unci at 3: 39.3 each	69: 53.775	211: 76.838
The upkeep of retainers is deducted according to the letter of the Governor General Erik Dahlberg, dated 5 December 1700: for 20.25 revision unci at 4: each		81: -
To the pastor: 8 leaps rye	4: -	
8 „ barley	4: --	8: -
Remuneration of the bailiff in cash and in kind		75: 51.725

Balance

The rental for 1700		760: -
	Total	1136: 38.563

CONTO NOVO

Debit

From the previous account	760: -

Credit

According to the placard of the Governor General, Count Erik Dahlberg, of 20 September 1700, the retainers are doubled and for 20.25 revision unci at 8: each the total is	162:-
Per balance the rental for 1700 is	598:-
Total	760:-

There are several minor errors in the multiplicatiom and in the addition. We notice that both estates held together 20.25 revision unci. After long deliberations the Chamber College on 9 September 1687 had decided that an uncus was equal to 60 riksdollars of the peasants' customary dues and statute work, calculated at conventional prices (ED 1950, p. 32). In our example for 20.25 unci we obtain 1215 Rd and in the above calculation the total of customary dues is 667 Rd 37 groschen. This means that the statute labour at Mujāni and Dūķeŗi was estimated at 547 Rd 53 groschen compared with the valued total of the land–469 Rd 2 gr. The discrepancy can be explained by the fact that in the original estimate of the uncus (at 60 Rd) the statio and upkeep of the retainers was included at a total estimate of 15 Rd (*ibid.*). If we deduct this amount from the value of the uncus, the total for 20.25 unci of Mujāni and Dūķeŗi is 911.25 Rd which leaves for the value of statute labour about 244 Rd. Actually in 1700 the Crown credited the leaseholder a total of 376 Rd 38.563 groschen or Rd 18.59 per uncus and, after doubling the retainers because of the war, even 26.59 Rd.

With the usual approach of shifting the expenses to the peasantry, these credited items were a bonus to the leaseholder. On the evidence of these figures one can conclude that the leaseholder of Mujāni and Dūķeŗi had a nominal profit of 297 Rd and after the doubling of the retainers (provided the upkeep of those could be shifted in the first year on to the shoulders of the peasantry) even of 459 Rd. The actual profit was even larger because the price of grain exceeded the nominal price at which the calculation was made up. On the other hand, during the Great Northern War, Livonia was completely devastated, and the amassed fortunes were lost. Ten years later during the plague in 1710/1711 Livonia lost 62 % of its population. In the former bishopric the loss was lower –approxim. 50 % (see map ED 1962, p. 192).

The catastrophe which struck Livonia at the end of the Swedish period was one of the most severe the country had experienced in its thorny path of history. Against these coming events the misfortunes of the Oxenstiernas af Södermöre pale into insignificance.

AFTER THE DEATH OF KARL GUSTAV OXENSTIERNA

Karl Gustav Oxenstierna died on 13 March 1686 in Vienna where he had been the Swedish ambassador since 1684. His Livonian estates passed on to his wife Hedvig Ebba De la Gardie. On 6 November 1688 King Karl XI issued a detailed explanation about estates subject to reduction. All estates which were an appurtenance to public estates and all estates exchanged against public estates had to be reduced. It seems that on the strength of this resolution the so-called comparative wacka-book was prepared (formerly KA, Handlingar rör. Sveriges balt. o. tyska prov., no. 45. Livland, Förteckningar). In this document Ropaži is listed as 'cronogodz som bero på lösen' (estate of the Crown subject to redemption of pledge) with 22 old and 17 new (of the revision of 1688) unci. Further, in the document we find thirty former estates of Oxenstierna af Södermöre with 392 old and 517 new unci, which are listed as reduced estates. As private estates from the Oxenstierna af Södermöre estates are listed: Vāle with 11 ½ and 26 unci, Lorupe with 1 ¼ and 1 ¼ unci, and Buxhövdenhof with ¾ and 1 ⅞ unci, or a total of 13 ½ old and 29 ½ new unci.

A scrutiny of the estates granted to Karl Gustav Oxenstierna had shown that Doctormoise, Skaņkalne, Kauguri, Jaunā muiža, Mujāni, Ēvele, and Braslava, which previously had belonged to Cēsis castle though granted to Karl Gustav Oxenstierna, were nevertheless subject to reduction (RA, Livländska Donationskontoret, B: 1, Konceptobservationer 1688–1692, Lit. C). On the request of the widow of Karl Gustav, Hedvig Ebba, the King permitted her to draw the income from Ēvele and Mujāni for her lifetime, but a new investigation showed that Ēvele was to be regarded as a public estate. On a renewed request by the Countess (1691) she was left the estate for five years (*ibid.*, D 1, C: 2). It seems that despite this decision the period was extended and the estates Ēvele and Mujāni were left to the Countess for her lifetime. On 20 March 1693 she leased Ēvele, Mujāni, and Lenči to Johan von Reutern (RA, TA 134, fol. 253–263). Then in 1696 the decision regarding Ēvele was again rescinded.

The reduction commission was approached by heirs of the previous possessor of Ēvele Valentin von Höveln: Robert Philip von Wenzlow who had married the daughter of Höveln, his sister Dorothea von Wenzlow, and Robert Philip von Wenzlow's daughter, Maria Polixena, married to Gerhard von Palmstruch. They claimed Ēvele together with Ķeiži and Jērcēni as their inheritance (Stryk, p. 427). The reduction commission found that Ēvele had been granted on 5 January 1622 to Fieldmarshal Hermann Wrangel assuming that its possessor Höveln had sided with the enemy, which could be proved to be wrong. On the contrary, two sons of Höveln had allegedly served the Swedish Crown.

On the strength of this claim King Karl XI resolved on 7 April and 5 June 1696 (RA, RR) that Ēvele was a private estate and had to be restituted to the heirs. Consequently Countess Hedvig Ebba lost Ēvele. In March and April 1703 the claim that Ēvele was a public estate was once more raised (RA, Livonica II, vol. 713) but without results. It remained the possession of Maria Polixena Palmstruch.

The fate of the other former Oxenstierna af Södermöre estates after the reduction was chequered. Even before the reduction, already in 1676, Ropaži was handed over (immiterat) to Governor General Krister Horn (RA, TA 172, fol. 593) and later passed on to the following governors general—Jakob Hastfer and after his death to Erik Dahlberg. Major General Erik Soop asked that Ropaži be leased to him, but the King rejected his request (RA, RR: 8 May 1696) and the estate remained the possession of the Governor General. In the final years of Swedish rule in lieu of remuneration for an amount of 6130 Rd also Burtnieki with Bauņi, Vecate, Vilzēni, and Jaunburtnieki, were granted to the Governor General (RA, Livonica II, vol. 696). About 1694 Vecate had been leased to Major Schreiberfeld and at the same time Bauņi had been leased to assessor Sternfeld.

Kauguri and Mūrmuiža were subleased by Johan Reutern to Christofer von Dunte. In 1699 the latter was involved in a court case with the heirs of Johan von Reutern because of his mistreatment of the peasant Jānis Skangalis whom he illegally had evicted from the farm (*ibid.*, vol. 704). Nevertheless, on the farm of Skangalis a manor was established, which still existed in the twentieth century (Endzelīns, p. 98).

Kokmuiža was also subleased by Johan von Reutern. The leaseholder was the previous bailiff of Oxenstierna, Zacharias Holde. During a court case in 1698 it was revealed that, by ruthlessly exploiting the peasants of Kokmuiža, Holde had amassed a fortune of gold and silver, had led a luxurious life and aspired to and finally achieved ennoblement (RA, Livonica II, vol. 701). Holde lost his case in the court and Kokmuiža was subleased to Count Mellin.

In 1699 the leaseholder of Valmiera, with 57 peasant farms, was Peter Bachmann.

FINAL DESTRUCTION OF THE BISHOPRIC

The Great Northern War started with a triumph for the Swedish arms. After the victory over Russians at Narva in 1700 King Karl XII spent the winter at a camp at Laiuse in Estonia. In June 1701 he marched with 18,000 men through Valmiera and Cēsis to Riga. On 9 June at Spilve near Riga the Swedes defeated the allied Saxonian and Russian forces. Before this battle the Saxonians had marauded in Livonia up till Cēsis. Karl XII continued his march through the Duchy of Kurzeme and spent the following winter at Virga. In 1702 he continued his fateful march to the south.

To destroy the Swedish base in Livonia the Russians organized raids. The exaggerated report of 1702 by Fieldmarshal General Boris Petrovich Sheremetiev is well known: '. . . Between Tallinn and Riga all has been weeded out. Settlements are now only to be found as dots on maps. . .' The former bishopric Valmiera was indeed devastated and the castle burnt down, but otherwise the Russian fury had struck mainly at Estonia.

Already at the beginning of the war in addition to the doubling of the number of retainers (see page 218) Governor General Dahlberg started to organize Latvian hunters (who were famous as marksmen) into military units (patent letter of 12 February 1700). In the autumn of the same year he ordered to proclaim from the pulpit that farms of peasants who were prepared to defend the country should be freed from statute labour while they are volunteers in the Swedish forces. On 10 January 1701 the King decreed the formation of Latvian and Estonian battalions. He ordered that peasant farmers should be enlisted 'because one cannot rely on farmhands' (ED 1962, p. 160 ff.).

Implementing the King's order the Governor General prepared an organization plan which was confirmed by the King. On 24 April 1701 the Governor General published an order to establish Latvian and Estonian battalions and as a result six Latvian battalions were set up: the battalions of Alūksne, Cēsis, Koknese, Turaida, Tirza, and Valmiera.

Of the former bishopric the Latvian battalion of Cēsis was commanded by Lieutenant Colonel Friedrich Wilhelm Liphard. The battalion consisted of the following companies (in brackets number of men): Cēsis (58), Rubene (54), Trikāta (68), Sigulda (58), Āraiši (52), and Rauna (59). The Valmiera battalion was commanded by Lieutenant Colonel Reinhold von Linau. The companies were those of Valmiera, Ēvele, Burtnieki, Dikļi, Valtenberģis, and Rūjiena.

The battalions were fighting under the blue Swedish colours with the initials of the King and a crown on one side and the Livonian coat of arms on the other side. The reports about their fighting spirits are contradictory. For instance, the commander of the Tirza company reported: 'My lads are excellent soldiers as those enlisted by press-gangs never were and never will be' (26 September 1701) and 'My lads are keen to meet the enemy the sooner the better' (24 October 1701 from Alūksne). Contrasting with these reports is what was written by the commander of the Cēsis battalion on 8 September 1702–that he was not able to provide food for his battalion and 200 had left with all the weapons; only 80 soldiers had remained in the battalion. The unfavourable report of Major General Wolmar von Schlippenbach about the Latvian soldiers and their officers, in contrast to his favourable testimonial about the Estonians, finds its explanation in the poor supplies to the Latvian forces. Schlippenbach recommended to disband the Latvian battalions and to establish enlisted formations instead. Despite this recommendation, the Latvian battalions were not disbanded and continued to fight till the bitter end in 1710.

The peasants of the former bishopric supported the Swedish war efforts not only by providing soldiers but also in another way. Smīde, a peasant from the Cēsis estate, lent to the Swedish government 430 Rd, Iņķis from the same estate–615 Rd, Zēmelis from Jaunburtnieki–650 Rd, Juris Voitiņš from Spāre –225 Rd, and the publican of Amata– an undisclosed amount. These peasants were granted the status of freemen by the King.

All the heroic efforts and the sufferings were in vain. Livonia was lost to Sweden and became a *gubernia* of Russia. The estates of the former bishopric at first remained under the control of the Russian government, but then they one by one were given away. The first to go was Trikāta which was donated by Catherine (I) to the corporation of the Livonian nobility in 1725. The other estates were donated to courtiers and favourites of the rulers: Mujāni in 1727, Burtnieki in 1736, Cēsis in 1747, and Valmiera in 1762.

In this way the former bishopric finally was split up. There was no longer the entity which over the centuries had been called the bishopric. There was not any longer the dynasty of the Oxenstiernas af Södermöre. The last member of this distinguished family, the son of Karl Gustav, also Karl Gustav, died on a march in Poland with the forces of Karl XII in the year 1706.

APPENDIX 1

THE UNCUS

Sources: Tidö Archive–The private landrevision of the Oxenstierna estates 1671/1672 (RA, TA 321). Edgars Dunsdorfs, *Actus revisionis Livoniae 1638* (Riga 1938–1941), Introductory volume. See also: Edgars Dunsdorfs, 'Zum Hakenproblem', *Commentationes Balticae* I, 1953 (Bonn 1954).

With the term 'uncus' the land-unit is denoted which is called in Swedish *hake*, in German *Haken*, in Latvian *arkls*, in Polish *radlo*. The Latin term *uncus* was used in Livonia at an early stage and also in the Polish–Lithuanian period. For instance see: Archivum skarbu koronnego, Warscawa, Dz I, no. 64, fol. 46–55. The *pobor* (tax) in Trikāta was levied in unci–'Casparus Tepel nomine sui parentis solvit de 6 uncis 6 fl. . .'.

Because of incorrect interpretation of the sources by historians, it was wrongly assumed that the uncus was a land measure of a definite size, only with variations as to various types of unci. Thus, after elaborate calculations, a Livonian uncus was assumed to be 88.5 ha, the Plettenberg uncus–48 ha, the Archbishop's uncus–33 ha, the Polish uncus–60 ha, the German uncus–15 ha (see Aghte, p. 25). There is a grain of truth in the relative size of the various types of unci, but the absolute figures are spurious.

In the estates which came into the possession of Axel Oxenstierna, land had been surveyed before he acquired the estates. For instance, in Ēvele, land was measured on the order of Melchior Höveln in the years 1593 and 1597. In Burtnieki and other estates of the bishopric, land was measured on behalf of Bishop Otto Schenking who assumed the see in 1587. Among Oxenstierna's staff in the Livonian estates, a land surveyor was on the payroll as early as 1629. The first technical data are from 1643 when the surveyor Jakob Schultz measured Bānūži. He measured the land in morgen and converted them to unci calculating 60 morgen on one uncus. In 1646 Sverker Josephsson compiled a landbook for Valmiera town and according to his information the quantity to be sown on one uncus was 60 tons of grain. Assuming that the tons were Swedish tons and the grain was rye, the 60 tons in modern measures could be estimated at 90 hectolitres.

The nature of the uncus becomes clear from the land surveys in the Oxenstierna estates conducted in 1671 and 1672 (referred to in Chapter Eight). As a further example we select some farms which existed up to the Second World War. According to the survey, on the peasant farm Baķi (see Endzelīns, pp. 17–18: Liepmuiža) were found 38 tonsteads of average quality land and 76 tonsteads of sandy land and swidden (cultivated in rotation for several years on burnt down woodland with ashes ploughed in and then left for a considerable time to recuperate; see page 81), or a total of 114 tonsteads. This total was then reduced taking into account the quality of the land as follows: the 38 tonsteads were estimated to be equivalent to 26 tonsteads of good land, and the 76 tonsteads to be equivalent to 38 tonsteads of the same. The total of 64 tonsteads thus calculated was regarded to be one uncus. Similarly for Ķerpis the measurement gave 40 tonsteads average quality arable and swidden. This was estimated to be equal to 26 tonsteads of good quality land. In addition Ķerpis had taken up Sermiņa sala with 70 tonsteads average quality land which was estimated to correspond to 46 tonsteads of good land. The total of 110 tonsteads was estimated to be equivalent to 72 tonsteads and regarded as one uncus. Strunķis had good infields at his farm of 23 tonsteads which were estimated as 23 tonsteads. Along the rivulets he had 45 tonsteads swidden estimated at 22 ½ tonsteads and near the lime-kiln 30 tonsteads good and average arables which were estimated to be equivalent to 20 tonsteads. Thus 98 tonsteads were reduced to 65.5 tonsteads and regarded as one uncus. As a rule, the surveyor regarded 64 tonsteads of estimated land as one uncus. In the case of Ķerpis the surplus of 12 tonsteads was not included in the uncus because he had not sufficient meadows. These examples illustrate the meaning of the uncus. It was not an area measure, but cadastral measure taking into account the quality of the land, the situation as to proximity to the markets, the capacity of the peasant to render statute labour and to pay customary dues, and other economic considerations.

There are further complications. The uncus was used for different purposes. In the first place, manors demanded from the peasants customary dues according to the uncus figure of each farm. Secondly, the government levied taxes according to the unci of each manor. These taxes had to be paid exclusively by the peasantry, but were usually collected by officials of the manor from the peasants on behalf of the Crown. The different purposes of the unci resulted in different totals of the same.

For the manors' own purposes records were prepared listing the names of the farms, the uncus, customary dues, and statute labour. The German name of these manorial rolls was 'Wackenbuch', a term of Estonian origin. The uncus number in these documents were the traditional ones. In cases where it was established that the farm was not able to pay dues and present statute labour according to its uncus number, either after a formal survey or after inspection of the farm the manor reduced the uncus number. Thus farms had two different uncus numbers–the traditional one and the actual one. The German term for the former was 'Besitzhaken', for the latter 'Zahlhaken'–possession uncus and payment uncus. The totals of these unci did not correspond to numbers of unci from which the manor received revenue. The reeves were exempt from payment of customary dues, so were peasants who were destitute, farms temporarily abandoned and recently settled, freemen privileged from ancient times, also hunters, fowlers, blacksmiths, and others. A number of farms were granted to the clergy (prebend), retainers, judges, and manorial officers. All these unci were called subtracted unci (Swedish: avkortad) and what remained were termed kept (behållen) unci.

To establish the number of unci from which taxes were taken by the Crown, official inquiries were held called uncus revisions (see page 90). After the comprehensive revision in 1638, for fifty years there was no change in the established official or revision uncus number. Actually there were considerable changes because of the increase of the population and expanded settlement of the country during peace time. The result was that the manors collected taxes from the actual unci, but paid to the Crown only according to the revision unci thus benefiting from the surplus. An exception happened in the bishopric when peasants were ordered to deliver the statio direct to the Crown.

While farms paid customary dues according to the payment unci, statute labour was levied according to man-power for which the Swedish term mantal was used. Because the mantal was taken into account in calculating the uncus, actually the yard-stick for establishing the level of statute labour to be rendered to the manor was also indirectly the uncus. Peasants from a whole uncus, as a rule, had to supply a man and a horse for five days a week to work as directed by the manor on own food and with own implements. For a lesser uncus number the statute labour to be performed varied. This variation was not in proportion to the uncus number but usually in excess. In addition farms had to provide a second labourer (see page 100), on occasions commuted. In the Oxenstierna estates the second labourer was taken from the mantal figure, either actually or commuted. In 1634 it was explained that the second labourer (the *otrinieks*) had to be sent according to the mantal, and a quarter of an uncus was to be calculated as a half mantal. The exception was Mujāni where an *otrinieks* had to be sent from each farm disregarding the uncus number. Furthermore the mantal was applied to levy payments of some customary dues at an equal rate of all farms. In such cases the total mantal meant the total of farms. One could not say that the picture was simple.

A sort of definition of the various unci and mantal was given in an explanation prepared in connection with the reduction at the end of the seventeenth century (RA, former KA, Revisionsjordebok 1690, Riga och Wendens krets, fol. 12–13): 'In the Oxenstierna's estates possession unci are called the old traditional unci, which were used before the survey and before it had been established as to how much peasants had to pay. Oxenstierna had ordered the survey of the unci and his conclusion was that they had been estimated too high. The unci established after the survey are called payment unci and the peasants perform statute labour and pay their dues according to the payment unci. The mantal is a title according to which equal statute labour and payment of some dues are performed from various uncus numbers (1, ¾, ½, ¼ uncus), for instance, legal dues, money in lieu of honey, etc.'

Possession unci and payment unci were units of land in internal use of the estates. The unci established by the government were the revision unci. The following illustrates the changes between the official revisions of 1638 and 1688 as to the revision unci. The data refer to the total districts of Burtnieki, Cēsis, Ēvele, Mujāni, Trikāta, and Valmiera, i.e. not only to the Axel Oxenstierna's estates, but to other estates situated in the same district as well. Because of changes in boundaries the comparison is not exact, but nevertheless it brings out differences which occurred during the 50 years from 1638 to 1688.

COMPARISON BETWEEN UNCI OF LAND IN 1638 AND 1688

	Land of peasant holdings (uncus number)									Total	
	1/16	⅛	¼	⅜	½	⅝	¾	1	over 1	farms	unci
1638: number	7	19	343	–	560	–	19	106	–	1054	489
%	0.8	1.8	32.5	–	53.1	–	1.8	10.0	–	100.0	
1688: number	161	50	339	7	475	1	232	279	3	1547	798
%	10.4	3.2	21.9	0.5	30.7	0.1	15.0	18.0	0.2	100.0	

From the comparison firstly we notice an increase in the number of farms and an even larger increase in the unci for taxation levies as well. The number of farms had increased from 100 to 147, but the total of unci from 100 to 163. Secondly changes in the composition of the distribution of the unci show an increase of the smallest as well as of the largest categories. Nevertheless, the modal value in both series was the half uncus farm, which in 1638 constituted 53 %, but in 1688–31 %.

In Chapter Four it was mentioned that there was a discrepancy between the number of farms listed in the 1638 internal register of the Oxenstierna estates and the 1638 official revision. If we compare the various categories of unci which can be identified in both documents for 873 farms out of the total 881 farms, we obtain the following table.

INTERNAL LIST OF FARMS COMPARED WITH OFFICIAL REVISION OF THE OXENSTIERNA ESTATES IN 1638

	Land of peasant holdings (uncus number)							Total	
	?	⅛	¼	½	¾	1	over 1	farms	unci
Internal records									
Number:	2	–	49	466	46	304	6	873	595 ¼
%	0.2	–	5.6	53.4	5.3	34.8	0.7	100.0	
Revision									
Number	6	1	265	491	17	93	–	873	417 ½
%	0.7		30.4	56.2	1.9	10.8	–	100.0	

The comparison shows that the revision reduced the number of unci, listed in the internal manorial records. This result had been achieved by considerably increasing the number of quarter uncus peasants and reducing the number of one uncus farms. In both series the modal value remains the half uncus peasants.

Of considerable interest is the relationship between the various categories of uncus. The peasants who were holding one uncus land according to the manorial records and remained also one uncus peasants according to the revision, had on the farm on average 2.67 men over 15 years of age (standard deviation: 0.83), 2.17 horses (0.71), and they were sowing 4.66 tons of grain (1.47). The one uncus peasants reduced in the revision to half an uncus had on the average 2.29 men over 15 years of age (0.89), 1.82 horses (0.73), and 3.69 (1.6) tons of sown grain. Peasants with half an uncus in both documents had 1.98 (0.71) men, 1.6 (0.61) horses, and 3.0 (0.85) tons of sown grain. Peasants with half an uncus in the manorial rolls and a quarter of uncus in the revision had 1.76 (0.77) men, 1.28 (0.55) horses, and 2.48 (0.77) tons of sown grain. Peasants with a quarter uncus in both documents had 1.73 (0.81) men, 1.05 (0.44) horses and 2.00 (0.68) tons of sown grain.

The high standard deviation (in brackets) shows that the scatter of the data around the average is very large. Nevertheless, from this comparison it emerges that there were objective reasons for reducing the uncus of a large number of farms. From the discussion on page 187 we further learn that peasants with a smaller uncus had more wealth than one could expect in proportion to peasants holding larger farms.

APPENDIX 2

LIVONIAN ESTATES OF THE OXENSTIERNAS AF SÖDERMÖRE

Abbreviations of districts: Bu–Burtnieki (Burtneck); Cs–Cēsis (Wenden); Ro–Ropaži (Rodenpois); Si–Sigulda (Segewold); Tr–Trikāta (Trikaten); Va–Valmiera (Wolmar).

Axelshof	Jaunā muiža	Va
Bauenhof	Bauņi	Bu
Blankenfeld, Blankenfeldshof	Blanka	Bu
Breslau	Braslava	Bu
Burtneck	Burtnieki	Bu
Buxhövdenhof, Offerlachs	–	Bu
Doctormoise, Doctorshof	Kunğēns	Bu
Ducker, Duckern	Dūķeŗi, Dukurmuiža	Mu
Freudenberg	Priekuļi	Cs
Gertzenhof	Jērcēni	Va
Kapunenhof	Kapūns	Bu
Karlshof	Kārļa muiža	Va
Kaugerhof	Kauguri	Va
Keysen	Ķeiži	Va
Kokenhof, Kokemuische	Kokmuiža	Va
Kolbergshof	Skaņkalne	Bu
Königshof, Konningshof	Ķoņi	Bu
Kronenberg, Chroneborg, Wilderhusenshof, Briefmarshallshof	Lorupe	Si
Kudling	Bānūži	Cs
Landsberg	–	Bu
Landtsbergshof, Widsen	Vijciems	Tr
Lenzenhof	Lenči	Va
Leymat Zehmat	–	Cs
Lindenhöfchen, Durenhof	Liepmuiža	Cs
Lodenhof, Groß	Vaive, Veismaņi	Cs
Lodenhof, Klein	Vaive, Veismaņi	Cs
Luthershof, Lutermoise	Rentmeistera muiža, Luturmuiža	Bu

Mojan	Mujāni	Mu
Muremoise	Mūrmuiža	Va
Nagelshof, Sissigall, Siselkaln	Naglumuiža	Ro
Nougurskihof	Negurska	Bu
Ottenhof	Vecate, Ate	Bu
Ranzen	Rencēni	Bu
Rodenpois	Ropaži	Ro
Sackenhof, Alt-Sackenhof	Vāle, Vecvāle	Tr
Schiltkornshof, Silkarentz Hof	Šilkoris	Va
Schmöllingshof, Groß	Rūte	Bu
Schmöllingshof, Klein	Baloži	Bu
Steinenhof	Stiene	Bu
Sternhof	Jaunburtnieki	Bu
Strikenhof	Strīķi	Va
Trikaten	Trikāta	Tr
Turneyhof	Tarnisa	Va
Völkersams Hoflage		Va
Welckenhof	Veļķi	Va
Wenden	Cēsis	Cs
Wilkemoisa	Vilkamuiža	Bu
Wilsenhof	Vilzēni	Bu
Wolfahrt, Hövelshof	Ēvele	Va
Wolmar	Valmiera	Va
Wrangelshof	Brenguļi	Tr

INDEX

Note: Å, Ä, and Ö, which are at the end of the Swedish alphabet, have been placed under A and O respectively.

39, 42, 82, 90, 91, 103, 104, 112, 140, 152, 165, 168, 169, 174, 182, 184, 189, 199, 202, 220–223, 226; church (drawing 1691), 37; plan, 183
Buxhövden, Johan († before 1632), possessor of estate, 15
Buxhövdenhof, also Offerlachs, estate, 16, 210–212, 219
Caduc goods, 17, 18, 165, 169
Calvinists, 5
Capital value of the bishopric and Swedish and Finnish estates, 86–89; of the bishopric in 1624–1654 (graph), 87
Cartage, 41, 48, 100, 101, 104, 128, 163, 180, 181
Cascheinius, Joachim (†1657), magister, pastor at Valmiera, dean since 1637, 24, 137, 140
Cash: payments to the Crown (trend), 129; income and expenditure, 170
Castle districts, 7, 214
Catherine I (1684–1727), empress of Russia, 222
Cēsis (Wenden), circuit, district, castle, estate, 1, 3, 4, 6, 8, 10–12, 18, 19, 22–26, 29, 32, 36, 42, 43, 45–50, 83, 90–92, 103, 105, 109, 110, 112–114, 122, 133, 134, 136–138, 140, 145, 149, 152, 155, 159, 161, 165–168, 174, 176, 182, 184, 186, 187, 189, 192, 196, 199, 202, 203, 208, 210, 219–222, 226; in 1842, 47; plan, 115; view of castle, 115
Cesvaine (Sesswegen), district and estate, 2, 25, 130, 160
Ceumern, Kaspar von (1613–1692), secretary of Livonian nobility, 191
Chamber College (Kammarkollegium), 98, 195, 205, 213, 214, 218
Charcoal, burning of, 85, 167
Children of soldiers and colonists, 114, 116
Christburg, starosty of Prussia, 157, 158
Chroneborg–see Lorupe
Churches, 6, 25, 37, 134, 165, 174
Churchward, 138
Clergy, clerics, 4–7, 9, 24, 25, 30, 35, 43, 50, 85, 134, 135, 137–139, 162, 185, 201, 207, 211, 225
College of Commerce (Kommerskollegium), 160, 162
Colonists–see Finland, Finnish
Commandant, 162, 163, 169, 174
Commercial court of Riga, 106
Commerowski, Matthias, Polish petty nobleman, 19
Commons and wastes, 20
Commutation, 34, 39, 42, 83, 100–102, 118, 123, 179–181, 184, 193, 200, 225
Conflagration, 48
Consistory: overconsistory, subconsistories (church courts), 6, 7, 36, (43), 134, 135, 137, 138, 145, 165, 211
Consumption of grain, 98, 99
Copyholder, 93
Corporal punishment, 142, 143
Corpus juris Livonici, 140, 142
Council: of Cēsis town, 49, 136–138, 145; of the Livonian nobility (Landesrat), 4; of Riga, 8, 84, 86; Swedish state, 141; of Valmiera town, 43, 47, 48, 138
Courland–see Kurzeme
Courts, 4, 7, 16, 19, 36, 43, 129, 132–149, 163, 165, 167, 192, 194, 201, 203, 204, 207, 208, 211, 212, 220
Crop failure, 154, 181, 182, 211
Crown, 58–75, 85, 92, 109–131, 133, 134, 136, 140, 149, 163, 172–174, 176, 199, 201–203, 205, 206, 208, 210, 211, 218, 219, 224, 225; share of the revenue of the bishopric (graph), 128
Cruus, Johan (†1644), husband of Katarina Oxenstierna, 150
Cruus, Lars Jespersson (1621–1656), husband of Agneta Horn, 150.
Currencies: Albert riksdollars, 130, 202, 216; carolines, 123; ducats, 162; groschen (gr.), 55; guilders, 23, 124; öre,55,

45–48, 83, 84, 86, 87, 91, 108, 110, 112–114, 120, 130, 140, 144, 156, 160–162, 164, 166, 170, 174, 191, 193 –196, 199, 203, 214
First Northern War–see Wars
Fischer, Johann (1633–1705), superintendent (1674), superintendent general (1675–1700), 6
Fishing and hunting, 40, 169
Flax and hemp, flax spinning, 105, 106, 163, 179
Fleming, Jakob (1640–1689), councillor, 195
Folksongs, 45, 101
Fonal–see Vohnja
Forestalling and regrating, 47, 48, 76
Fowlers, 225
France, French, 156
Frauenburg, town in Prussia, 157
Freemen, 26, 30, 31, 104, 176, 185, 222, 225
Freudenberg–see Priekuļi
Friberg, Adrian von, merchant, 86; his widow, 165, 167
Friedrich von Hessen-Homburg (1633–1708), landgrave, 204
Fries, Ellen (1855–1900), historian, xiv, 32, 157, 160
Frölich, Karl Gustav Hansson (1689–1748), acting governor general, 3
Frost, Gerhard, Dr, burgess of Cēsis, 49
Fugitives, refugees, 8, 9, 20, 99, 146, 156, 191, 192, 195, 211
Fünen, 156
Galenhof–see Pučurga
Gallan, peasant, 190
Gardberg, John, historian, xiv, 159, 161
Garrison, 25, 35, 36, 41, 43, 46, 48, 57, 109–116, 120, 139, 152, 155, 156, 161–163, 168, 176, 194, 202, 203, 207
Gauja (Aa), river, 17, 22, 28, 109, 110, 147, 149
Gaujiena (Adsel), district and estate, 2, 130
Georgi, Siegfried, preacher of Wrangel's regiment (1631), Finnish pastor at Valmiera (1636), 24
Germany, Germans, German, 4, 8, 46, 54, 112, 113, 122, 139–141, 157, 160, 166, 174, 190, 191, 223, 224
Gertzenhof–see Jērcēni
Gezelius, Johan Georg (1615–1690), superintendent (1660–1664), 6
Giging, Mathias, possessor of Lorupe, 146
Gilsen–see Patkule
Glass manufacture, 85
Glück, Ernst Johann (1654–1705), pastor, dean, translator of Latvian Bible, 6
Gotland, 2
Governor general, 3, 4, 36, 116, 118, 124, 125, 133–136, 146, 149, 154, 165, 187, 191, 195, 220, 221
Grain: sales, consignment, 86, 166, 172, (179), 200, 202; sown by peasants, 91, 184
Granaries, granges, 40, 44, 54, 84, 110, 111, 113, 169, 180
Grants of land by the Oxenstiernas af Södermöre, 24–27, 178
Great Northern War–see Wars
Greek Orthodox 'Old believers', 5
Greifswald, town, 160
Grothusen, Henrik (†1666), captain, 131
Grysenberg, Jörgen, bailiff, burgess of Cēsis, 169
Guardians of the heirs of the Oxenstiernas af Södermöre, 84, 85, 145, 146, 158–169, 175, 176, 180, 182, 184, 195, 196, 202, 204, 212
Gubert, Salomon (†1653), pastor and author, xiv, 51, 78; title page of his book, 53
Guilds, 8, 50
Gulbene (Schwanenburg, Gulben), district and estate, 2, 130
Gulbrandsson, Lars, accountant, 54
Güldenstern, Sigismund (Zygmunt, 1598–1666), possessor of estates, castellan of

169, 179, 186; 1624–1654 (graph), 79
Maps, 13, 29, 111, 115, 153, 178, 183, 188
Marienburg–see Alūksne
Marienburg (at present Malbork), castle and town in Prussia, 157
Market, 47, 102, 106
Martensson, Klas, retainer, ensign, 26
Matzson, Markus, retainer, ensign, 26
Maur, Johan, wood-ward at Trikāta, 104
Meadows, 39, 47, 49, 82, 83, 100, 101, 104, 142, 178, 179, 186, 188
Meklenburg, 1
Mellin, count, 220
Mellupe, river, 28
Mengden, Engelbrecht von (1587–1648), county judge, 140, 141
Menzenkamp, Justus (1628–about 1694), secretary, lawyer, 156
Merchants, 8, 10, 50, 55, 76
Merchet, 9
Merkel, Garlieb (1769–1850), writer, 144
Meurling, Anna Christina, author, xv, 133, 145, 157
Meyer, Bartolomeus (†1656), pastor of Valmiera (1625–1626), of Cēsis (1626–1656), dean 1637–1656), 24, 137
Meyer, Heinrich (1590–1645), merchant at Riga, 34, 125; his widow, 41, 86
Mežkrievi, peasant farm, 18
Mežkunğēns–see Kunğēns
Michael, executioner, 147
Militia, the military, 112, 165, 176, 214, 217; billeting, 211; units, 221
Mills, millers, 40, 42, 43, 49, 84, 92, 112, 137, 167, 214, 217
Missweber, Jurgen–see Janis Jörgen
Mitau–see Jelgava
Mode hundred (wacka), 196, 198, 199
Moisneks, etc., displaced peasants, 23; -moise, abandoned peasant farms, 23
Mojan–see Mujāni
Möller, Wilhelm (also Wellam Meller), retainer (1625–1633), son-in-law of Walter von Duhren, possessor of Dūre (since 1637), 27, 116
Morgen, measure of land, one sixtieth part of an uncus, 223
Mortenson, Berend, retainer, lieutenant, 14, 25, 110
Mujāni (Mojan), district and estate, 11, 12, 14, 22, 25, 26, 29, 90, 91, 103, 105, 112, 114, 152, 168, 174, 182, 185, 189, 196, 198, 199, 202, 208, 210–219, 222, 225, 226
Müller, Hans (†about 1668), merchant, 166
Munck, Anders Andersson (†1678 or 1681), possessor of Rāmuļi, 19, 156
Munck, Anders Jonsson († 1634), captain, steward, 14, 15, 19, 30, 34, 75, 76, 78, 110, 135, 136, 166, 169
Muremoise–see Mūrmuiža
Mūrmuiža (Muremoise), estate, 12, 22, 28, 112, 182, 184, 198, 210, 220
Mūsiņš, peasant, 189, 190
Nagel, Johan, merchant, bailiff, 86, 164–167, 172; his widow, 186
Nagelshof–see Naglumuiža
Naglumuiža (Sissigall, Siselkaln, Nagelshof), estate, 186
Narva, town, 220
Natural economy and money economy, 57, 75, 76, 129
Negurska (Nougurskihof), estate, peasant farm, 15, 210
Neu-Isenhof–see Püssi
New-settlers, 20, 26, 30, 36, 48, 93, 103, 104, 180, 185, 192, 201
Neydenburg–see Herrmann
Nietau–see Nītaure
Nilsson, Olof, accountant, 165, 168, 169
Nītaure (Nietau), district and estate, 2, 130
Nobility, noblemen and their servants, 4, 5, 7–9, 48, 49, 102, 104, 116, 120, 123, 130, 132, 133, 140–142, 144–146, 149, 168, 169, 178, 191, 192, 196, 205,

208, 210; Riksregistratur, xv, 145, 157, 191, 213, 220; Tidö arkivet, xvi, 15–19, 23, 28, 31, 32, 34, 39, 41, 42, 44, 46, 49–51, 54, 76, 78, 83–85, 90, 93, 94, 100–102, 104, 111–114, 118, 120, 122, 131, 136, 137, 139, 140, 142, 145, 146, 151, 152, 154–159, 161–165, 168, 170–173, 175, 176, 181, 182, 187, 194–196, 198, 199, 202–204, 212, 219, 220, 223
Raine, estate in Estonia, 130
Ramelshof–see Rāmuļi
Ramotzki–see Ieriķi
Rampart of Valmiera, 38, 46, 48, 101, 113, 114
Rāmuļi (Ramelshof), estate, 19, 169
Ranzen–see Renceni
Rauna (Ronneburg), district and estate, 2, 109, 130, 221; Rauna gate of Cēsis, 49
Rautenstein, Heinrich, steward (1643–1646), 34, 44, 46, 75, 76, 104, 105
Reduction (expropriation of estates by the crown), reduction commission, 14, 16, 98, 148, 149, 160, 161, 205–208, 210, 211, 213, 219, 220
Reeves, 26, 30, 40, 44–46, 92, 185, 188, 214, 217, 225
Reformed church, 5
Refugees–see Fugitives
Reichandres, town and estate in Prussia, 158
Reichard, colonel, 158
Reimers von Rosenfeld, David (†1664), steward (1646–1649), 19, 34, 35, 39, 75, 76, 101, 102, 113
Reiniken, Franciscus (about 1601–1665), judge (1638–1663 or 1664), 136, 137, 139, 140, 145, 166, 169
Remuneration of manorial officers, 56–75, 172, 173, 198–201
Rencēni (Ranzen), estate, 15, 23, 28, 167, 168, 174, 185, 199, 202
Rencis, peasant farm, 23
Rent, calculation of, 200–202, 211–220
Rentmeistera muiža, also Luturmuiža (Luthershof, Lutermoise), estate, 15, 30, 185, 210
Repina, estate in Estonia, 130
Retainers (troopers, militia men), 4, 5, 14, 25, 26, 28, 31, 38, 91, 116–120, 125, 141, 162, 165, 167, 174, 176, 185, 211, 212, 214, 217, 218, 221, 225; 'retainers' statio', retainers subsidy, 124
Reutern, Johan von (1635–1698, ennobled 1691), merchant in Riga, 202, 208, 210–212, 219, 220
Reutz, Jakob, steward (inspector), judge after 1663, 145, 146, 164–169
Reval–see Tallinn
Revision of unci, 7, 14, 16–18, 22–26, 45, 90–93, 98, 103, 116, 122, 123, 175–178, 182–186, 188, 192, 196, 205, 214, 219, 225–227
Rēzekne (Rositten), town in Latgale, 154
Rhine-lands, 2
Richter, Alexander von (1803–1864), jurist, historian, xv, 118, 133, 134, 141, 142
Ridder, Mikel, creditor; father-in-law of merchant Adrian Friberg, 167
Ridēns, peasant farm, 16
Riga (Rīga), capital of Livonia, later capital of Latvia, 1, 3–6, 8, 10, 11, 15, 18, 36, 42, 48, 50, 51, 54, 76, 82–86, 91, 103–106, 122, 126, 128, 129, 133–135, 141, 147, 149, 155, 156, 162–167, 169, 186, 199, 205, 206, 214, 220, 221, 226; Riga dollars, 55; Riga marks, 55 Riga measures, 91, 94, 124
Riga, Municipal Library of, 143
Riksarkivet–see RA
Ringenheim, Johan Georg von, steward, later retainer, 161, 165, 168
Rodenburg, Johan von, engineer, 113
Rodenpois–see Ropaži
Roela (Rögel, Royel), estate in Estonia, 151, 152, 198

Rögel–see Roela
Rome, 3
Ronneburg–see Rauna
Ropaži (Rodenpois), district, estate, 17, 18, 24, 26–28, 42, 43, 84, 85, 90, 91, 125, 152, 154, 164, 165, 167–169, 172, 182, 186, 189, 192, 196, 199, 202, 210, 219, 220; ruins of castle (1791), 119
Rositten–see Rēzekne
Rostock, town in Germany, 1, 160
Royel–see Roela
Rubene (Pappendorf), parish, 25, 36, 140, 221
Ruhendorf, Johann (†1686), pastor at Trikāta since 1662, dean, 145
Rujen–see Rūjiena
Rūjiena (Rujen), district and estate, 2, 221
Russia, Russians, 3, 5, 8, 49, 103, 124, 130, 131, 144, 154, 155, 191, 192, 204, 220–222
Rūte (Gross Schmöllingshof), estate, 15, 27, 210
Ryning, Erik Eriksson (1592–1654), governor general, 3
Saaremaa (Ösel), island, province of Estonia, 2, 6
Sabach, Saback–see Zābaki
Sacken, Otto von, nobleman, 16, 17
Salaca, river, 16, 28, 149
Salaspils (Kirchholm), district and estate, 130
Sales of produce, 58–75, 86, 101, 162, 212
Salisburg–see Valtenberģis
Saltpetre, cooking of, 114
Samson, Hermann (1579–1643), ennobled Himmelstierna, superintendent general, vii, 5, 6, 25, 148
Saulhof–see Sauļi
Sauļi (Saulhof), estate, 16
Saxonia, 220
Schenking, Otto (†1632), Catholic bishop, 17, (23), 28, 30, (31), 223
Schiltkornshof–see Šilkoris
Schinckel, Herbert, baron, v
Schirren, Carl (1826–1910), historian, professor, xvi, 148, 149, 193
Schlippenbach, Wolmar von (died before 1678), judge, 14, 165
Schlippenbach, Wolmar von, major general, 221, 222
Schmöllingshof, Gross–see Rūte
Schmöllingshof, Klein–see Baloži
Schnack, Jakob (1625–1697), ennobled Sneckenberg, guardian of the heirs of the Oxenstiernas af Södermöre, 84, 159, 160, 165–168, 175, 176, 195, 196
Schools, 4, 43, 49, 83, 134, 138, 145, 207
Schreiberfeld, major, 220
Schroop, estate in Prussia, 157, 158
Schujen–see Skujene
Schultz, Jakob, surveyor, 223
Schwanenburg–see Gulbene
Schwembler, Hermann (ennobled 1653 with the name of Lossenau), assistant judge, 19, 29, 30
Scots, 112
Secretary, 35, 41, 49, 54, 132, 163, 191
Segewold–see Sigulda
Semgallen–see Zemgale
Serben–see Dzērbene
Serfs, serfdom, bondage, 9, 10, 20, 104, 175, 192, 196
Sesswegen–see Cesvaine
Seuberlich, Erich (1882–1946), genealogist, xv
Sheepfolds, 42
Sheremetiev, Boris Petrovich (1652–1719), fieldmarshal general, 221
Sheremetiev, Vasilij Petrovich (†1659), Russian general, 154
Sidelines, 83
Sigulda (Segewold), district and estate, 2, 7, 130, 146, 221
Silkarentz Hof–see Šilkoris
Siselkaln–see Naglumuiža
Sissigall–see Naglumuiža

Skangalis, Jānis, peasant, 220
Skaņkalne (Kolbergshof), estate, 14, 25, 210–212, 219
Skujene (Schujen), district and estate, 2
Skult, burgomaster of Cēsis, 169
Skundrich (also Kurich), Andres, peasant, 18
Skütte, Klas († about 1668), notary, 166
Skytte, Johan Bengtsson (1577–1645), governor general, 3, 19, 103, 122, 132, 134, 135
Slaves, 9, 193
Slicher van Bath, B. H., historian, xvi, 76
Smīde, peasant, 222
Smilten–see Smiltene
Smiltene (Smilten), district and estate, 2, 130, 147
Sneckenberg–see Schnack
Sneckensköld, Jakob, governor of royal domains, 211
Södermöre, county in Kalmar län, Sweden; counts: Oxenstiernas af Södermöre, v, 2, 151, 159, 202
Soldiers, troops, 38, 48, 84, 85, 91, 105, 109, 110, 112–114, 116, 125, 131, 137, 176, 194
Soom, Arnold, archivist, author (1900–1977), v, xvi, 83, 159
Soop, Erik (1643–1700), major general, 220
Sorcerers, 148
Sowing of grain, 39, 43, 98–101, 110, 181, 186, 208, 213
Spāre, estate, 222
Spiering, Arend and Isak, financiers, 87
Spilve, location near Riga, 220
Spinning and weaving, 39, 46, 83, 101, 194; correlation between spun flax and woven linen cloth, 56
Sprengport (before ennoblement: Roland), Jakob († 1688), captain, commandant of Valmiera, steward, 34, 35, 41, 42, 75, 76, 101, 114, 120, 131, 154–156, 161–165, 167–169, 172–174, 194, 195; sketch drawn by him for a demesne in the Ropaži district, 29
Spruks (Spruck), Toms, peasant, 179–181
St. Catharina (Katherinen)–see Kadrina
St. Jacoby (St. Jakobi)–see Viru-Jaagupi
St. Jürgen–see Jurğumuiža
Stalen, Johan (1590–1651), professor, superintendent (1648–1649), 6
Stapel, Johann, grantee, 15, 27
Starosty, term denoting district, used during the Polish-Lithuanian period and also later, 12, 157, 202
Statio–see taxes
Statute labour, 5, 9, 20, 34–36, 38, 39, 42, 45, 48, 51, 74, 82, 83, 85, 92, 100–102, 104, 118, 120, 142, 167, 169, 173, 174, 179–181, 184, 193, 200, 201, 211–213, 218, 221, 224–226; norms to be performed: 39, 101; work journals, 51, (100)
Stefan Batory (1533–1586), king of Poland and Lithuania (from 1575), 11
Steinenhof–see Stiene
Sternfeld, Kasper (?), assessor, 220
Sternhof–see Jaunburtnieki
Stettin (at present Szczecin), town, 133
Stewards, 5, 19, 20, 25, 31, 32, 34–43, 45, 47, 48, 51, 78, 83, 85, 92, 94, 101, 102, 112, 133, 136, 138–140, 142, 144, 145, 161, 166, 168, 175, 194
Stiene (Steinenhof), estate, 15, 210
Stiernsköld, Nils (1583–1627), admiral, 2
Stipends of clergy, 7
Stockholm, 15, 41, 44, 51, 54, 83, 133, 136, 145, 159, 161, 162, 165, 168, 176, 179, 196, 210
Stralsund, town in Germany, 14, 208
Strikenhof–see Strīķi
Strīķi (Strikenhof), estate, 14, 210
Strokirk, Michael, governor of the economy, 98
Strömberg, Nils (1646–1723), governor general, president of Chamber College, 3
Struckman, Kord, merchant, 86

Völkcrsams Hoflage, estate, 12, 25, 210
Wacka, annual muster of peasants, 40, 44, 45, 101, 163, 169
Wacka-book (Wackenbuch), land roll, terrier, 34, 51, 176, 219, 224, (227)
Wahlen, Johann von, assessor, joint possessor of Sauļi, 16, 135; his widow, 26
Wahlenhof–see Vāle
Wainsel–see Vainiži
Walk–see Valka
Walter de Henle (13th century), author, 35, 43
War, articles of, 114; First Northern War (1655–1660), 35, 85, 86, 112, 125, 129, 131, 134, 145, 146, 148, 154–157, (163–165), 176, (186), 191, 195; Great Northern War (1700–1721), 218, 220, 221; Polish and Swedish War (1600–1635), 120; ravages of, 90, 179, 203; war tax, 130
Water-meadows, 39, (42), 81, 100
Wattküll– see Vatku
Weavers, 50, 83, 194
Weber, Heinrich, secretary, bailiff, 35, 101, 163
Weber, Matthias, retainer, 26
Webster, *Webster's Third New International Dictionary of the English Language*, xvi, 81
Welckenhof–see Veļķi
Wemes–see Vöhma
Wenden–see Cēsis
Wenzlow, Dorothea von, claimant of Ēvele, 219
Wenzlow, Maria Polixena–see Palmstruch
Wenzlow, Robert Philip von, claimant of Ēvele, 219
Whipping-post, 147, 148
Widsen–see Vijciems
Wiek–see Läänemaa
Wiggiben hundred, 17
Wijrland–see Virumaa
Wilderhusenshof–see Lorupe
Wilkemoisa–see Vilkamuiža
Wilsenhof–see Vilzēni
Wirrenorm, village in Estonia, 161
Wismar, town in Germany, 157, 208
Witches, 35, 147, 148
Wittenberg, town in Germany, 1, 6
Wohlfart–see Ēvele
Wolgal–see Völe
Wolmar–see Valmiera
Woodland, 178, 215, 216, 224
Wrangel, Hans, colonel, possessor of Lugaži, 2
Wrangel, Herman Hansson (1587–1643), fieldmarshal, governor general, 2, 3, 14, 219
Wrangelshof–see Brenguļi
Wrangelshof–see Prangli
Wulfenschild, Heinrich, merchant, 86
Yield: peasant crops, 98–100; of rye and barley, 1624–1654 (graph), 77; of rye dependent on manure, 1664 (graph), 80; trend line, 76; yield ratios, 76–79, 81–83, 96, 98, 100, 102, 179–181, 188, 213
Zābaki (Saback, Sabach), peasant farm, 18, 168, 170
Zēmelis, peasant, 222
Zemgale (Semgallen), province of Latvia, 3
Zilūzis, farm name, 22
Zobel, Konrad, merchant, 86
Zuckerbecker, Johann, merchant, 167, 186
Zweibrücken, von–see Adolf Johann